New Auditor's Guide to Internal Auditing

Bruce R. Turner, AM, CRMA, CISA, CFE

Sponsored by

The Institute of Internal Auditors
Toronto Chapter

INTERNAL AUDIT
FOUNDATION™

Published by the Internal Audit Foundation
1035 Greenwood Blvd., Suite 401
Lake Mary, Florida 32746, USA

Limit of Liability: The Internal Audit Foundation publishes this document for informational and educational purposes and is not a substitute for legal or accounting advice. The Foundation does not provide such advice and makes no warranty as to any legal or accounting results through its publication of this document. When legal or accounting issues arise, professional assistance should be sought and retained.

The IIA's International Professional Practices Framework (IPPF) comprises the full range of existing and developing practice guides for the profession. The IPPF provides guidance to internal auditors globally and paves the way to world-class internal auditing.

The IIA and the Foundation work in partnership with researchers from around the globe to conduct valuable studies on critical issues affecting today's business world. Much of the content presented in their final reports is a result of the Foundation-funded research and prepared as a service to the Foundation and the internal audit profession. Expressed opinions, interpretations, or points of view represent a consensus of the researchers and do not necessarily reflect or represent the official position or policies of The IIA or the Foundation.

ISBN-13: 978-1-63454-054-4
23 22 21 20 19   1 2 3 4 5 6

Dedicated to my family
for their unconditional love, inspiration, and support.

To my loving wife, Bea, for being the NICEST –
Nurturing, Inspiring, Caring, Empathetic, Supporting, Transforming –
partner throughout our more than 40 years of marriage.

To my children, Nicole, Jacqueline, and Glen, and their partners
for sparking the GLOW – through Generosity, Love, Objectivity, Wisdom –
that guides my route to "aspiring the heights."[1]

To my grandchildren, Elina, Elijah, Lucinda, Zachary, and Ashton,
for creating the SHAPE – Sparkle, Humor, Amiability, Purity, Energy –
that feeds my passion for making the world a better place.

"A good company delivers excellent products and services, and
a great company does all that and strives to make the world a better place."

—Bill Ford Jr., Great–Grandson of "Captain of Industry" Henry Ford
and Business Leader in His Own Right

Disclaimer

Each chapter contains a story on "perspectives," which is largely the work of fiction. The stories are intended to provide an introduction to the technical areas covered in the chapter. While the stories are informed by true-life events, all personal and organizational identifiers have been removed. Names, characters, businesses, events, and incidents are either products of the author's imagination or used fictitiously. Any resemblance to organizations or actual persons, living or dead, is purely coincidental.

Contents

List of Exhibits

Executive Summary

There has never been a better time to be an internal auditor!

Internal auditors help their organizations accomplish their objectives and improve their operations through an independent and objective approach designed to add value. Their approach is systematic and disciplined in evaluating and improving the effectiveness of the organization's risk management, control, and governance processes. Internal auditors undertake these activities within the organizations for whom they work.

The twenty-first century is offering up many fresh challenges as a consequence of rapid business changes, global connectivity, emerging technologies, and increasingly complex economic, regulatory, and operating environments. The internal audit profession is responding by evolving significantly to meet the growing demands. Internal auditors are now well positioned to help their organizations deliver excellent products and services, while doing all that they can to make the world a better place.

Internal auditors undertake a broad variety of interesting work, gain a holistic understanding of the business, are usually well compensated, are often early adopters of evolving technology, and can enjoy the opportunity to travel the world to undertake their offsite work. The importance of having a capable and well-equipped internal audit activity has become increasingly recognized. In some parts of the world, this has been accelerated by governments and regulators moving to make internal auditing mandatory. Coincident with these changes, boards, audit committees, and senior management are expecting more from their symbiotic partnership with independent internal auditors.

This book incorporates insights, stories, and tips for new auditors in their first few years in the profession. It has been shaped in such a way that it:

- Provides essential reading for new auditors navigating the auditing landscape for the first time
- Introduces stories that will help to extend the auditor's thinking beyond the basics
- Illustrates why audit workpapers need to be prepared to withstand intense external scrutiny
- Offers team leaders and educators tools to help train new recruits
- Links the basics of internal auditing through a series of sequenced events to the broader context
- Accommodates the many different pathways that people follow to move into an internal audit role at all levels, from auditors through to chief audit executives (CAEs)
- Recruits highly skilled people from other professions, such as engineers and lawyers, through to health-care professionals, such as nurses

Internal auditors are currently transforming their mindset from one of hindsight to delivering insights and ultimately sharing foresight. Traditionally, they had a hindsight perspective (assessing what happened in the past to provide control assurance). Today, management increasingly expects internal auditors to also deliver fresh insights (perspectives on risks facing the organization and control assurance in the here and now). Soon, this will increasingly shift to also expecting foresight (helping organizations prepare for the future).

Auditors need to understand the changing environment if they are to provide foresight. The pace of change in the twenty-first century is unparalleled in history; notably, while it took 38 years for radio to reach 50 million users, Facebook took just nine months to reach one billion users. Radical digital transformation will continue over the next decade with a consequent significant impact on the business risk landscape through artificial intelligence, big data analytics, biometrics, blockchain, conversational commerce, dark web, internet of things, and robotic process automation, among others.

The book has been developed in a style that is educative in nature by:

- Splitting chapters into six distinct parts, covering the who, why, how, when, what, and where of internal auditing
- Explaining more than 140 terms in a comprehensive glossary
- Providing almost 70 exhibits with practical illustrations, examples, and diagrams
- Including more than 50 references to useful published materials in the notes section

Former U.S. First Lady Barbara Bush once commented, "I had the best job in America. Every single day was interesting, rewarding, and sometimes just plain fun." This is a sentiment shared by many internal auditors, so each chapter includes insights from expert practitioners on what they love about internal auditing.[1]

Business leader Bill Ford Jr. provides great context for internal audit's role of enhancing and protecting organizational value through his reflection, "Creating a strong business and building a better world are not conflicting goals—they are both essential ingredients for long-term success."

Several high-profile luminaries—global leaders of the profession—also share a slice of their personal wisdom before each of the six core parts of the book and on the following page.

> **Wisdom of a Global Luminary**
>
> "After more than twenty years of experience as an internal auditor and as a chief audit executive, my personal advice to a newcomer will be to find a mentor. This could be a senior internal auditor within the audit team or the department head, someone possessing an integrated and open mindset, knowing the business and internal audit techniques, with excellent leadership and communication skills, demonstrating highly ethical behavior, and is willing to provide you with regular feedback and advice. Find *your* personal role model for your career as an internal auditor!"
>
> —Angela Witzany
> Head of Internal Audit, Austria
> Past Chairman of IIA Global Board of Directors 2016–2017

Part 1 (chapters 1 through 4) explores the *who* of internal auditing. It reflects on the importance of connecting with other professionals, introduces auditing frameworks and standards, reflects on the value proposition, and charts the various pathways into the internal audit activity. Once the realm of accountants, internal audit teams now consist of multidisciplinary skillsets ranging from engineers and educators to lawyers, health-care professionals, and technology experts. It also emphasizes that, as the expectations of boards, audit committees, and senior executives increase, the capabilities of internal auditors need to constantly expand to fulfill their contemporary role. Chapter 1 reflects that while the broad methodologies of internal and external auditing have common features (planning, fieldwork, reporting, and follow-up), the scope, objectives, approach, time frames, and nature of reporting are vastly different.

Part 2 (chapters 5 through 8) looks at the *why* of internal auditing. It explores the concepts of governance, risk management, and control, how these are influenced by the culture and tone at the top, and the foundations they provide for risk-based auditing. An important facet discussed in chapter 8 is The IIA's International Professional Practices Framework (IPPF), which is the conceptual framework that organizes authoritative guidance, including the *International Standards for the Professional Practice of Internal Auditing*. The standards related to each topic in the book are then recapped in each chapter.

Part 3 (chapters 9 through 12) dives into the *how* of internal auditing, covering key preparatory stages where new auditors shape their professional skills. It details how each part of the internal audit work fits together, from audit planning and defining the audit objectives, to interviewing using SMILE techniques, assessing risk and control (including key management reports), and developing an audit program that assesses hard and soft controls and shapes better ways of working.

Part 4 (chapters 13 through 17) covers *when* the rubber hits the road and the auditor applies practical auditing skills of undertaking fieldwork and testing. This includes data analytics, developing recommendations from observations, preparing and finalizing the audit report and determining an audit rating, maintaining quality control, and, ultimately, following up and reporting on the resolution of audit recommendations.

Part 5 (chapters 18 through 20) addresses the *what* of internal auditing, reflecting on the importance of quality assurance and improvement arrangements and the measurement of performance. The final chapter concludes with a series of practical stories from the frontline that aim to bring to life the mission of internal auditors to enhance and protect organizational value. The short stories reflect the ABCs of auditing (being attuned, balanced, and credible).

Part 6 draws together the *where* of information that helps to expand on the overall content, including appendices, notes, and glossary.

Preface

Foundations for Successful Learning

This book meets the specific needs of new auditors as well as educators and others who support them. It delivers powerful and practical content by structuring chapters according to the common elements of learning of the first Australians—Aboriginal people—one of the world's oldest continuous cultures.[1] The illustration on the following page reflects the recognized ways of learning at the bottom, then flows upward to connect with the structural flow of each of the chapters (noting that, in some cases, sections within a chapter can potentially address more than one way of learning).

Chapter Structure Aligned to Recognized Ways of Learning

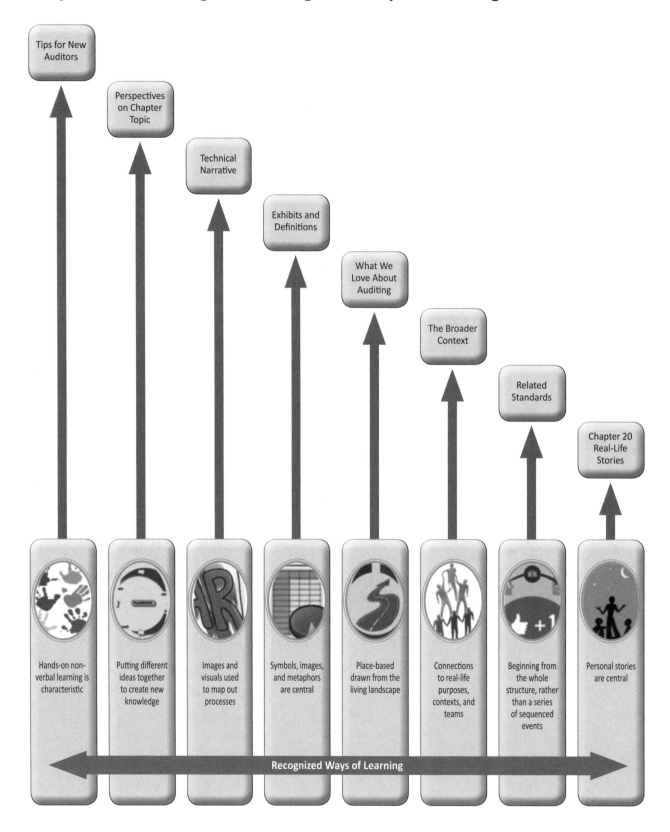

Tips for New Auditors

Perspectives on Chapter Topic

Technical Narrative

Exhibits and Definitions

What We Love About Auditing

The Broader Context

Related Standards

Chapter 20 Real-Life Stories

Hands-on non-verbal learning is characteristic

Putting different ideas together to create new knowledge

Images and visuals used to map out processes

Symbols, images, and metaphors are central

Place-based drawn from the living landscape

Connections to real-life purposes, contexts, and teams

Beginning from the whole structure, rather than a series of sequenced events

Personal stories are central

Recognized Ways of Learning

There are now many pathways for moving into an internal audit role, with individuals being appointed at all levels through to CAEs. In addition to drawing in talented people from within the business, internal audit is also drawing in highly skilled people from other professions, such as engineers and lawyers through to health-care professionals such as nurses. The technical practices, storytelling, practical examples, research insights, stories from the frontline, and comprehensive glossary will aid significantly in their transition.

In the following narratives, four professionals reflect on their respective journeys into an internal audit role over the last couple of years and the challenges they confronted.

Challenges of Practitioners Confronting the New Frontier of Internal Auditing

Example 1: Shifting from Nursing and Law to Auditing
Cathy Cox

The Challenges of a Mature and Experienced Legal and Health-Care Professional Moving into Internal Auditing

"Over 30 years of experience as a registered nurse in an acute health-care setting (operating theaters), a couple of years as a lawyer (commercial law), and a rebound back to health care in a corporate health setting gave me a valuable background and footplate in which to undertake audits within the health setting. The challenges were numerous. Self-doubt, knowing I am no longer the expert in my field, yet with my maturity the client has an expectation I am. The realization and understanding of the hierarchy of priorities. The difference in lines of communication and the language utilized (informal versus formal). Forming new working relationships and building up trust and confidence with my (new) colleagues. Building a new network and being recognized as a valued member of the team. Being humbled by the wealth of knowledge and expertise in the world of auditing and knowing I only possess a tiny portion of this knowledge."

Example 2: Shifting into Internal Auditing from a Business Role
Sarah Humphris

The Challenges of Moving from a Business Role into Internal Auditing

"Working in a financial institution and health fund, I took up the opportunity to move into internal audit with the intention of building my knowledge and providing assurance to the business on best practice. There is sometimes stigma attached to audit, governance, and risk, and overcoming that has been my biggest challenge in moving into the area. I have found that when I tell people what I do for a living, they instantly become a bit nervous and make the same remarks, 'So you find the people who do the wrong thing' or 'What's that?' Once you're here though, it's easy to see the benefits both professionally and personally."

Example 3: Shifting from Nursing to Auditing
Malou de Bruin-Rijs

The Challenges of a Young Nurse Moving into Internal Auditing
"After starting my career as a nurse, I recently chose to become an auditor in the Netherlands to help maintain the quality of patient care at the hospital at the highest possible level. I find conducting the interviews to be a great challenge, and want to understand what I can do in an interview to make the client feel comfortable and to reflect that I am not there to question their personal integrity but to figure out how the system works ... or doesn't work. The challenge for me lies in shifting from being a user of the system to identifying opportunities for making the system work even better."

Example 4: Promoted into an Auditing Role at a Commercial Bank
Daniel Whiteman

The Challenges of Moving from a Banking Support Role into Internal Auditing
"I developed a passion for the auditing profession during my first banking position when I was just 18, having learned a lot from one of the auditors during a routine bank audit and through my university studies. My current employer supported my career aspirations, and, following the growth of the bank, I was promoted into my current role as an internal auditor. The challenge of moving into the audit arena is the notion that you feel that you must know everything ... internal policies and procedures, standards, and legislation. Indeed this was not what is expected; however, it was a pressure I placed on myself very early in my transition to the internal audit role."

Acknowledgments

To my many professional colleagues, past and present, who continue to motivate others in our shared pursuit of excellence aimed at making the world a better place. And to IIA–Australia for permission to use its suite of published materials, including a series of topical white papers, the Auditing in Australia handbook, and training course materials for interviewing skills. Selected content has been interspersed throughout this book.

To the first Australians, with great respect, as the traditional ways of the Aboriginal people provided a recognized ancestral framework (of knowing, being, doing, valuing, and learning) that was used to establish the eight ways of learning framework (i.e., eight interconnected pedagogies), which, in turn, informed the structure of the book.

To the Internal Audit Foundation and The IIA for their commitment to developing the internal audit profession across the globe. Special thanks to Candace Sacher of the Foundation for her exemplary publishing support and encouragement throughout the project; to Lee Ann Campbell of the Foundation for her keen eye in editing the manuscript; and to the panel of subject matter expert reviewers from the Foundation's Committee of Research and Education Advisors (CREA) and The IIA's Standards and Guidance team for providing invaluable advice and ideas:

Anne Mercer

Debi Roth

Jane Traub

Judy Grobler

Kıvılcım Günbattı

Tania Stegemann

I am especially indebted to the 53 expert practitioners (including global leaders and potential future leaders) from around the world who contributed their constructive insights, what they love about the profession, features of their favorite audit, and their pathway into the profession. The response exemplified the commitment of audit professionals to The IIA's motto "Progress Through Sharing."

Expert Practitioners Who Contributed Personal Insights to the Book

Alex Hardy	Angela Witzany*	Andrew Cox	Andrew Dix	Angie Bezandes
Anthony Robinson	Anton van Wyk*	Bob McDonald OAM*	Bruce Sloan	Carol Holley
Cathy Cox	Christie O'Loughlin	Christina Phillips	Clarita Imperial	Daniel Whiteman
Daniela Danescu	Danson Nadarajah	Farah Araj	Geoff Campbell	Glen Howard
Jessica Chiang	Joe Bell	Larry Harrington*	Dr. Len Gainsford	Linda Veronese
Malou de Bruin-Rijs	Mark Harrison	Melanie Kelly	Melissa Grantham	Michael Parkinson
Michael Valitutti	Narelle Sheppard	Noelene Reed	Norman Marks*	Oliver Dieterle*
Paul Sobel*	Peter Jenkins	Peter Kennedy	Phil Meredith	Pretty Pritika
Rizwana Ali	Ross Tyler	Sandra Lenarcic	Sarah Humphris	Simon Woo
Siri Thongsiri	Stephen Coates	Stephen Horne	Sue Morrison	Suzy Stamatonikolos
Tina Baker	Tracy Piscopo	Wendy Preston	* Denotes Global Luminaries	

The insights were provided from expert practitioners in regions as diverse as Africa, Australia, Europe, Middle East, North America, and through to Fiji and Tuvalu, which are smaller South Pacific nations. Representation was from all active working generations with a wide spread of years of experience covering all levels, from audit committees and CAEs through to auditors. The statistics are included in appendix A (for the 50 practitioners who supplied demographic information).

About the Author

Bruce R. Turner, AM, CRMA, CISA, CFE, remains active as an audit and risk committee chair and company director. He is just the second professional internal auditor in Australia to receive Order of Australia honors. He was appointed a Member (AM) in the Queen's Birthday Honors of 2015 in recognition of his significant service to public administration through governance and risk management practices and to the profession of internal auditing.

Bruce has held board and independent audit committee roles over the last decade in 25 diverse organizations, including central government, construction, environment, finance, health care, infrastructure management, local government, natural resources, not-for-profit, parklands, parliamentary services, state revenues, supreme audit institution, telecommunications, and transport. He is a past chair of The IIA's Global Public Sector Committee 2014–2015, spent six years on the IIA–Australia Board to mid-2018, and remains an active executive coach, mentor, and white ribbon ambassador (denouncing violence against women).

He has more than 40 years of practitioner and leadership experience in internal auditing across the globe, traversing the energy, financial services (commercial, merchant, and central banking), government, manufacturing, and transport sectors. He has recruited dozens of new auditors into internal audit roles throughout his career and watched proudly as their careers blossomed. He is well positioned to share his wisdom in this book.

Bruce was the 2008 recipient of the Bob McDonald Award, which is the highest honor that can be conferred by IIA–Australia on an internal auditor. In the same year, he was a Penrith City Wall of Achievement recipient in his hometown (one of Australia's top 20 cities by population), recognizing his success in influencing the efficient, effective, and ethical operation of organizations critical to the local community.

Bruce retired from full-time work in 2012 after five years as chief internal auditor at the Australian Taxation Office, one of the largest public sector organizations in Australia. He previously held CAE roles at commercial service delivery organizations—Integral Energy Australia and StateRail. Under his stewardship, StateRail was just one of two Australian recipients ever of IIA–Global's Commitment to Quality Improvement Award. He has presented papers at conferences across the world and is an accomplished author, having been awarded an IIA–Global Outstanding Contributor Award in 2014.

Recognizing that he would have more time to smell the roses in retirement, Bruce developed a retirement plan founded on the acronym FLOWERS – Family, Leisure, Overseas, Writing, Events, Roles, (and other)

Stuff. He continues to pursue his passion for inspiring the development of others and advancing the profession through his storytelling. In his first seven years of retirement, he authored more than 30 publications (books, white papers, practice guides, guidelines, and articles) and co-authored an additional 12 more.

He lives in Australia at the Blue Mountains, west of Sydney, with his wife of more than 40 years, Bea. Their children and grandchildren live close by and gather each Sunday night for family dinner at the familial home, where there is always much fun, humor, laughter, and a good yarn.

New Auditor's Guide
to Internal Auditing

PART 1
THE *WHO* OF INTERNAL AUDITING

Chapters 1 through 4 consider the people who make up the profession, their pathways into internal auditing, and the development of capabilities that help them fulfill their roles and responsibilities.

Profession	Pathways	Capabilities	Roles

Wisdom of a Global Luminary

"Everyone starting a career should understand the value of personal branding. We all have a brand, whether we know it or not. But those who proactively manage that brand will see their career accelerate faster than those who don't manage their brand. Some of the attributes one wants to consider include intellectual curiosity, continuous learner, integrity, passion, humility, critical thinking, strong verbal and writing skills, executive presence, inspiring, innovative, patient, open-minded, transparent, and positive."

—Larry Harrington
Chief Audit Executive, U.S.
Past Chairman of IIA Global Board of Directors 2015–2016

Chapter 1
The Internal Audit Profession

Understanding the value proposition of internal auditing is pivotal to delivering the vision and mission of the internal audit mandate through effective assurance and consulting services. This chapter explores each of the elements of the definition of internal auditing, introduces the concept of internal audit stakeholders, and emphasizes the importance of understanding the business.

Understanding the Basics

What Is Internal Auditing?

Internal auditing is, in essence, checking to make sure the business is operating according to accepted standards; for example, checking that financial data is valid and verifying that business risks and legal obligations are being properly managed. Internal auditing involves doing these activities for the organization you work for, such as an energy firm, versus an accounting firm. The technical definition of internal auditing is included later in this chapter.

The IIA

Founded in 1941, The IIA is the global professional body for internal auditors. It has more than 190,000 members with affiliated institutes and chapters in more than 170 countries and territories throughout all populated continents of the world.

The IIA's mission is to provide dynamic leadership for the global profession of internal auditing. It serves as the chief advocate of the internal audit profession, is the profession's international standard setter, delivers globally accepted internal auditing certifications, and provides thought leadership, research, and education.

The IIA sets the bar for internal audit integrity and professionalism around the world with its International Professional Practices Framework (IPPF), a collection of guidance that includes the *International Standards for the Professional Practice of Internal Auditing* and the Code of Ethics. The IPPF is explained later in this chapter and elaborated upon in chapter 8. The way that standards are established is explained in chapter 8.

Common Body of Knowledge (CBOK)

The Global Internal Audit Body of Knowledge (CBOK) is the world's largest ongoing study of the internal audit profession and includes insights from internal audit practitioners and their stakeholders. The CBOK study is conducted by the Internal Audit Foundation.

A key component of CBOK is a global practitioner survey that provides a comprehensive look at the activities and characteristics of internal auditors worldwide. CBOK studies are undertaken every four to five years and can be downloaded free of charge from the CBOK Resource Exchange on The IIA's website (www.theiia.org). They are useful for new auditors interested in gaining a broader perspective of contemporary audit topics, key issues, and fresh ideas.

Recognizing the Differences Between External Auditing and Internal Auditing

It is important to understand the significant differences between the internal auditing and external auditing disciplines in *what* is done and *how* it is done. The differences are not always well understood. While the broad methodologies of internal and external auditing have common features (planning, fieldwork, reporting, and follow-up), the scope, objectives, approach, time frames, and nature of reporting are vastly different.

Many external audits are a repeat of prior annual audits (notwithstanding there will be occasional changes to the business and its financial control system), whereas most internal audits (beyond the traditional assurance-based audits depicted in exhibit 3-3) are first-time reviews or are undertaken on longer review cycles (several years). The key differences between an external audit and an internal audit are illustrated in **exhibit 1-1**.

Exhibit 1-1: Fundamental Differences Between External Audit and Internal Audit[1]

External Audit		Internal Audit
Appointed from outside the organization (independently appointed in the public sector)	**Status**	Employees of the organization, or can be an independent entity through outsourced/co-sourced arrangement
Independent of management and the governing body (including the board of directors)	**Independence**	Independent of activities audited but able to respond to the needs of management and the audit committee
Serves third parties that need reliable financial information, including shareholders (corporate sector) and parliament (public sector)	**Serving**	Serves the needs of the organization

Board of directors, and answers questions from shareholders at AGM	**Reports to**	Audit committee functionally for operations and CEO for administration
True and fair view of financial statements	**Objective**	Varies according to the audit; focused on evaluating controls designed to assure the accomplishment of the organization's goals and objectives
Historical events as expressed in financial statements	**Focus**	Forward looking
Reviews records supporting the financial statements (periodically, usually annually)	**Coverage**	Reviews governance, risk management, and control processes according to risk-based need
Opinion on financial statements	**Outcome**	Helps the organization to enhance and protect organizational value and accomplish its objectives
Incidentally concerned with prevention and detection of fraud and corruption in general, but is directly concerned when financial statements may be materially affected	**Fraud and Corruption**	Is directly concerned with evaluating the potential for the occurrence of fraud and how the organization manages fraud risk
Shareholders, regulators, board of directors, and audit committee	**Reports go to**	Management and audit committee
External audit standards	**Standards**	Internal audit standards
Mandatory	**Qualifications**	Not mandatory, though there is a recent shift in some jurisdictions to require the chief audit executive (CAE) to have appropriate certifications and qualifications or demonstrated high-level experience

Professional Designations

Primary Certifications

As the main global professional body covering internal auditors, The IIA offers the Certified Internal Auditor (CIA) professional designation.

> **Key Features of a Certified Internal Auditor**
>
> The IIA recognizes that:
>
> - The CIA is the only globally accepted designation for internal auditors, and involves education and experience eligibility requirements.
> - The CIA remains the standard by which individuals demonstrate comprehensive competence and professionalism in the field of internal auditing.
> - Earning a CIA helps to sharpen skills and proficiencies; enhances credibility and respect; increases potential for advancement and earning; and demonstrates understanding and commitment.
> - The CIA process involves candidates taking exams covering three distinct parts, which are offered year-round through computer-based testing at more than 500 locations worldwide.
> - CIAs are required to complete and certify each year the required continuing education hours.

There are also two other global professional bodies supporting the main sub-disciplines for internal auditors: information technology (IT) and anti-fraud. These are, respectively, ISACA and the Association of Certified Fraud Examiners (ACFE). The primary certifications of each of these professional bodies are:

- Certified Information Systems Auditor (CISA) – ISACA
- Certified Fraud Examiner (CFE) – ACFE

Each professional body has explicit continuing professional education requirements for certification holders requiring validation each year. Given the multidisciplinary nature of internal auditors (see chapters 2 and 3), there are many accounting and other professional bodies that provide thought leadership and support.

The Value of Professional Certifications and Ongoing Professional Training

The CBOK 2015 global internal audit practitioner survey found that time, focus, and discipline required to achieve an internal audit certification can be a big help when it comes to the skills needed for the profession.[2]

Notably:

- Those with an IIA certification of any type assess themselves as having a higher level of competency—across all competency areas—than those with no certification of any type.
- Competencies with the greatest rating elevation among those with an internal audit certification include the IPPF (rated 28% higher) and the technical expertise competencies of internal audit management and ethics (rated 13% and 16% higher respectively).

• Having a certification makes a difference at all age levels. Practitioners in their 30s and 40s show the same 11% to 12% jump in ratings as the practitioners in their 20s. The rating elevation continues for respondents who are over the age of 50, albeit at a lower level.

The CBOK study also reported that when investing in training for employees, organizations want to see that their efforts bring results. Self-assessment ratings increase as training hours increase, peaking at 60 to 69 hours of training per year. Self-assessment ratings for this group are 21% higher than for those without annual training. The ratings dip down somewhat after 70 hours of training.

Professional Activities

Features of a Profession

There are five common features of a profession that create the SPACE in which it operates—status, power, autonomy, capability, and ethics. **Exhibit 1-2** summarizes these features using the SPACE acronym and reflects how these features apply to the internal audit profession.

Exhibit 1-2: Common SPACE Features of a Profession

Feature	Description	How Applied to Auditors
Status	Enjoys high esteem in society given that the value and professional expertise of the work is crucial to society as a whole, both individuals and companies	Governments and regulators recognize the internal audit profession through laws, regulations, and policy.
Power	Draws from its prestigious societal position to control its membership, champion its advocacy agenda, and generate esprit de corps among its membership	Professional bodies (e.g., IIA, ISACA, ACFE) deliver wide-ranging services and advocacy for their members.
Autonomy	Controls their own affairs and are free to exercise professional judgment, with a professional body to oversee professional entry, standards, and compliance	Professional bodies have clear entry requirements, standards, and compliance obligations.
Capability	Delivers high standards of professional and intellectual excellence through specific technical and professional requirements and ongoing education	Certified auditors are required to maintain and report continuing professional development.
Ethics	Maintains ethical standards of behavior designed to protect their clients and drives practices and conduct that reflect a higher duty	Professional bodies for internal auditors require compliance with their codes of ethics.

Note: Author's creation based on consolidation of research.

Internal Audit Value Proposition

The three core elements of the internal audit value proposition are assurance, insight, and objectivity, which are outlined in **exhibit 1-3**.

Exhibit 1-3: The Value Proposition of Internal Auditing

The value proposition of internal auditing is based on three core elements of value delivered by internal audit to an organization:

Assurance = Governance, Risk, and Control

Internal audit provides assurance on the organization's governance, risk management, and control processes to help the organization achieve its strategic, operational, financial, and compliance objectives.

Insight = Catalyst, Analyses, and Assessments

Internal audit is a catalyst for improving an organization's effectiveness and efficiency by providing insight and recommendations based on analyses and assessments of data and business process.

Objectivity = Integrity, Accountability, and Independence

With commitment to integrity and accountability, internal audit provides value to governing bodies and senior management as an objective source of independent advice.

Governing bodies and senior management rely on internal audit for objective assurance and insight on the effectiveness and efficiency of governance, risk management, and internal control processes.

Source: Supplemental Guidance: Value Proposition of Internal Auditing and the Internal Audit Capability Model (2012).

The Practical Meaning of Assurance

For internal auditors, "assurance" is not just a matter of telling management verbally that "things are okay." It is, in essence, the conclusion of a meaningful and systematic evaluation of credible information to deliver a well-informed level of comfort over the organization's governance, risk management, and control arrangements (or elements of these arrangements). Assurance could be provided internally within the organization by operational managers and/or their staff, or by internal auditors. Where business processes are outsourced to a third-party contractor, there may also be assurance reporting requirements.

For instance, to provide assurance over an organization's workplace health and safety arrangements, an internal auditor might consider credible information on its purpose (e.g., legislation; policies; procedures), capability (e.g., results of staff awareness surveys; risk register; experts in key oversight and influencing roles), commitment (tone at the top; meaningful engagement of worksite health and safety committees; availability of trained personnel; trends in key performance indicators; interviews), and monitoring and learning (e.g., inspections; management reporting of lost time injuries, near misses, and other common key performance indicators; induction arrangements; online training modules). [This is a condensed example.]

The technical definition of assurance is reflected in exhibit 1-3.

International Professional Practices Framework (IPPF)

Conceptual Framework

The IPPF is described in its glossary as "The conceptual framework that organizes the authoritative guidance promulgated by The IIA. Authoritative guidance is composed of two categories—(1) mandatory and (2) recommended."[3] The IPPF is explored in more detail in chapter 8.

Internal Audit Activity

The internal audit activity is described in the IPPF glossary as "A department, division, team of consultants, or other practitioner(s) that provides independent, objective assurance and consulting services designed to add value and improve an organization's operations. The internal audit activity helps an organization accomplish its objectives by bringing a systematic, disciplined approach to evaluate and improve the effectiveness of governance, risk management and control processes."

Vision and Mission of Internal Audit

Defining the *vision* of the internal audit activity helps to shape the preferred future state of the activity. The vision is usually developed in consultation with the audit committee, internal audit staff, and other key stakeholders to provide a clear and succinct description of what the activity will be once the CAE successfully implements the strategies to achieve the aspiration. The vision should complement organizational strategies and values, and align with the mission of internal audit.

Contemporary internal audit charters are increasingly incorporating the *mission* of internal audit defined from the IPPF (see chapter 8), which is "To enhance and protect organizational value by providing risk-based and objective assurance, advice, and insight." New auditors should embrace internal audit's vision and mission when planning, designing, and conducting their work.

Meaning of Stakeholder

The persons, groups, or organizations that can affect, or be affected by, the internal audit activity are collectively called stakeholders. The most critical stakeholders are typically the board, audit committee, CEO, and external auditors. Operational staff and managers are the primary stakeholders with whom internal auditors have dealings throughout their fieldwork.

Note: Author's creation based on consolidation of research undertaken by The IIA's Public Sector Committee.[4]

Assurance and Consulting Services

Assurance services are described in the IPPF glossary as "An objective examination of evidence for the purposes of providing an independent assessment on governance, risk management, and control processes for the organization. Examples may include financial, performance, compliance, system security, and due diligence engagements."

Consulting services are described in the IPPF glossary as "Advisory and related client service activities, the nature and scope of which are agreed with the client, are intended to add value and improve an organization's governance, risk management, and control processes without the internal auditor assuming management responsibility. Examples include counsel, advice, facilitation, and training."

> **Example of the Differences Between Assurance and Consulting Services**
>
> Global data protection regulations are one of the heightened risk areas according to a 2018 IIA Global Perspectives and Insights report.[5] The report reflects on the increased regulation over the privacy of data and highlights a series of serious data privacy breaches (in one case, impacting 711 million individuals worldwide) and the significant fines and other sanctions that organizations could face. Given the heightened data privacy risks due to global connectivity, the CAE could ask an internal auditor (under the supervision and direction of their team leader) to:
>
> - Assess the organization's overarching privacy regime initially, in collaboration with business management (consulting services); and
> - Develop an ongoing internal audit assurance program to make sure the business has the right processes in order to continue complying with privacy requirements (assurance services).

Definition of Internal Auditing

The *definition of internal auditing* as described in the IPPF (see chapter 8) is as follows, "Internal auditing is an independent, objective assurance and consulting activity designed to add value and improve an organization's operations. It helps an organization accomplish its objectives by bringing a systematic, disciplined approach to evaluate and improve the effectiveness of risk management, control, and governance processes."

The difference between assurance and consulting services is illustrated in the prior example. Other elements of the definition are defined below.

Element	IPPF Glossary Definition
Independence	"The freedom from conditions that threaten the ability of the internal audit activity to carry out internal audit responsibilities in an unbiased manner."
Objectivity	"An unbiased mental attitude that allows internal auditors to perform engagements in such a manner that they believe in their work product and that no quality compromises are made. Objectivity requires that internal auditors do not subordinate their judgment on audit matters to others."
Add Value	"The internal audit activity adds value to the organization (and its stakeholders) when it provides objective and relevant assurance, and contributes to the effectiveness and efficiency of governance, risk management and control processes."
Source: International Professional Practices Framework.	

Exhibit 1-4: The Four-E's – Providing the Platform for Adding Value

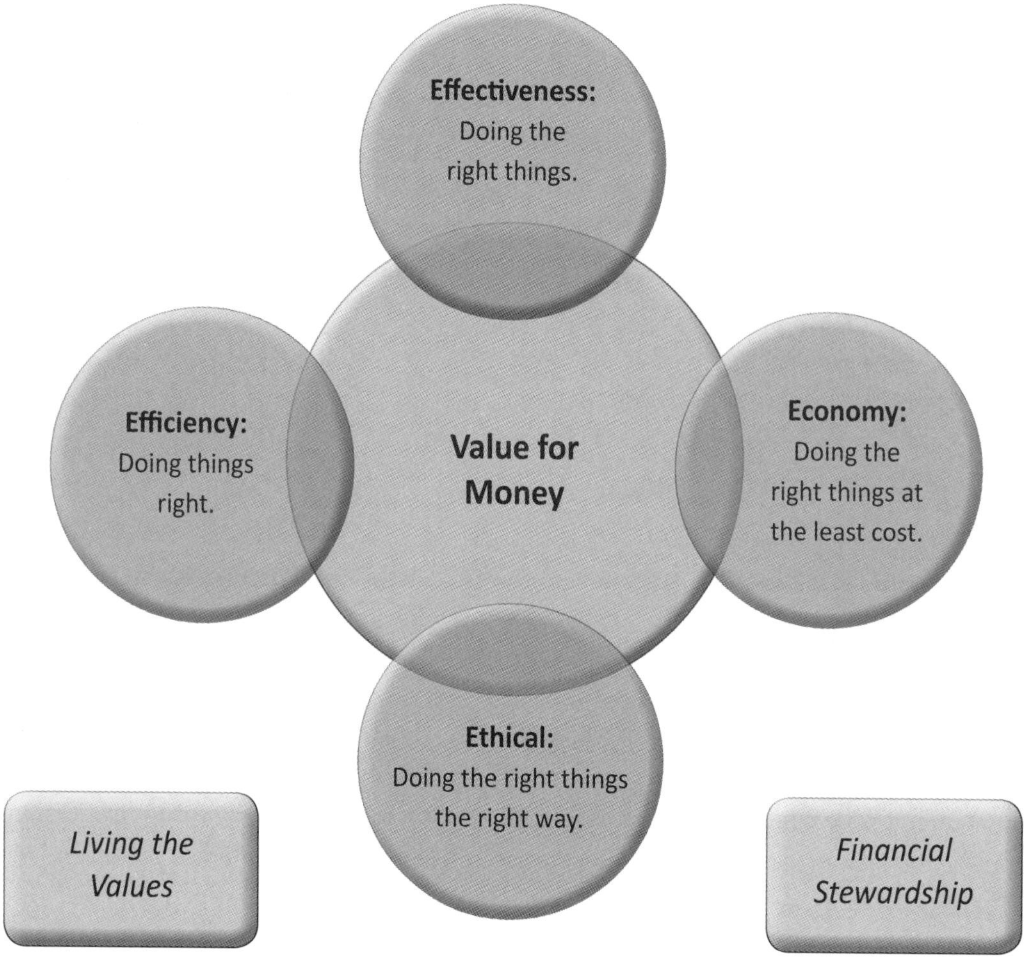

Effectiveness:
Doing the right things.

Value for Money

Efficiency:
Doing things right.

Economy:
Doing the right things at the least cost.

Ethical:
Doing the right things the right way.

Living the Values

Financial Stewardship

Note: Author's creation based on consolidation of research.

In adding value and demonstrating business acumen, it is important for auditors to understand the concepts of efficiency, effectiveness, economy, and ethical—the "Four E's." This is illustrated in **exhibit 1-4** and expanded upon in exhibit 12-3.

The Broader Context

Stakeholder Relationship Management

The success in conducting internal audits is highly dependent on the support and influence of key stakeholders, with some stakeholders having greater influence than others. A CBOK 2015 stakeholder study identified two primary areas of focus for internal auditors in effectively dealing with stakeholders[6]:

- Become masters in knowing the mission, strategy, objectives, and risks of your business.
- Help stakeholders recognize that you understand the business, framing your communication with them within the context of strategy and objectives.

Perspectives on Professionalism

Ronnie and Maria were on the trip of a lifetime. They had flown into Ontario, Canada, and were about to spend a few days at the majestic Niagara Falls, which is often described as one of the natural wonders of the world. They caught glimpses of Horseshoe Falls from their 19th floor balcony, and felt quite exhilarated after an energizing experience sailing under the waterfalls on the Maid of the Mist boat tour.

Ronnie and Maria had one more treat to tick off their bucket list. They had booked a helicopter flight. The professional pilot, Hal, took them up into the sky above the turbulent rapids and cascading waterfalls where they saw the Whirlpool Rapids, America Falls, Bridal Veil Falls, and the Horseshoe Falls. Hal provided his expert commentary as they flew over the nearby wine country, rugged landscape, and historic sites.

Ronnie and Maria discovered that Hal had undertaken extensive training to become a commercial pilot, and had worked for a major international airline for nearly 30 years. He was still required to complete 40 hours of continued professional development each year, needed to maintaining minimum flying hours to keep his pilot's license, and had to abide by a strict code of ethics. They were in awe of Hal's experience as a professional pilot! Ronnie remarked that seeing the waterfalls from above provided a much clearer perspective than he could have ever imagined.

Internal auditing is also a recognized profession requiring special knowledge, skills, attributes, and adherence to a code of ethics. Internal auditors' mandate is very broad, requiring them to cover governance, risk, control, and compliance arrangements over all significant activities and operations across an organization. In some cases, internal auditing is a little like being the professional pilot in the helicopter, as it provides a much clearer perspective of the business than anyone could imagine.

What Practitioners Love About Internal Audit

"Every day you can help to improve your organization. And with your insight and ideas, you get access to the number 1 decision-makers in your organization."			
CAE	Baby Boomer	Over 20 years' auditing experience	Economics

Tips for New Auditors

- Do not see internal auditing as a temporary solution to your employment needs while you search for that dream job. Embrace internal auditing as a life changing and strategically positioned opportunity that will open endless windows for you as you develop and grow in the profession.
- Recognize that the perceived importance of internal auditing is still evolving, with reform to mandate internal audit activities from a corporate regulator or similar likely to speed up this evolution and create more opportunities in the profession moving forward.
- Understand the business, its drivers and areas of focus, and what is most important to the leadership and then base your work, advice, and recommendations around that. The goal of the internal audit profession is to support organizations to achieve their objectives.
- Be curious and have an open mind. Actively listen and investigate issues through multiple lenses so you can see things from different perspectives. Seek a mentor to guide you and don't be afraid to ask questions. This is how you learn best.
- Be sure to balance ongoing technical knowledge with relationship-building skills to be effective.

Related Standards

IPPF and ITAF

This book provides information at the end of each chapter on the related standards from The IIA's International Professional Practices Framework (IPPF), which covers the majority of internal audits (sourced from the IPPF). For information systems auditors, the ISACA standards as part of the Information Technology Assurance Framework (ITAF) may be more relevant.

Chapter 2
Pathways into Internal Audit

Internal audit activities are increasingly introducing flexible pathways to entice the best talent so that the internal audit activity is well equipped to enhance and protect organizational value. This chapter discusses a range of contemporary pathways for short-term to longer-term internal audit roles.

Understanding the Basics

Common Types of Audits

The drivers for enhancing and protecting organizational value include internal audit's value proposition and the Four E's. These concepts were introduced in chapter 1 as exhibits 1-3 and 1-4 respectively. The why and how of internal auditing are discussed in parts 2 and 3.

There are varying types of internal audit activities geared to adding value to the business, and all of them require talented people. For instance, common types of audits include:

- *Compliance audits* that ascertain the extent of compliance with policies, procedures, legislation, standards, and good practice, and the related governance, risk management, and control arrangements.
- *Performance improvement audits* that evaluate the efficiency, effectiveness, economy, and ethics of the organization's systems, processes, and resources, and the integrity of information.
- *Consulting and advisory activities* that evaluate and inform on appropriate controls and processes and advise on a range of issues as a consequence of specific requests from the board, audit committee, senior management, and other stakeholders.

These types of audits can then be further divided into specialist audit engagement types covering areas such as health, safety, and the environment.

Being Interviewed for an Auditing Role

Most options for securing an internal audit role involve the standard processes for applying for positions, including the preparation of curriculum vitae (CV). The position objectives and specific requirements are usually outlined in the position advertisement. Preparing a well-developed CV is crucial to getting an interview, which then allows you to elaborate on your credentials for the role.

If you are granted an interview, it is also extremely important to prepare diligently beforehand. This might include anticipating the type of questions (as a minimum) or arranging a mock interview with a friend or relative. Those conducting interviews will usually assess whether an applicant is the right person for the job by asking situational, motivational, and/or behavioral questions.

Situational Questions	Motivational Questions	Behavioral Questions
A situation is presented and the applicant is asked to talk through potential solutions so the interviewer can assess how the applicant would tackle possible workplace issues and challenges.	The interviewer will aim to unearth the applicant's drive, enthusiasm, and engagement to assess whether the values of the applicant and the organization are in reasonable alignment.	Given that past behavior is usually a good predictor of future behavior, the interviewer will seek to understand how the applicant has handled different prior experiences and challenges.

Core Competencies for Auditors

The CBOK 2015 global internal audit practitioner survey reflected upon the 10 core competencies for internal auditors, which are[1]:

1. Improvement and Innovation
2. Internal Audit Delivery
3. Communication
4. Persuasion and Collaboration
5. Critical Thinking
6. IPPF
7. Governance, Risk, and Control
8. Business Acumen
9. Internal Audit Management
10. Professional Ethics

The Meaning of 10 Core Competencies

The IIA Global Internal Audit Competency Framework (see adjoining diagram) defines 10 competencies needed to meet the requirements of the International Professional Practices Framework (IPPF) for the success of the internal audit profession.[2] The framework has been crafted to reflect the following elements:

Source: Global Internal Audit Competency Framework.

- To provide an effective service, internal auditors need to operate according to high ethical standards and coordinate the resources and activities of the internal audit activity. Professional ethics and internal audit management provide a firm foundation for the delivery of internal audit.
- The principal points of focus of an internal auditor's expertise are the IPPF; governance, risk, and control; and business acumen. The IPPF is the primary source of professional standards for internal audit that The IIA provides to all internal auditors around the world.
- Additionally, internal auditors require technical expertise in governance, risk, and control to inform their work and help organizations accomplish their objectives. Business acumen in the form of understanding the client organization, its culture, the way it works, the sector in which it operates, and the local and global factors that act upon it is another essential prerequisite that enables internal auditors to provide effective assurance and advisory services and so add value to the organization.
- Internal auditors need to be competent in communication, persuasion and collaboration, and critical thinking in order to deliver internal audit engagements and drive improvement and innovation in an organization.

Flexible Pathways

There are many pathways for moving into an internal audit role. Individuals can be selected at all levels, from CAE through to an auditor, and involve people across different generations, from baby boomers to millennials (and, soon, Generation Z). Examples of common pathways include:

- From a chartered accounting firm
- From an operational role
- Through a graduate program
- From external auditing
- Formerly the company chief financial officer (CFO)
- From a business role (was studying part-time)
- Formerly an information and communications technology (ICT) specialist

Moves into an internal audit role can be longer-term (i.e., ongoing or permanent) where internal auditing becomes a career path, through to shorter terms of a few years or several months. The more common pathways are illustrated in **exhibit 2-1** and explained in the next few paragraphs.

Exhibit 2-1: Options for Moving into an Internal Audit Role

Recruitment
- Recruitment from outside the organization
- Internal promotions
- Internal transfers

Guest Auditor Programs
- Specific audits
- Longer-term temporary assignments

Graduate Program
- Rotation through internal audit
- Permanent appointment

Recruitment

Recruitment from Outside the Organization

There may be occasions when auditors need to be recruited or where specialized skillsets are required, such as ICT experts, or the myriad specializations, like safety auditors, lawyers, teachers, detectives, engineers, or bankers (see further information on the capabilities of internal auditors in chapter 3). The appointments are usually made through a merit-based recruitment process and are ongoing (permanent) in nature. In some cases, a recruitment agent might be used. The appointments could also be made on a longer-term contract basis (for, say, 12 months to five years) while the homegrown talent has the opportunity to develop through knowledge transfer and experience.

Internal Promotions

An applicant within the organization or within the internal audit activity with the requisite skills for the role could apply for an advertised position and be successful in securing a promotion through merit-based selection. They will typically have a track record within the organization, which can be less risky than appointing someone unknown from outside the organization.

Internal Transfers

Appointments to an auditing role can be made at any level. Senior management might do this as part of their longer-term succession planning and/or employee development arrangements, recognizing the value of a practical working knowledge of governance, risk, and control.

In some cases, senior management could appoint an experienced business manager to a CAE role and surround them with experienced auditors, with the aim of providing business acumen to drive closer alignment between the work of internal audit and the needs of the business.

Guest Auditor Programs

What Are Guest Auditors?

Guest auditors may be brought into the internal audit activity for a defined period of time before they return to their normal role. This provides a unique experiential training and development opportunity.

Guest auditors benefit from the insights they gain with respect to corporate governance, risk management, and internal control; skills that they will need as they move into future senior leadership positions. They are also influenced to become ambassadors for internal audit.

Specific Audits

There will be times when it is beneficial to draw guest auditors into specific audits where their technical skills are needed. The aim is to deliver subject matter experts from technical business areas to the internal audit activity to bring expertise to particular audit engagements. For example, someone with a nursing background would be of great value for conducting an audit of medicines in a health-care setting; a mining company could use engineers to great effect. These programs run for a relatively short duration and allow guest auditors to assess specific components of audits, rather than experience the whole audit process.

Longer-Term Temporary Assignments

There will be occasions where an internal audit capability assessment identifies a need to leverage the expertise of business staff. This program facilitates assigning operational staff from business areas to the internal audit activity for defined periods (usually several weeks or months). It helps to drive improvement strategies through technical advice on audit planning, fieldwork, and reporting.

Graduate Program

Rotation Through Internal Audit

Many organizations have graduate recruitment programs where university graduates are recruited to the organization. The organization then invests in their transition from university to business through structured training over 12 to 24 months, including three- to six-month rotations to gain experience in different parts of the business.

A rotation through an internal audit activity has benefits for the graduate because it introduces them to governance, risk, and control fundamentals through experiential learning and, ultimately, helps to shape their career. It also delivers practical insights on auditing and a holistic appreciation of the core activities of the organization. Graduates can come from many different disciplines, not just the traditional backgrounds of finance and accounting (see exhibit 3-1).

Permanent Appointment

It is common practice for CAEs to establish a career path through varying levels across the organizational structure (the various roles are discussed in chapter 4). Participants in the organization's graduate recruitment program provide a road-tested feeder group. When graduates have had a successful rotation through the internal audit activity, they will often be targeted for formal permanent appointment to an auditing role. The graduates might use this as a steppingstone into other roles within the business, or they might decide to make internal auditing their career.

The Broader Context

Building Your Personal Brand – Know What You Stand For

If there are apolitical community issues that you stand for that are not in conflict with those of your organization's leadership and values, you can leverage those interests in a positive way to influence the behavior of others. In doing so, you will be recognized for your efforts and can start building a multidimensional personal brand.

Leaders of our profession have used their roles to great effect for a range of important causes. For instance:

- A former global chairman of The IIA spoke with passion about diversity. The message resonated, respect for him grew, and progress was achieved.
- An audit committee chairman spoke fervently about the need to close the gap between indigenous and non-indigenous health, well-being, and employment. The message resonated. He has had an enduring impact on many decision-makers who also now champion the issue and promote practical solutions.
- A senior manager connected with an auditor and built a powerful professional working relationship when he discovered they shared a common interest—they were both White Ribbon Ambassadors (recognizing the need to end violence, abuse, and inequality faced by women). The public profile of the auditor was boosted through joint events and media with the senior manager. This, in turn, helped to build a stronger professional profile among internal audit's stakeholders.

Perspectives on Pathways

Ron and his brothers, Rob and John, had arranged a three-day camping trip for their eight sons, aged 15 through 18. The annual trips were great for parental bonding at an age when the boys were vulnerable to other influences; the cousins had forged an inseparable lifelong friendship. The boys arranged the menu and supplies, and collaborated on an itinerary with the objective of safe, fun adventures. It was a dry camp (no alcohol) and this year they had traveled to Abercrombie Caves in Australia's Southern Highlands.

They set up camp near a river and enjoyed a refreshing swim, canoeing, football, and a barbecue dinner with good humor and conversation. They were looking forward to a caving adventure the next morning.

The group met the ranger at the opening of the cave and he provided them with a safety briefing. He mentioned that they would be walking along narrow tracks, cross several slippery streams, and, in some places, would have to crawl through narrow spaces to get into different cave structures. The boys were excited, whereas the three fathers were apprehensive given the strenuous activity, unknown terrain, and tight spaces—all in the dark. A couple of the fathers, Ron and John, were big men, over six foot four and weighing around 280 pounds.

After four hours of underground fun, they finally made their way out of the cave system and into the open rainforest. Ron was exhausted as he had triumphantly struggled through narrow claustrophobic rock corridors where he could barely fit. Ron wondered how John could be so fresh and clean as he was slightly bigger. John laughed, explaining that the ranger allowed him to use a parallel track that took him through bigger caves that rejoined the smaller caves, and nobody had noticed in the darkness that John had taken a different path.

Similarly, there are many different pathways that can lead people into an internal audit activity. For many years, an accounting pathway provided a natural route, but that has changed as internal auditors in the twenty-first century are expected to have a blend of multidisciplinary skillsets.

What Practitioners Love About Internal Audit

"Every day is a new adventure that is always filled with changes in people, processes, and technology."			
CAE	Generation X	Over 20 years' auditing experience	Accounting

Tips for New Auditors

- Internal audit is management's friend, and there should be a collaborative partnership between internal audit and management. The internal auditor works for the same organization, so we all have an interest in seeing the organization do well.
- Dare to try and dare to learn! When you are willing to learn and explore, you will find yourself gaining a lot more from both the technical and nontechnical sides of internal auditing.
- Internal auditing is a really great foundation for many future careers, and having good knowledge of using internal controls effectively and knowing how to spot red flags is invaluable.
- Even if you do not stay in internal auditing, the time you spend exposed to reviewing processes, understanding controls, mitigating risks, and understanding how the business operates is both worthwhile and useful in your future career.
- Internal auditing can be used as a stepping-stone into business areas you wish to pursue. There is a good chance the breadth of skills you acquire as an internal auditor will open doors into a business management role down the road.

Related Standards

Standard 1200 – Proficiency and Due Professional Care
Engagements must be performed with proficiency and due professional care.

Standard 1230 – Continuing Professional Development
Internal auditors must enhance their knowledge, skills, and other competencies through continuing professional development.

Chapter 3
Capabilities of Internal Auditors

Contemporary internal audit teams are typically multidisciplinary. This facilitates the value and credibility of assurance, advice, and insight they provide to stakeholders. This chapter introduces the core principles for the professional practice of internal auditing and how they are applied in practice.

Understanding the Basics

Core Principles for the Professional Practice of Internal Auditing

One of the capabilities that the new auditor needs to develop quickly is a technical and practical knowledge of the International Professional Practices Framework (IPPF), which is discussed in more detail in chapter 8. The core principles present a strong basis for the standards and other parts of the IPPF in guiding and shaping the internal audit profession; they provide guidance on how internal auditors can be effective.

IPPF Definition of Core Principles for the Professional Practice of Internal Auditing

The Core Principles for the Professional Practice of Internal Auditing are the foundation for the International Professional Practices Framework and support internal audit effectiveness.

Source: International Professional Practices Framework.

The 10 core principles are:

- Demonstrates integrity
- Demonstrates competence and due professional care
- Is objective and free from undue influence (independent)
- Aligns with the strategies, objectives, and risks of the organization
- Is appropriately positioned and adequately resourced
- Demonstrates quality and continuous improvement
- Communicates effectively
- Provides risk-based assurance
- Is insightful, proactive, and future-focused
- Promotes organizational improvement

In considering their personal professional development needs, auditors are encouraged to self-assess against the core principles to identify gaps in their capability where they could benefit from specific training and development over the ensuing six to 12 months. These opportunities can then be discussed with the team leader, perhaps as part of the performance evaluation process discussed in chapter 19.

Depending on an auditor's role and responsibility (see chapter 4), the capabilities typically expected within the internal audit activity span services, people management, professional practices, performance management, organizational relationships and culture, and governance.

Multidisciplinary Auditing Teams

There was a time when internal audit teams were made up solely or substantially by professionals with an accounting qualification. Times have changed. These days, internal audit teams have multidisciplinary skillsets, as illustrated in **exhibit 3-1**. Where multidisciplinary skillsets are established, it is important for new auditors to be open to the opportunities for knowledge transfer on the industry and auditing skills from these specialists.

Exhibit 3-1: Example of an Audit Team Discussing Their Base Qualifications

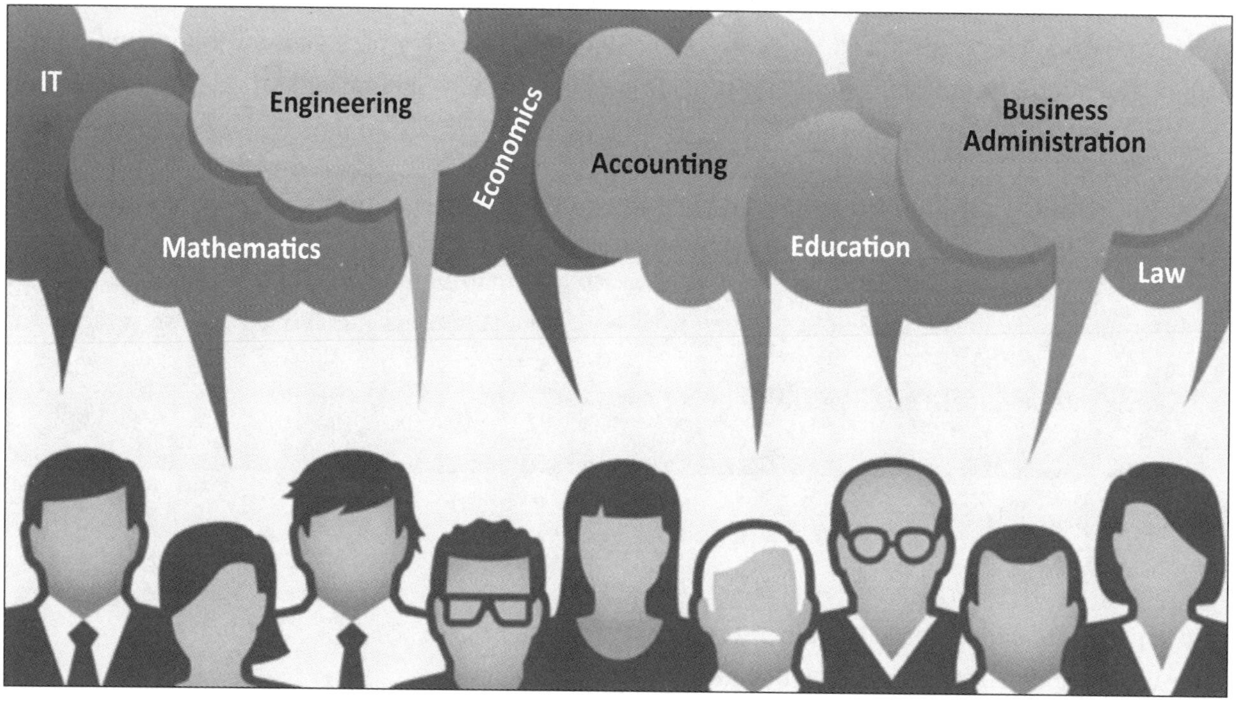

The change in the mix of base qualifications of auditors recognizes the expansion of the role and responsibilities of the internal audit activity over the past 10 to 20 years, coupled with the increasing expectations of key stakeholders. **Exhibit 3-2** provides examples of multidisciplinary skillsets commonly incorporated into contemporary internal audit teams, the drivers for recruiting them, and the outcomes that they have the potential to deliver. The establishment of the team composition and capability will be determined based on the vision and strategies of the internal audit activity.

Exhibit 3-2: Examples of Multidisciplinary Skillsets for an Internal Audit Activity

Specialization	Type of Entity/Role	Insightful, Proactive, and Future-Focused Outcomes
Common Specialist Areas		
Accountants	All	See exhibit 3-3.
Information, communication, and technology (ICT) specialists	All	Deliver constructive insights on the organization's digital strategies and the emergence of social media and cyber risks.
Areas Unique to Some Industries (Examples)		
Safety auditors	Health-care services and industrial-like railways, mining, and energy companies	Shape a safety culture to avoid injury and death through poor workplace practices.
Lawyers	Proportion of a company's spend on contractors is increasing where they have significant levels of third-party suppliers and, therefore, many contracts.	Deliver insights on whether the rights and obligations of the respective parties are fulfilled in contractual arrangements and that management has established appropriate internal mechanisms to monitor.
Teachers (adult education)	Public sector entities that are at significant risk of fraud and corruption	Champion proactive fraud and corruption prevention learning activities so that such events are avoided rather than just responded to.
Former police officers/detectives	Undertake investigations of wrongdoing where the volume of allegations requires expertise and experience.	Protect workplace morale and productivity by delivering timely and thorough investigations of alleged wrongdoing, recognizing that, typically, half of the allegations are unsubstantiated but impact adversely on employee engagement.
Business process engineers	Where companies expect internal auditors to have an improvement focus	Drive efficiency, effectiveness, economy, and ethics improvements rather than delivering assurance only.

Extending Financial Audit Coverage from Assurance to Insights

CAEs need accounting and finance (and other) people who can think outside the box to provide foresight. Accounting and finance specialists appointed to auditing roles need to embrace the full ambit of their capabilities to meet contemporary expectations of stakeholders. **Exhibit 3-3** contains examples that illustrate the transition of financial auditors from delivering assurance-based outcomes to delivering insightful, proactive, and future-focused outcomes.

Exhibit 3-3: Examples of Financial Audits that Deliver Different Outcomes

Traditional Assurance-Based Audits	Insightful, Proactive, and Future-Focused Outcomes
Revenue and expenditure cycles	Accounts payable audit would extend analysis into metrics, like the average processing costs, in order to present benchmarking as part of the audit report.
Procurement and contract audits	Audits of significant contracts would extend the analysis onto the supply chain and the periodic (at least annual) review of the contractor's continued reputation, service quality, and creditworthiness.
Major contracts after the contract execution	Potentially an independent observer on the selection panel for major contracts
Reasonableness of delegations and segregation of duties	For business efficiency, would balance the authorization controls (e.g., delegations and segregation) against potential processing bottlenecks
Suspense account reconciliations and assessment of un-cleared items	For transactions placed into suspense accounts, would assess the root cause and look for processing efficiencies
Assessing and management of "make good" provisions of leases	For negotiation of new leases, would champion new ways of working to optimize the use and cost of workspace
Occasional advice on accounting transactions	Would be expected to deliver strategic accounting advice
Opportunities for Nonfinancial Areas	**Insightful, Proactive, and Future-Focused Outcomes**
Verifying cash holdings at companies (other than banks) that handle significant volumes of cash	Draws on lessons learned from the financial services sector (recognizing that enhanced bank security has driven robbers to softer targets) to help shape a secure, safe, and efficient cash-handling culture that embraces the effective control practices of banks
Evaluating the environmental compliance and management system	Draws on global research to help shape a culture of sustainability that minimizes the risk of harm to the environment as a result of waste, noise, and harmful manufacturing processes

Auditors with an accounting and/or finance specialization also need to extend their skills beyond the norm to other areas. For example:

- Apply a range of business ratios in their audit work from current and liquid ratios and capital adequacy to more complex measures and indicators of company health.
- Promote the importance of risk management informing the company's strategic planning and ultimately the budget-setting process (the integration is still immature in most organizations).
- Assess, equally, financial and nonfinancial information (e.g., key performance indicators [KPIs]).

Meaning of Key Performance Indicators

KPIs are performance measures that evaluate the success of an organization against its business objectives, and are often applied to specific activities that an organization undertakes. KPIs for internal auditors are discussed in chapter 19.

Note: Author's creation based on research.

In some cases, nonfinancial KPIs are managed in specialist divisions outside finance. Auditors with accounting and finance skills should have the discipline and ability to ensure the controls are appropriate, from clarity of "counting rules" to calculations, systems, validation, and publishing protocols. For instance:

- A significant KPI for a rail entity is running on time.
- For recruitment activities, there are KPIs on areas such as time to recruit, candidate care, and attracting applicants from outside the entity.
- For work health and safety, there are measures on things like lost time injury frequency rates.
- Customer complaints can be an indicator of systemic issues.
- Staff engagement survey results can reflect cultural trends.
- Waiting times at hospital emergency rooms are politically sensitive.

Finding a Unique Niche

Successful internal auditors often find a unique niche that helps them to remain relevant and develop highly prized and transferable skills. An example follows in **exhibit 3-4**.

Exhibit 3-4: Insights for a New Auditor from a Millennial

Focus on filling the capability gaps within the internal audit activity, and aim to develop your unique skills in that area. Usually, it is in an area like data analytics where there seems to be an ongoing gap. These skills are transferable across all other industries as well.

The Broader Context

Maintaining Capability

While most of the core principles have underpinned the work of internal audit for many years, the ninth and tenth core principles challenge the status quo. **Exhibit 3-5** throws out challenges for new auditors in applying these core principles in practice.

Exhibit 3-5: Applying Core Principles 8 and 9 in Practice

Core Principles	Examples of How a New Auditor Can Embrace the Opportunity
Is insightful, proactive, and future-focused	Try to anticipate future business needs that are aligned to the organization's strategic direction; don't just look backwards at the controls that have been operating (which is the more traditional fieldwork approach). Understand what might be coming over the horizon by embracing a proactive approach such as global research, benchmarking, and trend analysis.
Promotes organizational improvement	Don't just focus on downside risks (i.e., determining whether controls are operating in practice); strive to achieve a balance with upside risks (i.e., identifying opportunities to improve the business and how it operates). Develop a mindset that shifts from purely "strengthening controls" to optimizing controls; this could well result in fewer controls, but ones that are more meaningful, cost-effective, and powerful.

Note: The concepts of risk-based auditing and internal controls are discussed in chapters 5, 6, and 7.

Building Trust

Auditors who are insightful, proactive, future-focused, and promote organizational improvement tend to offer strategic solutions to senior management and other stakeholders. In doing so, they position themselves as trusted advisors. Delivering meaningful advice is one part of the equation; the other part is building trust.

In an article in *Internal Auditor* magazine, Mike Jacka reflected on the power of internal auditors being seen as trusted advisors, commenting that, "To succeed as advisors, we need to understand what truly inspires confidence from stakeholders."[1] He went on to say, "Trust comes from actions, not words. It is what others see us do, what others discover we have done, and what others believe we will do. It comes from something as simple as meeting our agreed deadlines, and from something as complicated as having the integrity to report what is, rather than what everyone wants to hear. It represents the accumulation of activities that show we either back what we say or turn our backs on our promises, our clients, and ourselves."

Perspectives on Capability

Shiva was up in a hot air balloon above a winery with a dozen work colleagues celebrating a successful year. It was a peaceful experience as they floated across the sky on a sunny, cool, and calm day. The views were spectacular. After 20 minutes, the hot air balloon hit an air pocket and then dramatically dropped about 30 feet in a matter of seconds. It was an alarming experience, and the team was grateful to have a calm, experienced, and capable pilot.

The nervous reaction prompted a flood of stories about their taxi drivers en route to the winery, including overcharging, impersonal service, refusal to use the air-conditioner, dangerous driving, and getting lost. After more stories, Shiva mentioned that his driver was speeding out of town and had driven through two sets of red traffic lights. Then, when the driver was almost through a third set of red traffic lights, he screeched to a halt and had to reverse back to the line-marking as he was in the crossroad lane. When the lights changed to green, the driver had hit the accelerator hard only to realize the taxi was still in reverse!

The laughter subsided as the group spoke more seriously about the overall unacceptable level of customer service they had experienced, largely due to the poor attitude and lack of capability of their taxi drivers. When the team moved on to discussing the merits of disruptor competitors like Uber, the recent substantial loss of the taxi industry's market share was unsurprising.

Just as there are different modes of transportation available, there are different ways the internal audit activity can be delivered. If senior management is not satisfied with the in-house capability of the internal auditors, they might consider recruiting better credentialed and capable talent or use service provider firms. The value of internal auditing is derived from the overall capability of the internal auditors, and they need to be attuned, balanced, and credible.

What Practitioners Love About Internal Audit

"The work is very diverse and project driven. It is great if you are the type of person who enjoys understanding the whole, rather than just a narrow part, of a business and are prepared to stretch and challenge yourself to learn. It is a great career for those who are truly interested in continuous learning and do not want to do the same thing month-in and month-out."			
CAE	Generation X	10 to 20 years' auditing experience	Economics

Tips for New Auditors

- The key to being a successful internal auditor is to remain relevant; if you are not relevant, then you are no longer needed. Stronger collaboration with stakeholders requires highly capable communicators. If you're not building effective communication competencies (oral, listening, body language, written), you're probably falling behind.

- After relationship building and integrity, technical skills are very important. The various audit and risk management professional bodies provide many opportunities for learning and certification. Jump in and take full advantage of them; do not take the position that "I've got xyz qualification so I can now stop learning." Technology will provide increasing opportunities to facilitate higher-quality audits.

- Find the time (and headspace) to consider external insights through articles, webinars, and networking. This is critical for keeping your perspective open and staying fresh in the role. Make the time to "think outside your organization" and you will be a better auditor because of it.

- Having a mentor—be it within your career or personal—will be so helpful, as sometimes you need that one person to be there to listen, guide, and advise. And engage with one as early as possible.

- Don't stay in the same internal audit job, or as an internal auditor in the same organization, for a long time; move around and get experience. That way you will round out your experience and boost your capability, rather than having just one point of reference. Join The IIA and get involved in the internal audit profession.

Related Standards

Standard 1200 – Proficiency and Due Professional Care

Engagements must be performed with proficiency and due professional care.

Chapter 4
Roles and Responsibilities

This chapter covers the specific roles and responsibilities of the internal auditor and how success in the role is underpinned by business acumen.

Getting Started

First Steps

The first steps into an internal audit role can seem a bit daunting, but the internal audit profession embraces a systematic and disciplined approach in undertaking its work. It is one of the few roles in an organization that has a suite of information readily available to make the transition as smooth as possible. And communication skills sit at the heart of what internal auditors do, so engagement with the team should be reasonably painless.

The team leader will usually arrange a meet and greet as soon as practical. Because internal auditors often undertake fieldwork offsite, it may be a few days or weeks until the whole team is together.

The top 10 information sources for the new auditor are the internal audit charter, position description, internal audit's organization chart, staff profile, internal audit annual report, internal audit policies and procedures manual, internal audit plan, workpaper file, the IPPF (including the *Standards*), and The IIA's Code of Ethics. A description of each of the information sources follows. (*Note*: If an internal audit activity does not have all of these documents, obtain those that are available.)

Internal Audit Charter

It is essential to understand the internal audit mandate within the organization. The mandate is reflected in the internal audit charter, which sets the boundaries in which the internal audit activity operates. The charter defines the purpose, authority, and responsibility of the internal audit activity and establishes its position within the organization. Importantly, for auditors, it authorizes access to records, personnel, and physical properties and defines the scope of internal audit activities.

Position Description

It is helpful to read and comprehend the position objectives defined in the job description to understand the full range of responsibilities. While the primary role of auditors is to undertake audits, there may also be other position objectives associated with activity-wide tasks. Examples include managing stakeholder relationships, monitoring the follow-up of prior audit recommendations, undertaking the quality assurance and improvement program, monitoring time-management schedules, preparing progress reports on the forward audit plan, updating the audit manual, or helping to develop the forward audit plan.

Internal Audit's Organization Chart

It is helpful to understand where your role as an auditor fits into the broader structure of the internal audit activity and your specified reporting lines to the team leader and ultimately the CAE. Some internal audit activities have specific reporting lines to a team leader; others will have a pool of auditors that could work with any team leader depending on the breadth, depth, and complexity of an audit. You will especially need to tease out very early the performance management arrangements, including goal setting and performance evaluations; that is, who will be assessing your performance and how will they do it (performance management arrangements are covered in chapter 19).

Staff Profile

It is important to understand the background, years of audit experience, and qualifications of all members of the internal audit activity. The staff profile provides this information (where one is prepared).

Internal Audit Annual Report

It is helpful to understand the achievements of the internal audit activity, its value, the top five or 10 reflections of the past year, and its contribution to the strategies and objectives of the organization. Features of the internal audit annual report are described more fully in chapter 19.

Internal Audit Policy and Procedure Manual

Browse the audit manual to understand the policies, procedures, and methodology of the internal audit activity (the CAE is required under Standard 2040 to establish policies and procedures to guide the internal audit activity).

Internal Audit Plan

Obtain a copy of the forward audit plan to get a sense of the type of audits that are scheduled to be completed over the ensuing year or so. There may be areas of audit where you have a special interest or expertise and, if so, it can be worthwhile to highlight this to the CAE and team leader.

Workpaper File

It is worthwhile to scan a workpaper file for a recently completed audit to get a feel for how all parts of the audit come together and how the methodology is applied in practice. You will see the audit engagement plan, status reporting, fieldwork documentation, identification of observations, dealings with management, the audit report, evidence of quality assurance, and audit closeout materials.

> **Meaning of Workpapers**
>
> Workpapers are prepared by internal auditors to document the work performed in the planning, performance, and quality assurance review of audits. The workpapers for an audit engagement are filed together in a workpaper file, and this can be in electronic or hardcopy form. Further details on workpapers are discussed in chapter 13, which covers audit fieldwork and testing.

International Professional Practices Framework

It is important to browse through the IPPF (also known as the Red Book) to get a feel for its content, as professional internal audit activities across the world are required to comply with it. The IPPF is the conceptual framework that organizes the authoritative guidance promulgated by The IIA, and includes the *International Standards for the Professional Practice of Internal Auditing*. The IPPF is covered in more detail in chapter 8.

Code of Ethics

It is essential to read and understand the organization's code of ethics (or code of conduct) and particularly focus on the corporate values. An internal auditor is required to both live the values and champion them throughout the organization. A professional auditor will also be expected to comply with The IIA's Code of Ethics, which is included in the IPPF (see chapter 8). It promotes an ethical culture in the global profession of internal auditing.

Roles and Responsibilities Within the Internal Audit Activity

Chief Audit Executive (CAE)

The CAE is the head of internal audit and is responsible for the overall management of the internal audit activity, including the planning, execution, quality, reporting, and follow-up of all audits. CAEs are responsible for the effective management of the internal audit activity in accordance with the internal audit charter and the mandatory elements of the IPPF. They usually have a dual reporting role—to the audit committee functionally and to the CEO (or delegate) for administration.

Team Leaders

The team leaders lead the internal audit engagement on a day-to-day basis. They allocate and oversee the work assigned from the audit engagement plan and provide direction and support to the auditors as required. They are responsible for the budget, timeliness, quality, and value-add of individual audits. They maintain quality assurance over all stages of the audit with a particular focus on achieving the audit objectives, well-considered fieldwork, and meaningful reporting.

Team leaders may have a variety of titles (e.g., director of auditing, audit director, audit manager, audit supervisor) and there could also be different layers within the organizational structure depending on the size of the internal audit activity. Often, team leaders will also complete distinct segments of the fieldwork. They will keep the CAE apprised of progress on the audit against the audit engagement plan and highlight any significant observations or client engagement difficulties as they arise.

Internal Auditors

Internal auditors complete much of the legwork on audits once the audit engagement plan has been approved. They are usually allocated distinct segments of audit work and then undertake fieldwork in line with the planned audit objectives, scope, approach, and budget. They maintain close contact with the team leader on a regular, often daily, basis to report on the progress on their segment of fieldwork and highlight any potential observations or problems with client engagement. They may be called on to assist in planning the audit and will usually contribute to writing the audit report, particularly for their segment of work. Internal auditors may have different titles depending on their level of seniority, experience, and expertise (e.g., audit staff, audit services contractor).

The Broader Context

A Day in the Life of an Internal Auditor

An auditor's working day is quite varied. The following are common tasks when an audit is underway.

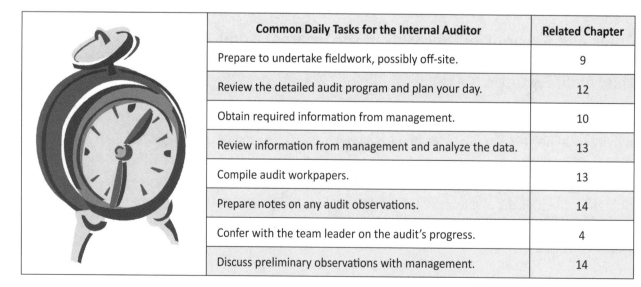

Common Daily Tasks for the Internal Auditor	Related Chapter
Prepare to undertake fieldwork, possibly off-site.	9
Review the detailed audit program and plan your day.	12
Obtain required information from management.	10
Review information from management and analyze the data.	13
Compile audit workpapers.	13
Prepare notes on any audit observations.	14
Confer with the team leader on the audit's progress.	4
Discuss preliminary observations with management.	14

An Auditor's Role Is Underpinned by Business Acumen

The 2015 Global Internal Audit Common Body of Knowledge (CBOK) Stakeholder Study reported "business acumen" as the most-mentioned competency for the internal audit activity for understanding what drives success for the organization and its associated key risks.[1] The key takeaways for new auditors in fulfilling their roles at the level expected are:

- Understand the essentials to the success of your organization—its industry, external environment, chosen strategies and business, and risks related to those strategies and business.
- Spend time with those in your organization who can help you think more like a business leader.
- Address issues from the stakeholders from their point of view, communicating with them using language that they understand.

New auditors can benefit from developmental programs (where they are available in their organization or through their local IIA institute) to develop business acumen, close skill gaps, and gain practical insights into the business and industry.[2] Two programs that provide a different perspective for audit work and fresh insights for the participants are mentoring and an alumni network.

Program	Design Goals	Primary Benefit	Secondary Benefit	Key Features
Mentoring	Achieve the full potential of internal auditors.	Fosters professional relationships where internal auditors have an opportunity to collaborate and share insights with experienced senior managers outside internal audit, or through a mentoring program run by an IIA chapter or institute.	Provides a forum offering constructive and frank advice to support internal auditors' career development.	A cost-effective way that internal auditors can acquire knowledge and skills, build business acumen, and understand how to operate in a challenging environment.
Alumni network (of the organization's former internal auditors)	Alumni are invited to internal audit functions and events to share ideas.	This approach enables new internal auditors to leverage a rich source of ideas, insights, and perspectives former internal auditors have gained in their new roles.	Achieves The IIA's motto "Progress Through Sharing" for professional counterparts.	Provides a basis for staying connected with experienced internal auditors who move into other parts of the business or to other organizations.

Keeping Within the Boundaries

The internal audit activity has a broad mandate to operate in an independent and objective manner. However, CAEs, team leaders, and internal auditors are still obliged to adhere to organizational policies and avoid activities that are not authorized under the internal audit charter and the approved forward audit plan. The consequences of ignoring these boundaries are illustrated in **exhibit 4-1**.

Exhibit 4-1: Cautionary Tale on Internal Audit's Authority to Operate

A CAE was terminated from his organization when he was found to have seriously breached the trust of the position. He had started spying on the governing body, senior executives, and the audit committee by monitoring all of their emails for no proper or authorized purpose. He was found to have breached organizational privacy, technology, and digital surveillance policies; was not undertaking authorized internal audit activities; and was operating outside the approved charter.

Perspectives on Roles

Phil was promoted to a senior management role with the state railways and had a great deal to learn. The state railways had an at-the-front development program requiring every senior manager to spend at least half a day every month in a customer-interfacing role shadowing the staff. Though apprehensive, Phil arranged visits and shadowed varied roles, including train driver, guard, ticket seller, revenue protection inspector, train and station cleaner—he even handled hospitality on the express train service to a remote regional city.

The at-the-front program was a great learning experience for Phil; he experienced firsthand the breadth and unique risks of each individual's responsibilities. It was clear that each role contributed individually and collectively to delivering the customer service motto of clean, safe, reliable, and affordable railway services:

- The train and station cleaners delivered clean services. Cleaning trains late at night during the summer is especially challenging when the temperatures are over 86 degrees and the air-conditioning is turned off. There are also unique safety risks arising from litter left on trains, including potential needle pricks.
- All roles are vital to the safe running of trains and passenger safety. It is evident that safety is the first consideration in everything the state railway employees do. Any mistake could have fatal consequences.
- The roles of train driver and guard (conductor) are vital to the on-time running of trains. In an integrated transport system, passengers do not want their trains to run late or be cancelled because of the congestion caused by other late-running trains.
- Train fares are kept at an affordable level when everyone pays their way, with ticket sellers providing the up-front cash collection role and revenue protection inspectors helping to minimize fare evasion. Both roles have unique dangers—ticket sellers hold large amounts of cash and are susceptible to robbery, and revenue protection inspectors sometimes deal with unruly and abusive passengers.

Similarly, each role within the internal audit activity is designed to link seamlessly together to deliver the internal audit value proposition of assurance, insight, and objectivity (see exhibit 1-3).

What Practitioners Love About Internal Audit

"We keep the wheels of the business moving smoothly."			
Audit Committee Chair	Baby Boomer	10 to 20 years' auditing experience	Accounting

Tips for New Auditors

- The role of the internal auditor is a privileged one—you have enviable access and influence. The challenge is to maximize that opportunity to the benefit of the organization.
- Don't get too focused on the audit methodology and process. You may lose sight of the desired outcome.
- Get involved in the wider organization; this could be serving on a committee (e.g., diversity, workplace health and safety, social, project governance).
- See yourself and your team as a partner to the business. Internal audit can help them achieve their goals.
- Your job is important, but you cannot expect to always be popular or respected. There are both good days and bad. Your reward has to be pride in a job well done, rather than the acclamation of other staff in the organization.

> **Related Standards**
>
> **Standard 2230 – Engagement Resource Allocation**
>
> Internal auditors must determine appropriate and sufficient resources to achieve engagement objectives based on an evaluation of the nature and complexity of each engagement, time constraints, and available resources.

PART 2
THE *WHY* OF INTERNAL AUDITING

Chapters 5 through 8 explore the internal audit profession and how all of the parts fit together. These chapters provide the bones to professional auditing standards by applying a range of practical examples and insights.

Governance	Risk-Based	Control	IPPF

Wisdom of a Global Luminary

"When entering the field of internal audit today, it is crucial that internal auditors keep up to date with change and have the ability to manage any credibility gaps. There are many attributes expected of internal auditors but key is the ability to be able to deal with all controls and processes that involve compliance, as well as strategy, sustainability, and stakeholder relationships. A lack of qualified and skilled resources will slow the internal audit process, in particular in closing the credibility gap. It has become a business imperative for organizations to attract and retain the best talent in the field of internal auditing."

—Anton van Wyk
Partner, Big 4 Firm, South Africa
Past Chairman of IIA Global Board of Directors 2014–2015

Chapter 5
Governance, Risk Management, and Control

Governance is the combination of processes and structures implemented by the board to inform, direct, manage, and monitor the activities of the organization toward the achievement of its objectives. This chapter covers how governance helps an organization to establish and maintain a proper tone at the top.

Understanding the Basics

Governance

Governance encompasses consistent values-based management and decision-making authority, coupled with cohesive policies, rules, guidance, and processes to provide proper oversight and accountability. In effect, it is the system by which an organization is controlled and operates, and reflects the relationships between an organization's management, board, shareholders, and other stakeholders.

IPPF Definitions for Governance, Risk Management, and Control

Governance is the combination of processes and structures implemented by the board to inform, direct, manage, and monitor the activities of the organization toward the achievement of its objectives.

Risk management is a process to identify, assess, manage, and control potential events or situations to provide reasonable assurance regarding the achievement of the organization's objectives.

Control is any action taken by management, the board, and other parties to manage risk and increase the likelihood that established objectives and goals will be achieved. Management plans, organizes, and directs the performance of sufficient actions to provide reasonable assurance that objectives and goals will be achieved.

Source: International Professional Practices Framework.

Tone at the Top

The tone at the top is a governance term that describes an organization's ethical climate. It reflects senior management's and the board's consistent behavioral example and their meaningful commitment to integrity through their modelling of open, honest, and ethical behavior.

It is an important element of the internal control environment and underpins all else. It should cascade through the organization to set its rhythm of integrity—tone at the top, tune in the middle, and chorus at the bottom. The tone at the top significantly influences the culture of the organization.

Risk Management

The risk management standard ISO31000:2018 defines risks as the effect of uncertainty on objectives. In effect, risk management is a means of understanding what might happen (uncertainty), determining how it could impact the achievement of objectives and goals, and then acting accordingly.

> **Meaning of ISO**
>
> ISO refers to activities of the International Organization for Standardization, which is an international body made up of representatives from various national standards organizations with the aim of setting and promoting a range of proprietary, industrial, and commercial standards across the world. ISO is not an acronym, rather it is derived from the Greek word isos, which means equal. Because the work of internal auditors focuses on an organization's risk management, control, and governance processes (see definition of internal auditing in chapter 8), one of the main ISO standards referenced by many internal auditors is the risk management standard ISO31000:2018.

The risk management standard provides customizable guidelines for managing risks, delivers a common approach to managing any type of risk, and can be used throughout an organization, including for decision-making at all levels.

Effective risk managers use the language of the business (rather than the language of risk) to help senior management succeed by:

- Making well-informed and intelligent decisions
- Taking on the desired amount of the right risks
- Maintaining focus on achieving organizational objectives (rather than just avoiding downside risks)
- Identifying potentially rewarding fresh opportunities
- Maintaining a dynamic and comprehensive risk management approach

Difference Between the Language of Business and the Language of Risk

A business manager might comment that he wants to "help make the risk of a fire in the factory smaller." A risk manager might refer to the same situation as "mitigation of incendiary risk" (i.e., incendiary refers to the means of starting fires).

Risk management is not a static process that you undertake and then leave. It has to be applied dynamically and embraced and integrated all levels of risk, as illustrated in the case study in **exhibit 5-1**.

Exhibit 5-1: Case Study on Risk Management for a Small Business

Alan was a successful small-business owner who had applied a risk management approach to running his business. He had maintained effective controls over financial and operational risks, concentrating on the revenue cycle, managing expenses, securing a long-term tenancy, delivering excellent customer service, training great staff, and maintaining high-quality inventories. He was very focused on delivering the objectives of the business.

He was astonished when his business went broke and he lost his family home!

Alan had been running a video store. He hadn't refreshed his risk assessment and had never completed an environmental scan. As a busy businessman, he did not have the time to contemplate what was coming over the horizon and the potential impact on strategic risks—with the proliferation of the internet, the improved quality and affordability of DVDs, relaxation of import taxes, and the introduction of streaming services.

Risk management is a dynamic process!

Meaning of Other Common Risk Terms

Risk appetite (statement) refers to broad parameters around the amount and type of risk that an organization's leaders are willing to take in order to achieve its strategic and operational objectives.

Risk register is a record of risks at all levels of the organization identified through a risk assessment process.

Note: Author's creation based on research.

Control

Auditors need to be equally conscious of soft controls and hard controls in tackling audit engagements. Soft controls are intangible in nature and include things like culture, tone at the top, living shared values, morale, integrity, trust, and empowerment. They are typically subjective and reflect implicit attitudes.

Conversely, hard controls are tangible, involve explicit activities, and are usually objective. Examples include approvals, delegations of authority, authorizations, verifications, reconciliations, segregation of duties, locks, and performance reviews.

Exhibit 5-2 illustrates the assurance work of internal auditors, including the culture that encircles risk and control activities. Chapter 11 explores in more detail the process internal auditors use for assessing risk, identifying internal controls to respond to the risk, and performing walkthroughs of internal controls.

Exhibit 5-2: Illustration of Internal Audit's Assurance Over Risks, Controls, and Culture

Internal Audit Assurance

Inherent Risks	Internal Controls	Risk is managed within defined risk appetite level.	Residual Risks
Higher impact/likelihood			*Lower impact/likelihood*
This is the raw or untreated risk that naturally occurs in an activity, operation, or function before checks and balances are applied.	These represent the checks and balances that organizations expect to be maintained to mitigate inherent risks and help to achieve objectives.		This is the threat that remains after treating an inherent risk through checks and balances that reduce it, avoid it, accept it, or transfer it.

Internal auditors provide assurance that the risk response (internal control) is operating in practice effectively and consistently.

Internal auditors provide assurance over risk management arrangements, including effectiveness of risk identification, evaluation, monitoring, and reporting processes.

Internal auditors should periodically assess and provide assurance for an organization's "lived" culture.

Organization's Culture

Note: Author's creation.

Culture

While policies and procedures identify the internal controls that management expects employees to follow, it is actually the "lived" culture across the organization that dictates what internal control practices are actually applied in practice. That is why the concept of culture is so important for the new auditor to comprehend and apply to the extent possible during fieldwork and in consultation with the team leader.

Boards and senior management play an important role in articulating the desired risk culture of the organization. They do so by defining the values and principles that promote sustainable success rather than a pure short-term profit motive. The defined values need to be reflected through the tone at the top (behaviors and/or statements of senior management) and through the organization's arrangements for governance, risk management, internal audit, remuneration and incentive, and feedback (including whistleblowing and customer complaints).

Internal audit should be given a mandate to comment on the organization's lived culture, including the tone at the top, the soft controls, whether the desired culture has been defined, and whether the actual culture and desired state are in sync.

Establishing the desired culture in an organization is driven from the board through different levels of the governance and business functions of the business, and involves driving the desired culture downward and then receiving reporting back upward on any divergence between the desired culture and the actual culture. **Exhibit 5-3** summarizes some of the downward and upward flows; it is intended to be illustrative rather than comprehensive.

Exhibit 5-3: Examples of Tone at the Top Downward and Upward Flows for Delivering the Desired Culture

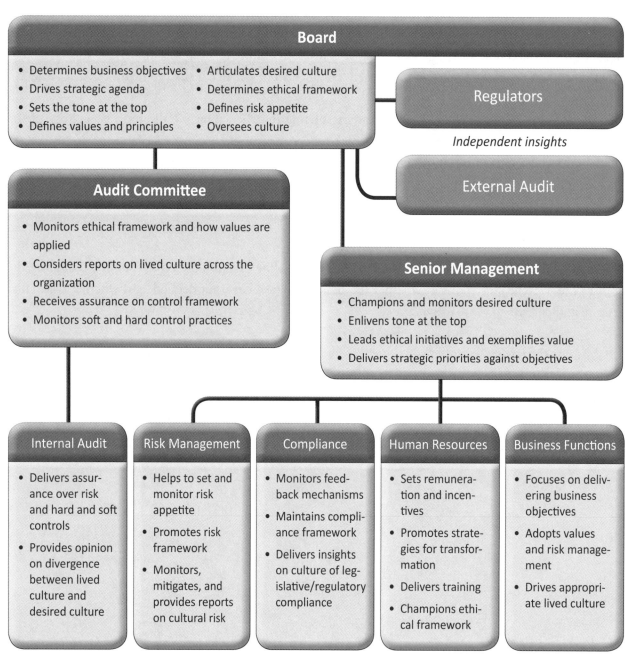

Board
- Determines business objectives
- Drives strategic agenda
- Sets the tone at the top
- Defines values and principles
- Articulates desired culture
- Determines ethical framework
- Defines risk appetite
- Oversees culture

Regulators

Independent insights

External Audit

Audit Committee
- Monitors ethical framework and how values are applied
- Considers reports on lived culture across the organization
- Receives assurance on control framework
- Monitors soft and hard control practices

Senior Management
- Champions and monitors desired culture
- Enlivens tone at the top
- Leads ethical initiatives and exemplifies value
- Delivers strategic priorities against objectives

Internal Audit
- Delivers assurance over risk and hard and soft controls
- Provides opinion on divergence between lived culture and desired culture

Risk Management
- Helps to set and monitor risk appetite
- Promotes risk framework
- Monitors, mitigates, and provides reports on cultural risk

Compliance
- Monitors feedback mechanisms
- Maintains compliance framework
- Delivers insights on culture of legislative/regulatory compliance

Human Resources
- Sets remuneration and incentives
- Promotes strategies for transformation
- Delivers training
- Champions ethical framework

Business Functions
- Focuses on delivering business objectives
- Adopts values and risk management
- Drives appropriate lived culture

Source: Author's creation.

Audit committees and senior management rely heavily on the daily application of internal controls that reduce the residual risk to an acceptable level within the organization's risk appetite. It is the collective insights delivered by those charged with providing assurance, including internal audit, which audit committees and senior management expect to identify any weaknesses in controlling the risks. Determining those charged with assurance is often done through an assurance map, which is a high-level document that identifies the holistic risk coverage across the organization by a range of assurance providers; it helps to identify gaps and duplication of assurance coverage.

Perspectives on Governance

For most of his life, Conrad had been training to swim the 800-yard freestyle at an international event. It was a proud moment to be representing his country, and, as he was at the peak of his prowess, Conrad thought he had a strong chance to secure a gold or silver medal.

During his warm-up swim, part of the ceiling fell into the pool and hit Conrad. He had lacerations to his head and arms, suffered serious concussion, and was unable to swim the event.

Inexplicable delays in decision-making had put pressure on timelines leading up to the event. Because the target date was immovable, the tone at the top was one of a sense of urgency... just get things done! The delays were overcome, in part, by obtaining waivers to standard governance arrangements and procurement procedures. A subsequent inquiry highlighted significant governance deficiencies, systemic failures, and infrastructural disasters, including:

- Infrastructural compromise was evident over safety, supplies, power installation, sanitation, and workmanship. Inattention to standards and poor quality assurance contributed to many problems.
- The compromises in workmanship led to a range of critical failures during the games, including part of the ceilings falling into the pool and weightlifting arenas; malfunctioning swimming filtration system and security barriers; and the collapse of a footbridge, beds, and scoreboard.
- Eliminating procurement competition led to a huge extra burden on the treasurer, with allegations of corruption and financial irregularities substantiated.
- The model of governance resulted in authority being dissipated, accountability defused, and unity of command being unclear or ignored.

The chair of the organizing committee was fired, arrested along with nine others, charged with corruption, and ultimately jailed. With the disappointment behind him, Conrad retired from swimming. He was inspired to complete an engineering degree to champion infrastructural integrity in all future major projects.

The governance failures and resultant turmoil of these international games could have potentially been averted through a strong tone at the top, including the engagement of internal auditors throughout the process. This reflects the opportunity for internal audit to bring a systematic, disciplined approach to evaluating and improving the effectiveness of governance, risk management, and control processes.

What Practitioners Love About Internal Audit

"I love the variety and complexity of what I do as an internal auditor and have a real sense that I can make a change for the better for my organization and people who work there."			
Technical Advisor	Baby Boomer	Over 20 years' auditing experience	Accounting

The Broader Context

Governance in the Spotlight

There are occasional crises and scandals across the world that put governance clearly in the spotlight. In 2018, an iconic bank (one of the top 50 banks in the world) reached agreement with a national regulator for a $700 million penalty relating to serious breaches of anti-money laundering and counterterrorism financing laws.[1] This represents the largest civil penalty in Australian corporate history.

An inquiry into the bank reported in 2018 that,[2] "Globally the financial crisis exposed a series of corporate scandals in banks. Governance weaknesses, serious professional misbehavior, ethical lapses and compliance failures have resulted in substantial financial losses and record fines and penalties. 'Conduct risk' has entered the lexicon of bank boards and regulators as a clear and present danger."

Cultural factors at the heart of the bank's stewardship lessened constructive criticism, led to slower decision-making, resulted in lengthy and complex processes, impeded accountability and ownership of risks, and resulted in a slippage in focus on outcomes. From an internal audit perspective, the report recommended, "The Executive Committee and Board improve their processes for monitoring issues raised by internal audit, regulators and other sources, and end any organizational tolerance for untimely and ineffective resolution of significant and outstanding matters of concern."[3]

Internal auditors benefit enormously from reading reports like this on crises and reflecting on the lessons learned. It is how they keep abreast of evolving governance, risk management, and control insights that help to inform their daily work and promote continuous improvement.

Chapter 17 explores the follow-up and resolution of internal audit recommendations.

Tips for New Auditors

- Understand the organization, the function, and the business area you are auditing. Understand what they are trying to achieve and the risks they face in achieving their objectives. You can achieve this through good stakeholder relationships with clients and keeping updated with their business plans.
- Keep developing your skills and technical knowledge to make sure you are relevant in your chosen profession. Invest in what matters to the profession and ultimately to the organization that employs you. Think of your skillset as an asset requiring regular review, just like any other asset that you own.
- As you work across business units, business functions, and staff levels throughout your career, strive to develop exceptional communication skills.
- Internal auditors deal in risk. Risk is present in every business. Leverage this position to make yourself exceptionally valuable in providing unique insights. Help the business to understand and manage the risks in delivering its business objectives.
- Pushing information onto people, no matter how well presented it is, has little positive impact if the message you are sending does not specifically interest or resonate with your audience.

Related Standards

Standard 2110 – Governance

The internal audit activity must assess and make appropriate recommendations to improve the organization's governance processes for:

- Making strategic and operational decisions.
- Overseeing risk management and control.
- Promoting appropriate ethics and values within the organization.
- Ensuring effective organizational performance management and accountability.
- Communicating risk and control information to appropriate areas of the organization.
- Coordinating the activities of, and communicating information among, the board, external and internal auditors, other assurance providers, and management.

Chapter 6
Risk-Based Auditing

The concept of risk is central to all facets of the internal auditor's work, from the resourcing model, communications with stakeholders, high-level planning, detailed-level planning, preparation of the program of work, fieldwork, prioritizing observations, reporting, and follow-up. This chapter provides a higher-level perspective and context for risk and control assessments discussed in chapter 11.

Understanding the Basics

Risk Assessment of Internal Audit

Internal audit activities that apply a risk-based auditing approach succeed at the first hurdle where they nurture a risk-aware culture for all facets of the activity and maintain an updated structured risk assessment of their own activity in line with an appropriate standard (such as the risk management standard ISO31000:2018).

Just as the business world is facing a changing risk landscape, so does internal audit with enhanced exposure to risks as diverse as brand, cybercrime, political risk, terrorism, and privacy of information. Risk assessments of the internal audit activity (where available) are helpful for new internal auditors to understand the context in which they are operating.

Risks affecting the internal audit activity can have consequences for the professional reputation of the activity and its outcomes. New auditors should recognize the risk assessment of the internal audit activity by applying identified controls in their day-to-day work and embracing risk management concepts in a practical sense to their work.

Risk-Based Auditing

Internal audit activities that apply a risk-based auditing approach succeed at the second hurdle when they apply risk to all elements of their approach consistently. For instance, they have a rigorous risk-based approach for their high-level planning and also apply a defensible risk basis to sample selection during fieldwork and the development of the work program, as illustrated in **exhibit 6-1** and expanded upon in exhibit 6-3.

Exhibit 6-1: Applying Risk to All Facets of Internal Auditing

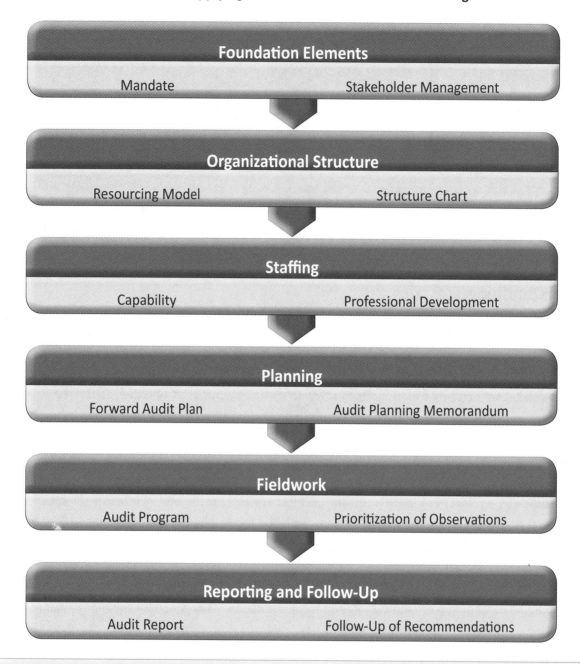

A Definition of Risk-Based Auditing

Risk-based auditing explicitly links the work of the internal audit activity to the organization's overall risk management framework. The internal audit methodology is aligned to the organization's risk appetite and other elements of the risk framework in order to provide independent assurance to the audit committee and senior management that the organization's risk management processes are effective in managing risks.

Applying Risk-Based Auditing in Practice

The new auditor will usually start a risk-based audit from the third stage, as illustrated in **exhibit 6-2** (the first two stages are included to provide context). The audit planning memorandum (audit engagement plan) is established based on the forward audit plan approved by the audit committee, and that, in turn, will reflect the organization's risk maturity level. Management completed its risk assessment and applied controls to reduce the risk; the internal auditor's job is to assess the reasonableness of the controls in reducing risks and check the performance of controls in practice.

Under the guidance of the team leader, the new auditor will undertake fieldwork that is aligned to the objectives and scope of the audit planning memorandum, and will typically focus on the higher-risk areas. It is important to recognize that risk-based audit fieldwork assesses the application of controls that are relied upon by senior management to move the inherent risk level to a more acceptable residual risk level. That is, an inherent safety-related risk might be rated high, but there are various controls in place that reduce the residual risk level to a lower level that is within the organization's risk appetite.

The audit result also prioritizes the observations through a risk-based lens and considers the impact of reported issues to the achievement of the organization's objectives. Where significant observations are raised, management may need to refresh its risk register to accord with actual practice.

Exhibit 6-2: Overview of a Risk-Based Audit Engagement

Stage 1: Establish Risk Maturity	Stage 2: Deliver Forward Audit Plan	Stage 3: Drive Audit Planning Memorandum	Stage 4: Focus the Audit Fieldwork	Stage 5: Report on the Audit Result
• Determine the level of risk maturity. • Establish the reliability of risk register. • Understand and apply the risk appetite.	• Use the risk register to inform the audit plan. • Prioritize audits per risk appetite. • Understand the control environment.	• Leverage forward audit plan for focus. • Consider specific operational risks. • Focus on key controls.	• Assess key control effectiveness. • Determine real residual risk level. • Risk prioritize observations.	• Focus report on areas of risk. • Accomplishment of objectives effects. • Management to refresh risk register.

Perspectives on Risk

A central bank's state manager was reviewing controls over the currency processing operation to provide an annual assertion to the CEO on how inherent risks were managed. Central banks have a unique role in manufacturing, distributing, and monitoring the integrity of currency (banknotes). Poor-quality banknotes are destroyed so they cannot be reused. They are written out of the central bank's records and are no longer a verifiable asset.

Banknotes are highly liquid in nature. The state manager confirmed the strong control framework, which included: impregnable physical security; employee vetting; code of conduct reminders; segregation of duties; movements under triple control (i.e., three persons) in locked cabinets; custodianship under triple control; senior employees hold keys and combinations; closed circuit television (CCTV) covering all banknote movements; ledger transactions computerized with passwords involving triple control; processing through sophisticated verification machines with automatic destruction of damaged banknotes; and regular surprise cash counts. The state manager signed the assertion and sent it to the CEO.

A few weeks later, the state manager received a whistleblower tip about the recent odd behavior and spending habits of David, who was a member of the cash processing team. David had been overlooked for a promotion and was bragging that he took his revenge by stealing $100,000 in banknotes. The state manager followed standard processes to assess the allegation. He invited David to his office and was shocked when David broke down and confessed to stealing $100,000, losing it on a gambling binge.

David explained how he stole the banknotes, notably:

- He derived the passwords of two other processing staff by discreetly watching their keystrokes when inputting transactions. He entered a false destruction transaction for $100,000 using the three password authorizations (two of whom he had stolen).
- When other operators were distracted, he removed $100,000 of banknotes, dropping them onto the floor where they could not be seen and where there was a gap in CCTV coverage.
- He changed the hardcopy reconciliation report after it was signed. The report then contained destruction transactions that corresponded with the transactions entered into the computer.
- He later returned to the processing room to collect the banknotes, concealing them under his loose clothing when he left the building.
- Because the falsified transaction showed the destruction of $100,000 in banknotes, nobody noticed the money was missing.

This scenario is loosely based on a true story that resulted in a conviction for the perpetrator. It emphasizes the importance for internal auditors to consider inherent risks in a manner where they always remain alert and suspicious, apply challenging "what if" scenarios, and never become complacent. That is the essence of risk-based auditing.

What Practitioners Love About Internal Audit

"Accept that you occupy a very important part of the organization's risk management and governance framework and that you always need to be proficient in what you do as an auditor."			
Audit Committee Chair	Baby Boomer	10 to 20 years' auditing experience	Economics

The Broader Context

Applying a Strategic Approach

Internal auditors should approach risk-based auditing from a very broad mindset and never be limited by what's always been done. By aligning their thinking to the objectives of an organization and its strategic direction, they can potentially deliver far greater value than a traditional assurance audit.

The following examples invite fresh thinking beyond the norm with a challenge to internal auditors to similarly apply creative and innovative thinking to their risk-based audit work:

- Health managers focused on reducing morbidity, mortality, and excessive health expenditure were grappling with high infection rates because doctors and other medical staff were too busy to stop at bathrooms to wash their hands, even though this was the best way to prevent the risk of health associated infections. Management installed alcohol-based hand wash at convenient locations throughout the hospital and in patient areas so that medical staff could conveniently wash their hands while in transit or with patients. Education, surveillance, and compliance reporting helped to change the mindset of health workers and visitors, reducing infection rates by up to 90%.
- A government needed to reduce the incidence of death and serious injury from traffic accidents to deliver on its road safety mantra. After wide consultation with the community and manufacturers, they made it mandatory for all drivers and passengers to wear seatbelts in all motor vehicles. Despite greater road use, the successful countermeasure reportedly helped to reduce the risk of death or serious injury by 50%. A generation of road users has always had to wear seatbelts, so a new habit has been established throughout the community.
- A bank with an objective of exemplary customer service wanted to reduce the administrative burden of reading all checks that ensured the regularity of dates, amounts, and authorization. They analyzed all the transactions to establish that 75% of the checks were for amounts of less than $300, very few transactions below this amount were problematic, and they had the potential to free up senior staff for more meaningful client-interfacing activities. They introduced streamlined check processing arrangements with check reading limits that balanced the downside risks (potential financial losses) with the upside risks (improved customer service).

Risk Considerations Across Audit Facets

Seven of the 12 audit facets illustrated in exhibit 6-1 are directly applicable to new auditors and the work they will typically complete. These are outlined in **exhibit 6-3** to illustrate that where risk is meaningfully considered in these facets, a credible, holistic, risk-based auditing arrangement is in place.

Exhibit 6-3: Examples of Risk Considerations Across Audit Facets

Audit Facet	Examples of Risks to Be Considered	Read More
Mandate	Need to recognize the boundaries of the internal audit work where there are subsidiaries and outsourced activities. Service provider contracts may have right-to-audit clauses.	Chapter 8
Forward Audit Plan	The longer-term audit activities should be focused on the higher-risk areas of the organization. Prioritization of audits (and the audit universe) should be based on risk.	Chapter 9
Audit Planning Memorandum	The time allocation on distinct phases of the audit will be influenced by complexity and inherent risks.	Chapter 9
Audit Program	There should be a strong focus on the risks to achieving the audit objectives and conformance to auditing standards when developing and executing the audit program.	Chapter 12
Prioritization of Observations	Not all observations are as important as each other, so they should be assessed in relation to the risk to the organization accomplishing its objectives. The assessment can be aided by root cause analysis.	Chapter 14
Audit Report	Greater attention should be given to the higher-risk observations, and recommendation should be prioritized according to the assessed level of risk, both upside (opportunities) and downside (weaknesses). Risk prioritization should recognize the entity's risk appetite.	Chapter 15
Follow-Up Recommendations	Priority should be given to at-risk recommendations and action being taken by management to address them. Interim control arrangements may need to be considered for high residual risk control weaknesses.	Chapter 17

Note: Author's creation.

Tips for New Auditors

- Don't sweat the small stuff too much—try to hone in on the key areas of risk.
- If you're stuck on an issue, just ask yourself what is the risk?
- Understand how the risk profession works and imbed risk thinking into your approach to internal auditing.
- Don't second-guess yourself—if you feel an area of risk warrants further investigation, then delve further.

• Be a lifelong learner. The world and business risk environments change so fast; what you know today may not be sufficient tomorrow. And sometimes you need to reinvent yourself to open new doors to the future.

Related Standards

Standard 2100 – Nature of Work

The internal audit activity must evaluate and contribute to the improvement of the organization's governance, risk management, and control processes using a systematic, disciplined, and risk-based approach. Internal audit credibility and value are enhanced when auditors are proactive and their evaluations offer new insights and consider future impact.

Chapter 7
Understanding the Internal Control Environment

The internal control environment is the attitude and actions of the board and management regarding the importance of control within the organization. The control environment provides the discipline and structure for the achievement of the primary objectives of the system of internal control. This chapter covers the various elements and examples of the control environment.

Understanding the Basics

Internal Control Environment

New internal auditors are better placed to evaluate controls during assigned audits when they understand key elements of the organization's overall control environment. According to The IIA's Practice Guide, Auditing the Control Environment, the control environment is the foundation on which an effective system of internal control is built and operated in an organization that strives to:

1. Achieve its strategic objectives;
2. Provide reliable financial reporting to internal and external stakeholders;
3. Operate its business efficiently and effectively;
4. Comply with all applicable laws and regulations; and
5. Safeguard its assets.[1]

IPPF Definition of Control Environment

The attitude and actions of the board and management regarding the importance of control within the organization. The control environment provides the discipline and structure for the achievement of the primary objectives of the system of internal control. The control environment includes the following elements:

- Integrity and ethical values.
- Management's philosophy and operating style.
- Organizational structure.
- Assignment of authority and responsibility.
- Human resource policies and practices.
- Competence of personnel.

Source: International Professional Practices Framework.

Internal Control Frameworks

A range of national internal control frameworks came to prominence across the world in the 1990s following many corporate failures. These frameworks included the Committee of Sponsoring Organizations' (COSO's) *Internal Control - Integrated Framework* in the United States, Canada's Criteria of Control (CoCo) Framework, and The Basel Committee on Banking Supervision's Framework for Internal Control Systems. Control models have since been updated and expanded (e.g., COSO in 2013 and the fourth revision of South Africa's King IV governance guidelines in 2016). Organizations have developed their own control frameworks, often leveraging the national models, with the nature of the framework depending on the countries or jurisdictions in which they operate, their industry, and the regulatory environment.

Meaning of Control Frameworks

Control frameworks are structured systems or processes that help organizations to achieve their objectives. They do so through better information, controls, risk management, compliance, and corporate governance that drive improved organizational performance and decision-making.

Note: Author's creation based on research.

New auditors are encouraged to understand the control framework established for their organization and read through their organization's associated policies and corporate information.

Applying a Control Framework in Practice

The Canadian control framework (CoCo) provides a simple and meaningful way for auditors to evaluate the reasonableness of controls that minimize risk and ensure the reliability of financial and other reporting. The framework emphasizes that control involves an organization in its entirety and begins at an individual level, with employees. Then the criteria focuses on four areas: purpose, commitment, capability, and monitoring and learning. These criteria remain meaningful for a new auditor when first considering the overall control framework for an organization, function, or activity.

In essence, an employee who performs a task does so with an understanding of why it is performed (its purpose). The employee applies resources to the efforts, which may include access to information, data, skills, knowledge, and supplies (capability). In accomplishing the task to a high standard, the employee will demonstrate dedication (commitment). Finally, the employee would evaluate his or her performance to determine improvements for next time (monitoring and learning).

Note: Author's creation based on Guidance on Control ©2018 CPA Canada. Criteria reprinted with permission of Chartered Professional Accountants of Canada, Toronto, Canada. Any changes to the original material are the sole responsibility of the author and have not been reviewed or endorsed by the Chartered Professional Accountants of Canada.

Assurance

Assurance is typically built in to an organization's established processes through delegations, risk management, compliance, management controls, and management systems (e.g., safety, environmental, and quality systems). An organization's overarching governance for assurance encompasses arrangements within the organization and externally (e.g., outsourced activities to third parties).

Chapter 1 identified assurance as a key element of the value proposition of internal auditing. Through their assurance work, internal auditors are able to provide a level of confidence to management that the organization's objectives will be achieved within an acceptable level of risk.

The IIA's Position Paper, The Three Lines of Defense in Effective Risk Management and Control, reflects the discrete areas relied upon to provide assurance.[2] The Three Lines of Defense model has been adopted by some organizations to distinguish between the internal audit role and that of other specialists within an organization.

To avoid duplicating the work of others, auditors need to understand all of the assurance providers, be aware of precisely what is being assured, the nature of assurance reporting, alignment between assurance and high-level risk exposures, consolidated risk and assurance profiles, and coordination of the reporting of assurance activities.

New auditors are encouraged to determine whether their organization has embraced the Three Lines of Defense (or similar) methodology and, if so, ask their team leaders how it affects their internal audit work.

Assessing Internal Controls

Auditors need to understand how all of the internal controls when working together can minimize adverse events. Weaknesses in internal control can result in avoidable risk events, as illustrated in **exhibit 7-1**.

Meaning of Controls

Controls are any action taken by management, the board, and other parties to manage risk and increase the likelihood that established objectives and goals will be achieved. Controls can be hard or soft. Hard controls are tangible in nature (i.e., physical, solid, real) and involve explicit and objective activities (e.g., approvals, delegations, authorizations, verifications, reconciliations, security procedures, check sums, hash totals, etc.). Conversely, soft controls are intangible (i.e., subtle), typically subjective, and reflect implicit attitudes (e.g., culture, tone at the top, shared values, morale, integrity, trust, and empowerment).

Example: Segregation (or separation) of duties is a typical control in most organizations that requires more than one person to be involved in a task. For instance, in the accounts payable function, there will be requirements for several different people to be involved in maintaining the vendor master file, preparing purchase orders, receipting for goods and services received, matching vendor invoices to the purchase order and the receipting report, paying the invoice, and monitoring the budget. The aim is to pay only bills for which the organization is liable based on invoices that are legitimate and accurate.

Note: Author's creation based on research.

Exhibit 7-1: Pothole Bowtie Diagram

There are usually three key elements that need to work together for effective internal control to be maintained: systems and processes, capability, and culture (leadership, behaviors, and attitudes). The risk event and risk impact in the bowtie diagram could have been avoided if the motorist maintained the tires on the vehicle to a proper standard (systems and processes), avoided unsafe road conditions—flooding that led to potholes (capability), or drove slowly at a safe speed (culture/behavior).

Evaluating the Adequacy and Effectiveness of Controls – IPPF Elements

Standard 2130 – Control

2130.A1 - The internal audit activity must evaluate the adequacy and effectiveness of controls in responding to risks within the organization's governance, operations, and information systems regarding the:

- Achievement of the organization's strategic objectives.
- Reliability and integrity of financial and operational information.
- Effectiveness and efficiency of operations and programs.
- Safeguarding of assets.
- Compliance with laws, regulations, policies, procedures, and contracts.

Perspectives on Control

Security across the country had been significantly tightened following unprecedented harmful events overseas. Accustomed to the change, Bjorn allowed more time when he traveled to meet clients in other parts of the city.

Bjorn arrived at a government building ahead of his appointment with a client on the 19th floor. The foyer was crowded with people lined up for security passes to enter the building through security gates monitored by several security guards. While waiting, Bjorn noticed a public area to the left of the foyer containing a range of interesting free publications. He walked over to grab several pamphlets. Noticing a set of stairs going up to the next floor, he tentatively walked up them and, once in the building, caught an elevator to the 19th floor. Nobody challenged him or asked for his security pass. Bjorn's meeting went well and he easily exited the building.

A few days later, Bjorn attended a major international sporting event with a sold-out crowd of more than 75,000 spectators. His backpack contained warm clothes, food, and water. He was accompanied by six nephews and nieces under the age of 12, all carrying similarly stocked backpacks. He arrived at the grounds and was alarmed by lines stretching more than 300 yards long, where security guards were stopping all spectators to inspect their bags. It was a slow process. Bjorn's family was worried that they would miss the start of the game, so he hurried them along past the lines, security guards, and inspection tables. Nobody stopped the group. They all showed their tickets, entered the stadium, found their seats, and joined in the supporter chant as their team entered the field.

Bjorn recognized the significant inherent risks requiring enhanced security arrangements and the steps taken to strengthen security control at both the government building and the stadium. He was, however, surprised, alarmed, and troubled that the controls at both locations had been easily circumvented.

There is a lesson here for internal auditors too. Despite what appear to be appropriate internal controls, internal auditors should never take for granted that an established control is working effectively and consistently in practice. They should challenge the robustness of the controls, including whether they remain effective when those primarily responsible for maintaining them are on leave or where individuals deliberately try to subvert them.

What Practitioners Love About Internal Audit

> *"If you love learning what other people do and how they deliver value to the business, it's great when you can help them do that more effectively while ensuring that the internal controls in place support good outcomes."*

Other: Business Manager	Generation X	5 to 10 years' auditing experience	Accounting

The Broader Context

Knowledge to Evaluate the Risk of Fraud

Under internal audit standards (IA Standard 1210.A2), "Internal auditors must have sufficient knowledge to evaluate the risk of fraud and the manner in which it is managed by the organization, but are not expected to have the expertise of a person whose primary responsibility is detecting and investigating fraud." Auditors also have a role to play in contributing (where possible) to the CAE's reporting to senior management and the board on significant risk and control issues, including fraud risks (covered under Standard 2060).

Fraud risk represents one of the key areas where organizations establish internal controls to detect or prevent fraud (and corruption) from occurring. The importance of doing so is highlighted in the ACFE Report to the Nations on occupational fraud and abuse, which reflected that internal control weaknesses were responsible for nearly half of all frauds, and organizations lose, indicatively, around 5% of their annual revenues to fraud.[3] The ACFE also reported:

- Only 4% of perpetrators had a prior fraud conviction.
- A majority of the victims recovered nothing.
- Tips are by far the most common initial detection method (40%), with employees providing over half of the tips and a further one-third coming from outside parties.
- Internal audit is the initial detection method for about 15% of frauds.
- Data monitoring analysis and surprise audits were correlated with the largest reductions in fraud losses and duration, yet only 37% of victim organizations implemented these controls.

Watch Point – Facilitation Payments

When reviewing the revenue and expenditure cycles for organizations active in foreign markets, auditors should be alert for any transactions that point to potential facilitation payments. These payments are illegal in most countries and are tantamount to bribes. They involve payments to public or government officials to incentivize them to complete an action or process that is beneficial to the party making the payment.

As an example, several senior managers in a manufacturing company have been accused of paying lucrative commissions to middlemen in order to secure government contracts in another country. They face a maximum of 10 years in jail and/or a $1.1 million fine under foreign bribery laws. The reputational damage to the manufacturing company and its parent has been significant.

The three primary categories of occupational fraud are asset misappropriations, corruption, and financial statement fraud, as illustrated in the ACFE fraud tree in **exhibit 7-2**. Internal auditors assessing controls need to be cognizant of the types of fraud that can occur where there are weaknesses in control arrangements.

Tips for New Auditors

- Always start an audit by carefully assessing the risks of the system under review, both from internal and external sources. Pay particular attention, with more audit scrutiny, in the areas where you believe that the risks are considered high. Most systems generally have controls in place; however, it is a matter of whether you can find a crack and accordingly drive a wedge at the right spot.
- Really dig deep and understand the business you are involved with. Most valuable insights come from a deep understanding of process and control and seeing a better way. It also makes new internal auditors valuable to the business, in that they are a well-rounded resource.
- At its heart, the role of the internal auditor is to objectively test and validate controls to provide assurance on their effectiveness. Seniority, authority, popularity, personality, and trust are not controls, but they are sometimes used to compromise or override due process, policies, or procedures. You need to recognize when this is happening.
- Internal auditors are often referencing what might happen because of detected weak controls, whereas managers are dealing with what will happen or has happened on a daily basis. So recognize that your risk tolerance, priorities, observations, and concerns as an internal auditor are not necessarily the same as those of your stakeholders.
- See it as a privilege to study how things work and to have an opportunity to help them work better. In particular, become competent with assessing soft controls and make considering culture one of your points of difference.

Exhibit 7-2: Occupational Fraud and Abuse Classification System (the Fraud Tree)[4]

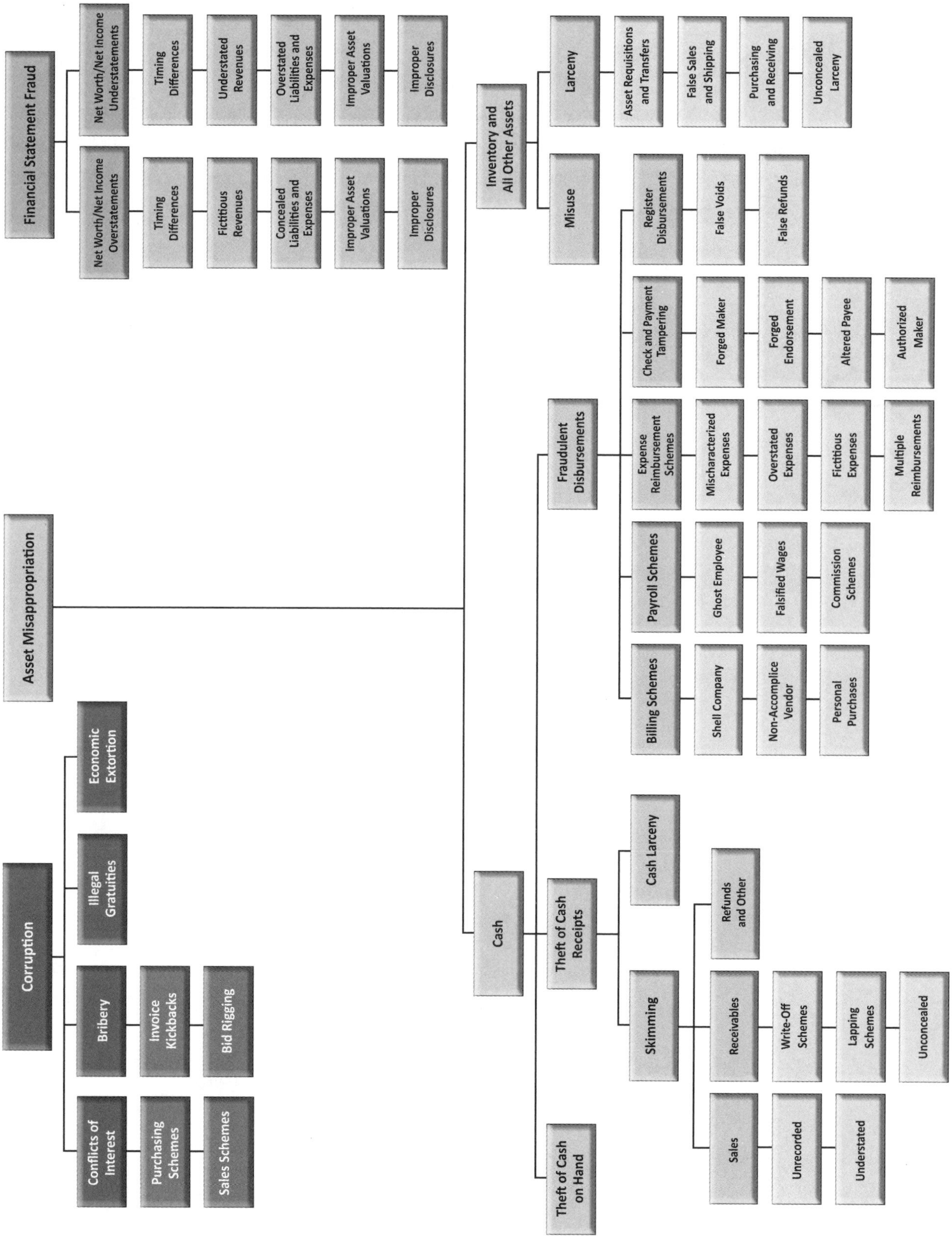
Financial Statement Fraud
Net Worth/Net Income Overstatements
Timing Differences
Fictitious Revenues
Concealed Liabilities and Expenses
Improper Asset Valuations
Improper Disclosures
Net Worth/Net Income Understatements
Timing Differences
Understated Revenues
Overstated Liabilities and Expenses
Improper Asset Valuations
Improper Disclosures
Asset Misappropriation
Cash
Theft of Cash on Hand
Theft of Cash Receipts
Skimming
Sales
Unrecorded
Understated
Receivables
Write-Off Schemes
Lapping Schemes
Unconcealed
Refunds and Other
Cash Larceny
Fraudulent Disbursements
Billing Schemes
Shell Company
Non-Accomplice Vendor
Personal Purchases
Payroll Schemes
Ghost Employee
Falsified Wages
Commission Schemes
Expense Reimbursement Schemes
Mischaracterized Expenses
Overstated Expenses
Fictitious Expenses
Multiple Reimbursements
Check and Payment Tampering
Forged Maker
Forged Endorsement
Altered Payee
Authorized Maker
Register Disbursements
False Voids
False Refunds
Inventory and All Other Assets
Misuse
Larceny
Asset Requisitions and Transfers
False Sales and Shipping
Purchasing and Receiving
Unconcealed Larceny
Corruption
Conflicts of Interest
Purchasing Schemes
Sales Schemes
Bribery
Invoice Kickbacks
Bid Rigging
Illegal Gratuities
Economic Extortion

Source: © Association of Certified Fraud Examiners. Used with permission.

Related Standards

Standard 2100 – Nature of Work

The internal audit activity must evaluate and contribute to the improvement of the organization's governance, risk management, and control processes using a systematic, disciplined, and risk-based approach. Internal audit credibility and value are enhanced when auditors are proactive and their evaluations offer new insights and consider future impact.

Standard 2130 – Control

The internal audit activity must assist the organization in maintaining effective controls by evaluating their effectiveness and efficiency and by promoting continuous improvement.

Chapter 8
International Professional Practices Framework

The International Professional Practices Framework (IPPF) is the conceptual framework that organizes authoritative guidance—including professional auditing standards—promulgated by The IIA. It is comprised of mandatory and recommended guidance. This chapter covers the mandatory and recommended elements of the IPPF.

Understanding the Conceptual Framework for Internal Auditors

Features of the IPPF

The IPPF (illustrated in **exhibit 8-1**) provides a globally accepted rigorous basis for the operation of an internal audit activity.

The key elements of the IPPF are described more fully on the following pages and encompass:

- *Mission Statement* reflects what the profession strives to accomplish.
- *Core Principles* highlight what effective internal audit looks like in practice as it relates to the individual auditor, the internal audit activity, and internal audit outcomes.
- *Definition* focuses on what internal audit is.
- *Standards* are relied upon by internal auditors to guide the profession and how the profession is practiced.
- *Code of Ethics* focuses on behavior.
- *Recommended Guidance* includes Implementation Guidance and Supplemental Guidance.

Mandatory provisions are the subject of public exposure, with formal consideration of comments received from IIA members and non-members.

Exhibit 8-1: Overview of the IPPF Elements

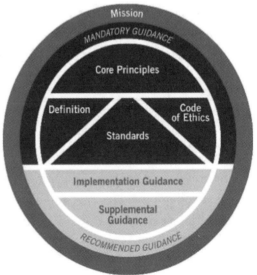

Source: International Professional Practices Framework.

Mission

"To enhance and protect organizational value by providing risk-based and objective assurance, advice, and insight."

Core Principles

The core principles articulated in the IPPF are explored in chapter 3 and summarized below.

- Demonstrates integrity.
- Demonstrates competence and due professional care.
- Is objective and free from undue influence (independent).
- Aligns with the strategies, objectives, and risks of the organization.
- Is appropriately positioned and adequately resourced.
- Demonstrates quality and continuous improvement.
- Communicates effectively.
- Provides risk-based assurance.
- Is insightful, proactive, and future-focused.
- Promotes organizational improvement.

Definition

"Internal auditing is an independent, objective assurance and consulting activity designed to add value and improve an organization's operations. It helps an organization accomplish its objectives by bringing a systematic, disciplined approach to evaluate and improve the effectiveness of risk management, control, and governance processes."

Standards

The worldwide standards for internal auditing are the *International Standards for the Professional Practice of Internal Auditing* issued by The IIA. There are two types:

- Attribute Standards: These are the internal audit foundations that establish the internal audit activity's position within an organization. They include clarity of the mandate in the form of an internal audit charter, the form-work for independence and objectivity, requirements for proficiency and due professional care, and quality assurance and improvement arrangements.

- Performance Standards: These encompass requirements for performing internal audit responsibilities from planning and performing the audits through to communicating the results.

There are 11 overarching and 41 underlying attribute and performance standards.

Setting International Internal Auditing Standards

The IIA serves as the internal audit profession's international standard setter (among other roles). It sets the bar for internal audit integrity and professionalism around the world with the International Professional Practices Framework (IPPF), a collection of guidance that includes the *International Standards for the Professional Practice of Internal Auditing* and the Code of Ethics.

Procedures for the mandatory provisions of the IPPF require public exposure and formal consideration of comments received from IIA members and nonmembers alike. The standards development process is supervised by an independent body, the IPPF Oversight Council of The IIA, which is appointed by The IIA's Global Board of Directors and comprises persons representing stakeholders such as boards, management, public and private sector internal auditors, regulators and government authorities, investors, international entities, and members specifically selected by the global board.

Code of Ethics

The purpose of the Code of Ethics is to promote an ethical culture in the profession of internal auditing. It states the principles and expectations governing the behavior of individuals and organizations in the conduct of internal auditing.

It describes the minimum requirements for conduct and behavior expectations through principles and rules of conduct, notably:

- Principles that are relevant to the profession and practice of internal auditing. They include integrity, objectivity, confidentiality, and competency. See **exhibit 8-2** for an overview.
- Rules of conduct that describe the norms expected of internal auditors. These rules are an aid to interpreting the principles into practical applications and are intended to guide the ethical conduct of internal auditors.

Exhibit 8-2: Overview of the Code of Ethics Principles[1]

Principle	Description
Integrity	The integrity of internal auditors establishes trust and thus provides the basis for reliance on their judgment.
Objectivity	Internal auditors exhibit the highest level of professional objectivity in gathering, evaluating, and communicating information about the activity or process being examined. Internal auditors make a balanced assessment of all the relevant circumstances and are not unduly influenced by their own interests or by others in forming judgments.
Confidentiality	Internal auditors respect the value and ownership of information they receive and do not disclose information without appropriate authority unless there is a legal or professional obligation to do so.
Competency	Internal auditors apply the knowledge, skills, and experience needed in the performance of internal audit services.

A fuller description of each of the above principles is provided in the Rules of Conduct contained within the Code of Ethics section of the IPPF. The Code of Ethics applies to both entities and individuals that perform internal audit services. Breaches may be the subject of disciplinary action by The IIA or local institute.

International Professional Practices Framework (IPPF)

The information in this chapter is designed to provide an overview of the key features of the framework, rather than a detailed description that is available in the Red Book (a common colloquial name for the IPPF publication). It is complemented by information at the end of each chapter that references back to the related standards in the IPPF. Every internal audit activity across the world should have an updated version of the IPPF, or at least ready access to it. All professional internal auditors should understand and apply the IPPF in their daily work. New auditors should seek access to the IPPF through their team leader or the CAE.

Note: The IPPF is available for purchase from the IIA Bookstore – https://bookstore.theiia.org

---

Implementation Guidance

Implementation guidance is designed to assist internal auditors in applying the standards and promoting good practices. It addresses the typical audit approach, methodology, and considerations, rather than detailed processes and procedures.

Note: Position Papers are issued by The IIA periodically to help stakeholders understand the significance of governance, risk, or control issues as they pertain to internal auditing.

Supplemental Guidance

Supplemental guidance is provided through a series of publications called Practice Guides, Global Technology Audit Guides (GTAGs), Guides for the Assessment of IT Risk (GAITs), and other detailed guidance for conducting internal audit activities. Supplemental guidance provides practical insights on topics such as:

- Programs and examples
- Tools and techniques
- Step-by-step approaches
- Processes and procedures
- Sector-specific issues
- Other topical areas

Applying the IPPF

This chapter is deliberately placed after the early chapters that provide the context for the role of an internal auditor and the foundations of governance, risk, and control. It sits before the later chapters that provide insights on how and when auditors undertake their audits. In doing so, this chapter provides the linkage between what auditors need to know and do by covering the things they need to apply. This is illustrated in **exhibit 8-3**.

Exhibit 8-3: Placement of This Chapter – Linking the Need to Know, Apply, and Do

Auditors Need to Know (Chapters 1 through 7)	Auditors Need to Apply (Chapter 8)	Auditors Need to Do (Chapters 9 through 17)
• About the profession • Pathways • Capabilities • Roles and responsibilities • Governance, risk, and control • Risk-based auditing	The IPPF: • Mission • Core Principles • Definition • Code of Ethics • Recommended Guidance	• Planning • Conduct interviews • Risk assessment • Audit program development • Fieldwork • Observations • Reporting • Quality • Follow-Ups
Who we are and the why of governance, risk, and control	**Why we do what we do** [linkage between auditors' need to know and auditors' need to do]	**How and when we do it**

Once auditors understand the context of internal auditing (covered in chapters 1 through 7), they need to gain a comprehensive understanding of the IPPF (and, in particular, the *Standards*) and how to apply it during their daily work. This understanding can be gained through a range of means, including self-study, on-the-job training, attendance at IIA courses, or completion of IIA certifications (e.g., Certified Internal Auditor).

Perspectives on Standards

The audit committee was reviewing the draft financial statements prepared by the acting chief financial officer (CFO). The accounts looked to be very different than in the past, so the audit committee was struggling to grasp the grounds for the changes and the reasonableness of them. The chair sought clarification on detailed aspects of the statements, and was alarmed when informed of an intricate "creative accounting" approach that the acting CFO had introduced.

After a lengthy conversation exploring all aspects of the draft financial statements, the chair exclaimed in exasperation that it was unbelievable that a qualified and certified accountant had little to no understanding of accounting standards. Indignantly, the CFO retorted that he had a very well-regarded marketing degree from a prestigious university and a strong background in creative roles.

Well-founded boards, management, regulators, and the community would never accept financial statements that were not prepared in accordance with established accounting standards. Similarly, they would expect the statements to be prepared by people who have the skills, experience, and qualifications, and ideally a credible financial certification.

It is a reasonable expectation that internal auditors would similarly conduct their work in line with professional auditing standards, and that the audit team has auditors with acceptable internal audit certifications. Anything less is unacceptable in the twenty-first century!

What Practitioners Love About Internal Audit

"Internal auditing is a job that is transferable, meaning you can change industries relatively easily; this is not generally an option available to people who select an industry early in their career and tend to remain in that industry for a long time. Internal audit is internationally applicable; meaning it is possible to remain an internal auditor and change geographic location to virtually anywhere in the world."			
Audit Committee Chair	Baby Boomer	Over 20 years' auditing experience	Business

The Broader Context

Importance of Applying the *Standards*

IIA President and CEO Richard Chambers is quoted as saying,

> "To carry out their responsibilities well, internal auditors must rely on the standards guiding the profession and have confidence that those standards reflect how the profession is being practiced.

The (2017) enhancements to the IPPF are designed to strengthen internal audit's position as an invaluable partner in business success."[2]

These sentiments are reinforced by regulators who retain a strong interest in the work of internal audit and compliance with professional auditing standards. Governments and regulators are increasingly mandating IPPF compliance as part of their laws, policies, and regulations. Understanding your organization's regulatory environment and the potential for regulators (and others) to access internal audit workpapers is covered in more detail in chapter 16.

From a regulatory perspective, the well-respected former chair of the Australian Prudential Regulation Authority (APRA) Dr. John Laker observed a decade ago:

"It is in difficult situations… The Institute of Internal Auditors comes to centre stage. Professional standards and support from the Institute can be a vital help in stiffening the spine of the internal auditors involved. On this score, we strongly commend the work of the Institute in Australia in improving the education and awareness of internal auditors and promoting the status of the internal audit function. That is work that, brick by brick, is helping to raise corporate governance standards in Australia, to the benefit of stakeholders and the community generally."[3]

Tips for New Internal Auditors

- Read and understand The IIA's IPPF and ask questions about its application.
- An internal auditor's success relies on relationship building and personal integrity. Strive to form trusted relationships if you want to have a long-term impact on an organization.
- Pursue formal qualifications in internal auditing. This will give you credibility and help you understand the technical aspects of what you do. Internal auditing is not black and white—there is a lot of professional judgment involved. (See further information on professional designations in chapter 1.)
- Always be sure to follow the highest ethical standards and behavior. Your clients have to know where you stand. This will foster trust, the fuel for your success as an internal auditor.
- Understand the current and emerging risk landscape as well as the client's value proposition well. This can be achieved through IIA and other courses, self-study, mentoring, and observations of the board and management. These insights will help you come up with pragmatic and commercial action plans that will improve the current control environment and future-proof the client's function.

Related Standards – Attribute Standards; Performance Standards

Information is included at the end of each chapter on the related auditing standards that apply to the audit steps described in that chapter. The information is sourced from the International Professional Practices Framework.

PART 3
THE *HOW* OF INTERNAL AUDITING

Chapters 9 through 12 break the internal audit preparatory processes down into distinct phases and outline how an internal auditor conducts each of these phases. Underpinning these chapters is the way that internal auditors conduct their work and the attitude they present. Many longer-term auditors reflect they have one of the best jobs in the organization, which they find interesting, professionally rewarding, and fun.

Planning	Interviewing	Walkthrough	Program

Wisdom of a Global Luminary

"Don't dive straight into looking at controls when starting an audit. Think that risk and control should be a mirror image, in that for major risks there should be controls in place and whether there are controls in place that no longer address risks. Risks without appropriate controls are not good, and controls not addressing risks are wasting resources."

—Bob McDonald
Audit Committee Chairman, Australia
Past Chairman of IIA Global Board of Directors 2003–2004

Chapter 9
Audit Planning and Opening Conference

Audit planning is the first phase of an audit. This chapter covers the common elements of a typical audit model: planning phase, preliminary client survey, defining audit scope and objectives, audit planning memorandum (also known as the audit engagement plan), reviewing existing documentation, audit opening conference, and creating or updating process flow documentation.

Understanding the Common Elements of Audit Planning

Research

The pace of business change throughout the twenty-first century is unparalleled in history, with rapid business changes, global connectivity, emerging technologies, and increasingly complex economic, regulatory, and operating environments. This emphasizes the need to undertake an environmental scan (further explained later in the chapter) as part of the research phase of audit planning to determine what has changed or is likely to change for the business activity being audited. By way of example, this could have occurred because processes changed upon implementation of a different business model; a new product line was introduced; processes were outsourced or computerized; the government changed legislation; or regulators imposed stricter compliance obligations.

The research phase includes consideration of other avenues of information that could aid in the audit:

- Thought leadership: to obtain fresh thinking on a range of topics and emerging issues from service provider firms; professional bodies like The IIA, ISACA, and the Association of Certified Fraud Examiners; and innovative government agencies.
- Cases studies: to glean insights from published reports on business failures. These might be available from special commissions of enquiry; regulators; investigative journalists and authors; law enforcement agencies; supreme audit organizations (auditors general); corruption prevention agencies; other government agencies; and local ethics and compliance institutes.
- Benchmarking: to identify what others are doing for related activities, including comparable measures and better practices.
- Stories: to consider practical ideas from the Internal Audit Foundation from a range of print or online reports, books, manuals, guides, and studies.
- Web chat and social media: to get a sense of community thinking on a range of topics.

- Organizational direction: to align the proposed audit with the organization's strategic drivers published through the vision, values, business objectives, strategic plan, business plan, codes of ethics, and published annual report.
- Prior audit results: to leverage results of prior audits and the improvement opportunities identified.

> **Use of the Term *Forward Audit Plan***
>
> Within this book, the term *forward audit plan* has been used to describe the high-level risk-based audit plan for the internal audit activity. This terminology reflects the evolving nature of audit planning in the twenty-first century where longer-term (three- to five-year) plans are becoming obsolete, and even annual plans are being refreshed more regularly to provide greater agility for internal auditors to meet emerging risk-based business needs.

Preliminary Client Survey

Once the research phase has been completed or is in an advanced stage, there will be many questions that need to be answered and specific documentation that will need to be accessed. The preliminary client survey is a structured approach that aids in the familiarization with an operation or activity through the transfer of information. Arrangements would be made for the delivery of the documentation through a secure means, ideally electronically.

> **Meaning of Preliminary Client Survey**
>
> In internal audit parlance, a preliminary client survey is a method of gathering information from business management. Given that some people experience survey fatigue, it is important to note that this type of survey is not a marketing type of statistical study or similar research method. It is more akin to the work of a property surveyor who examines and records the features of an asset so as to create a plan or description.

The preliminary client survey is particularly useful when the audit is being conducted at a different location from the auditor's home site, as it aids the development of the audit planning memorandum and optimizes the time the auditor has onsite to speak with stakeholders and review volumes of stored documentation (e.g., original contracts and invoices).

Examples of questions and documentation requests covered by the preliminary client survey include:

Areas of questions: future plans; dollar magnitude in assets, liabilities, transactional activity, salaries, revenues, expenditure, turnover, and volumes; problem areas and/or issues of concern/relevance that may be in play; peak work periods; leave arrangements for key stakeholders; transport and accommodation logistics; names of key contacts; list of key reports; previous regulatory noncompliance citations, including noncompliance incidents, root cause analysis, and remediation plans and their status.

Documentation: mission statement; organizational structure chart; position descriptions; published annual report (or operation-related sections); risk register; business plan; progress report against business plan; budget; contract register; product listing; client service standards; delegations; chart of accounts; financial statements; and staff engagement survey results.

In organizations with well-developed intranet and internet sites, some of the documentation will already be readily accessible by the auditor (e.g., organizational structure, published annual report, codes of ethics, product listing).

Budget

The audit objectives will be the starting point for determining the budget allocation for the engagement. The forward audit plan will contain the indicative budget for each audit. In most cases, the budget will be translated into the number of working days or hours allocated to the audit, or in the case of a service provider firm, the monetary budget.

There are many variables that may have occurred since the indicative budget was set. The final engagement budget will be influenced by the research undertaken, coupled with the defined audit objectives and scope and the audit approach. For instance:

- Research might indicate significant changes—internally or externally—that necessitate different audit coverage than originally intended.
- Audit objectives and scope might have been expanded or reduced, for instance, following the opening conference with management; as a consequence of the environmental scan undertaken as part of the research phase; or as a consequence of independent reviews undertaken by the external auditors, regulators, or other scrutineers.
- The audit approach might involve innovative practices that save time and effort to enhance effectiveness, such as collaboration with others; control self-assessment; risk workshop with operational staff; or greater use of technology. (*Note*: Control self-assessment is discussed in chapter 11; it is a structured process where management and auditors collaboratively assess the effectiveness of controls, the level of residual risk, and the achievability of business objectives.)

The final engagement budget will then be allocated across two distinct dimensions:

- Phases of the audit process such as research, planning, fieldwork, and reporting
- Resource allocation by auditor

An illustrative example of budget allocations is shown in **exhibit 9-1**.

Exhibit 9-1: Example of Budget Allocations

Audit Phase		Allocation for Auditors				Auditor Allocation	
		Pauline	John	Georgia	Richard		
Research	2	-	-	1	1	Pauline (team leader)	3
Planning	3	1	1	1	-	John (senior auditor)	5
Fieldwork	10	-	3	3	4	Georgia (auditor)	6
Reporting	5	2	1	1	1	Richard (auditor)	6
Total days	20	3	5	6	6	Total days	20

Note: This is an illustrative example. Allocations across phases and auditors will vary according to the topic being audited, skillsets, and availability of team members. The fieldwork phase would typically be broken down further into distinct segments (often associated with the audit objectives) assigned to each auditor.

The allocation of audit phases and distinct segments will be informed by the complexity of work and the availability, experience, and proficiency of team members.

Objectives

Audit objectives are broad statements that define *what* the intended accomplishments of the audit engagement will be. They are determined through a systematic and disciplined approach. There are typically between one and five audit objectives depending on the complexity of the activity and the breadth of the audit. There may be greater or lesser emphasis placed on different objectives.

Well-defined objectives sharpen the focus of the overall audit coverage, provide the basis of allocating the audit budget, guide the work throughout each phase of the audit, provide measurable audit criteria (for success or otherwise), and provide the basis for the overall conclusion of the audit and each significant facet of work.

According to *Sawyer's Guide for Internal Auditors*, 7th Edition: "Audit objectives state what is to be accomplished by the assurance engagement.[1] They provide direction for the audit team and, together with the scope and approach, create a common understanding between internal audit and business area management."

Examples of audit objectives include:
- A general objective for accounts payable might be: Determine the design adequacy and operating effectiveness of controls in accounts payable.
- A specific objective in a production environment might be: Determine the causes of high turnover in the production department.

Irrespective of whether audit objectives are general or specific (or a combination of both), the audit report is expected to provide clear conclusions for each objective.

Defining audit objectives requires consideration of expectations of all of the key stakeholders, including the audit committee, senior management, the CAE, local management, and operational staff. As an example, management might expect the auditor to address compliance and performance elements during an audit of the accounts payable activity. Discussions during the opening conference may reveal an expectation that the audit will provide insights from a comparative analysis of average transaction processing costs compared to peers, in addition to the more traditional approach of providing assurance over the design adequacy and operating effectiveness of internal controls in the accounts payable function. If acceptable to the CAE, these sorts of expectations would then be converted into specific and measurable audit objectives.

IPPF Definition of Engagement Objectives

Broad statements developed by internal auditors that define intended engagement accomplishments.

Scope

The audit scope defines the boundaries of the audit, what will be covered by the audit, and how much audit work will be performed. It identifies *where* the audit will be directed to achieve the objectives. This could involve places and people, activities, and time frames. For instance:

Places and People
- Specific locations to be visited or where walkthrough of a location or process is undertaken
- Specific key managers and/or personnel to be interviewed
- Locations to be covered remotely using computer-assisted audit techniques
- Specific control procedures to be tested
- Outsourced activities provided at a third party's premises or indefinable locations, including the cloud

Activities
- Specific areas of the business such as programs, technologies, products, and functions
- Specific components of a process such as manual processes, customer interfaces, computer application controls, or general IT controls (or a combination)

Time Frames

- The period of coverage (e.g., a specific date range, for example, between month/year, or a specified period like the previous fiscal year)

The scope will also record exclusions from the audit (i.e., areas that will not be covered). There may be good reasons for these exclusions, for instance:

- The audit topic may be too large to be done at one time.
- There may be insufficient resources available to complete the full audit topic.
- Assessed risks may not warrant the full audit topic being audited.
- Parts of the audit topic may have been audited previously.
- Management may be about to make significant changes in that area.

Criteria

Audit criteria are the measures used to gauge whether the audit objectives are achieved. Examples of audit criteria may be:

- Laws, regulations, policies, and contracts
- Procedures
- Guidelines
- Reports
- Expert advice
- Best practice guides
- Standards
- Administration instructions
- Plans
- Benchmarking
- Technical publications
- International literature

Sampling Strategy

The sampling strategy reflects the proposed approach for selecting fewer than 100% of the items being audited for the purpose of drawing an inference about a characteristic of the population. This will usually be determined during the development of the audit planning memorandum (and may sometimes be done as part of preparing the audit program). The topic is explored further in chapter 13.

Approach

The approach reflects *how* the auditors will accomplish the audit objectives and scope. The techniques could involve collaboration, checking, or analysis (or a combination). For instance:

Collaboration

- Conducting interviews with relevant stakeholders to determine the risks in the activity, identify the associated controls, and recognize significant changes or gaps
- Undertaking a risk workshop and/or control self-assessment workshop with operational staff

Checking

- Testing a sample of internal controls or transactions to evaluate how effectively operational risks are being controlled in practice
- Documenting control arrangements through techniques such as flowcharting and risk/control matrices
- Developing computer-assisted audit techniques to automate part of the audit work

Analysis

- Scrutinizing qualitative indicators such as staff engagement surveys, customer satisfaction surveys, complaints, and compliments
- Using data mining to automate the detection of relevant patterns in preexisting databases; using algorithms to examine significant amounts of data to identify hidden patterns, predict future trends, and generate new information
- Benchmarking against similar activities in other similar organizations

Timetable

The audit timetable reflects when the audit will commence and when it will conclude. It might include the dates of significant milestones.

There is little point in raising a significant control weakness with management and informing the audit committee six months after it was discovered. The timetable should be constructed to minimize the time between the start and finish of the audit so that opportunities for improvement are highlighted promptly.

There are many factors to be considered when determining the best time to conduct an audit. For instance:

- The peak workload periods for the area being audited (e.g., the end of the financial year is a busy time for a financial accounting area)
- The absence of key executives in the area being audited
- The weather patterns, major events, or other prohibitory factors in locations requiring travel (i.e., safety, exclusion zones, and availability of accommodation)
- Any other activities scheduled concurrently (e.g., visits by regulators or external auditors)
- Timing commitments to the audit committee, CAE, external auditors, or regulators
- Availability of auditors
- Allocation of the budget across auditors and audit phases (or objectives)

When auditors work on different teams for different team leaders, it is especially important that they gain release from each engagement within the agreed time frame. Otherwise, the flow-on effect could harm the outcomes and timing of the subsequent audit. This is a shared responsibility between the team leaders and the auditors.

A common key performance measure for internal audit is the duration of the audit, which reflects the time period between the start of an audit (commencement of fieldwork) and the delivery of the final audit report. This reflects the importance of delivering timely reports to management and the audit committee. Chapter 19 discusses techniques for measuring performance in more detail.

Audit Planning Memorandum

The audit planning memorandum articulates the terms of reference and outlines information about the audit, and the audit sponsor should be given an opportunity to provide input to its development. This assures appropriate coverage of the risks and issues associated with the audit topic. The auditor/s will have formed the basis of the terms of reference for the audit through the different planning phases already discussed in this chapter—research, preliminary client survey, budget, objective, scope, criteria, approach, sampling strategy, and timetable. The outcomes of the planning assessment are consolidated into a single document called an audit planning memo.

The common sections of an audit planning memo are:

- Background and overview: sourced from research and preliminary client survey
- Risk profile: sourced from research and preliminary client survey
- Audit objectives: defined as outlined previously
- Audit scope: defined as outlined previously
- Audit criteria: defined as outlined previously
- Approach: defined as outlined previously
- Sampling strategy: defined as outlined previously
- Previous audit work/known problems: sourced from prior audit file and opening conference
- Budget: determined as outlined previously
- Audit schedule: determined as part of the timetable assessment
- Approach: established as outlined previously, and will inform the audit program development and audit fieldwork and testing explored in chapters 12 and 13
- Approvals: provided by the team leader, audit manager, and CAE (and often endorsed by the client)

The audit planning memorandum should also document any actual, potential, or perceived conflicts of interest and how they will be managed during the audit.

Outcome

The primary outcome of most audits is documented in an audit report. While the traditional form of reporting is in a structured Word document, it is also acceptable to present the outcomes in a PowerPoint presentation. In a small number of instances, oral reporting is used. This is discussed further in chapter 15.

Documentation

Reviewing Existing Documentation

When an audit of an activity has been completed previously, there will be existing documentation. Documentation that is still topical and current should be reviewed as part of the planning effort. For instance, the prior audit report will remain topical, process flow documentation may remain current if there have been no significant changes, and other documentation such as annual business plans may have been superseded.

Creating or Updating Process Flow Documentation

Process flow documentation may be prepared by an auditor to outline the steps required to complete a task, activity, or process when it occurs. A process flow document details the steps of the process from end to end, including the inputs, the decision points, and the outputs. It may also be called a process flowchart or process flow diagram. In some instances, management will already have process flow documentation. The primary purpose of process flow documentation is to analyze the business process for improvement; it also provides a record that helps each worker understand how to perform a process correctly.

The development of process flow documentation should involve people who are experienced and knowledgeable in the process to ensure accuracy and integrity. It is best to document a single process or sub-process and then consolidate the whole picture to illustrate the connections between processes. A simple process could be documented in Word text or freehand flowchart, whereas more complex processes may require flowchart software. Whichever approach is adopted, the documentation needs to have version control and be accessible and editable. When an audit of the activity has been completed previously, the auditor should review and update the process flow documentation in collaboration with operational staff where changes have occurred.

Opening Conference

The opening conference (also called an entrance conference) provides an opportunity for the auditor(s) to connect directly with key stakeholders involved in the audit. It sets the tone for the audit and should be conducted in an open, cooperative, and professional manner.

Preparation is essential, with a well-ordered approach likely to provide the foundation of an effective engagement with value-added outcomes. Participants would include the audit team, management, key contacts, and operatives.

The first part of the opening conference typically involves small talk so the respective parties can get to know each other. The purpose of the opening conference is to:

• Introduce the internal audit team and outline their roles, build confidence, and establish an effective working relationship between the respective parties.

- Establish the type of audit that is being contemplated (e.g., compliance, financial, or operational).
- Discuss the risks and explain the proposed audit objectives, scope, and timing. These may need to be modified to suit the specific needs and expectations of management.
- Clarify any elements of the preliminary client survey (questions and documentation) that remain outstanding or require further discussion. Identify any specific issues that could impede the audit or require additional attention.
- Establish working arrangements, including frequency of periodic dialog with management as the audit progresses, onsite workspace, key contacts, access to documentation and files, and other logistics.
- Outline the audit process, including the steps to be taken to validate audit observations, determine recommendations, deliver a draft report, seek management comments and action plan, finalize the audit report, and follow-up recommendations.

Notes of the entrance conference are typically prepared covering the time, date, location, attendees, topics covered, and key matters that arise. Prior to finalization of the audit, the team leader should review the notes to ensure that key matters have been addressed and are covered in the report (where relevant) and/or the outcomes have been discussed with management. The notes are included in the workpaper file, which is discussed more fully in chapter 13. Further insights on communicating effectively are covered in chapter 10.

Perspectives on Planning

If you were considering a trip across the United States, through Europe, into Africa, or around Australasia, you would work your way through many options and narrow them down based on a range of intuitive criteria. You would do this to optimize the experience within your available resources. As an example:

- You would ask questions about the trip, including the locations, weather, peak times, availability of bookings, and culture. You could do this through consultation with a travel agent, in discussions with friends who have traveled, or an online web search.
- Based on your inquiries, you would probably compile a list of questions and identify further information that would help you finalize the details of the trip.
- You would work out how much you could afford, including travel, accommodation, and sightseeing.
- You would determine what you wanted to achieve from the experience, perhaps to produce a photograph gallery of the most exquisite natural scenery.
- You would determine the places you wanted to see and prioritize those that are "must not miss" and those that "would be nice to see."

- You would determine your mode of transportation, narrowing down whether it would be a road trip, cruise, luxury or budget coach, railway journey, other local transportation, or a combination.
- You would firm up the timing of your trip based on when you and your travel companions could take vacation leave, the season, transportation availability, and accommodation options.
- Once all of the details for the trip were finalized, you would prepare an itinerary to capture in a single document all of the key facets of the journey.
- You would capture your story in a digital album while sharing your favorite photos using social media.

Likewise, effective internal audit planning is fundamental to a successful outcome and the value you deliver. The travel example reflects fundamental elements of the planning for an audit, as shown in **exhibit 9-2.**

Exhibit 9-2: Travel Example Reflecting Fundamental Elements of Audit Planning

Steps in Travel Example	Audit Planning Element
Make inquiries about the trip	Research
Compile a list of questions and identify further information	Preliminary client survey
Determine affordability	Budget (including resource allocation)
What you want from the experience (i.e., photograph gallery)	Objective
Places to see	Scope
Mode of transport	Approach
Timing of trip	Timetable (including timing)
Itinerary	Audit planning memorandum
Social media/digital album	Outcome

What Practitioners Love About Internal Audit

"Some items appear as a task on the audit plan, while others arise as part of day-to-day business. These are the exciting audits to be involved in as you don't know what you will end up discovering."			
Auditor	Millennial	Almost one year auditing experience	Finance

Engagement Planning in the Broader Context

Environmental Scanning

Environmental scanning helps auditors understand changing business practices and what that means for internal audit coverage. In turn, this helps auditors deliver insights to management that are relevant to them, timely, and genuinely add value.

The importance of environmental scanning is reflected in the way that traditional business models have been disrupted and will never recover to their previous form. For instance:

- Retail: Online streaming services have seen the demise of video stores in many parts of the world. Similarly, online purchasing is jeopardizing the business models of large retail chains. Big data has profoundly altered marketing initiatives to better align with user behavior.
- Financial services: The use of electronic funds transfers and online banking have seen a significant drop in the use of checks. Cryptocurrency is now gaining momentum in some parts of the world.
- Manufacturing: Global competition and customer preferences have seen manufacturing companies close, alter their product lines, or reduce production. The motor vehicle industry is an example.

Tips for New Auditors

- Be imaginative in the engagement planning of internal audits. You are well positioned to provide fresh ideas through innovative thinking and by leveraging the power of technology.
- Stand in management's shoes when defining the audit breadth, as they might require more than a traditional audit scope delivers.
- Reflect on the learnings from your university, tertiary, and supplementary studies (as appropriate) when determining the best approach for conducting the audit. Perhaps there are techniques that you have been trained in that others in your internal audit activity do not know about.
- Cast your mind forward to the end result throughout each stage of your planning effort. Consider what outcomes you want to deliver to aid the business and what this will look like. If you can see this clearly, then you will undertake and document your work in a professional manner.
- Always look forward and exercise due professional care (i.e., apply the care and skill expected of a prudent and competent auditor, and in accordance with professional standards).

Related Standards

Standard 2200 - Engagement Planning

Internal auditors must develop and document a plan for each engagement, including the engagement's objectives, scope, timing, and resource allocations.

Note that the engagement plan will typically be drawn from a high-level risk-based plan (described as a "forward audit plan" in this book) in line with the following standard.

Standard 2010 – Planning

The chief audit executive must establish a risk-based plan to determine the priorities of the internal audit activity, consistent with the organization's goals.

Chapter 10
Conducting an Interview

Conducting interviews is an important aspect of the audit process. This chapter covers effective steps for conducting an interview, interview practices to avoid, and best practices for documenting the interview.

Understanding the Basics of Effective Interviewing

Purpose

Establishing the overall objective of the audit (see chapter 9) ensures you have the necessary focus to proceed to conducting interviews designed to help you understand the environment and operation (in the context of your audit objective). The internal audit interview helps to identify *what is* and provide a foundation for comparing to *what should be*. Auditors should hold off asking questions until they know enough to pose the questions and understand the answers.

Interviewing is a crucial step in the audit process, involving a structured and well-formulated conversation in a question-and-answer format typically undertaken in a relaxed environment. The main goal of an interview is to uncover new facts or confirm information discussed previously. Auditors need to be especially alert to nonverbal signals delivered through body language.

> **Explanation of Body Language**
>
> Body language refers to physical movements rather than words (e.g., hand gestures, facial expressions, eye movement, voice tone and volume, and postures) that communicate attitudes and feelings of people, and these can be either consciously or unconsciously. They represent a significant proportion of people's daily communication and are used to convey lots of information.

Interviewing is undertaken at different stages of the audit process, as illustrated in **exhibit 10-1**.

Exhibit 10-1: Interviewing at Different Stages of the Audit Process

Planning (Opening conference – see chapter 9)	Fieldwork (Fieldwork discussions – see chapter 13)	Reporting (Exit conference – see chapter 15)
Understand the strategic context and key business drivers.	Seek information on segments of the audit program to facilitate testing.	Confirm internal audit observations, validate the overarching root cause analysis, and provide preliminary audit opinion.
Obtain risk and other information to confirm audit objectives, scope, and approach.	Discuss outcomes of specific testing, clarify exceptions, share observations, and collaborate on solutions and root cause.	Agree on the reasonableness of audit recommendations and formulate an action plan.

To be successful in interviewing stakeholders as part of the audit, auditors need to reflect confidence, preparedness, and a professional approach. Because up to 75% of oral communication is said to be ignored, misunderstood, or quickly forgotten, it is imperative that auditors embrace structured interviewing techniques, such as the SMILE techniques outlined in **exhibit 10-2** and **exhibit 10-3**.

Exhibit 10-2: Overview of SMILE Techniques for Conducting Interviews

S tructured
M eaningful
I nsightful
L istening
E nding

Exhibit 10-3: SMILE Techniques for Conducting Interviews[1]

Structured

- Prepare a plan for the interview, including an overview of how you want the interview to go and what you want to cover.
- Preplanning ensures the interview focuses on the desired outcomes and helps to optimize time.
- Develop interview objectives.
- Brainstorm with other members of the audit team prior to the interview to anticipate all potential issues and allow topics to be explored thoroughly.
- Develop a questionnaire containing a series of preplanned questions (but allow for flexibility).
- Identify an indicative list of documentation to be obtained.
- Hold the interview at an appropriate place to allow for a demonstration and/or site tour (if required) and privacy (where necessary).
- Determine whether the interview will be tape recorded (unusual) and, if so, seek permission beforehand.

Meaningful

- Maintain focus on the primary objectives and expected outcomes of the interview.
- Ask questions that are short, clear, and objective, and ask them in logical order.
- Control the interview process so as to reach a timely and productive end.
- Use the preplanned questionnaire to guide the conversation.
- Take notes during the interview; this will form the basis of the record of interview (see exhibit 10-4).
- Behave professionally. Be relaxed and have open body posture; lean forward slightly if sitting; face people squarely at eye level; keep an appropriate distance; use simple acknowledgments; and make eye contact.
- If the interview seems to go off track, refocus the interviewee by referring to earlier discussions.
- Remember never to become accusatory as the interviewee is likely to become defensive.
- Never jump to conclusions if you appear to find irregularities; try to explore your assumptions.

Insightful

- Outcomes are optimized where care is taken to develop lines of communication and establish rapport.
- Insights can be discerned from more than words alone. It can be inferred from voice inflections, rate of speech, gestures, facial expressions, body language, or the emotional tone of the words spoken.
- Ensure that information is presented in reasonable quantities and arrange for another interview if you are having difficulty processing it (information overload).
- Wait until you have considered all information before forming judgments.
- Observe the interviewee's body language, voice inflections, posture, and eye contact. Also, be aware of your own so as not to give the wrong message.
- Stay silent after asking questions to allow the interviewee time and opportunity to process the question and gather their thoughts (if necessary).
- Notwithstanding preplanned questions, you will at times need to go with the flow as there could be unexpected, though meaningful, deviations from the plan.

Exhibit 10-3: SMILE Techniques for Conducting Interviews[1] (cont.)

Listening
• Put yourself completely in the moment. Focus energy and attention on the person communicating with you so that you hear both the spoken and the unspoken. • Listen actively, showing interest by occasionally reflecting answers back to ensure the answers you heard are the ones that were delivered. • Be aware of your own unconscious bias that may be operating during your interactions. • Active listening helps to clarify understanding, demonstrates interest and respect, and lets people know they have been heard. • Paraphrase important answers and get acceptance from the client. • Seek clarification of any points that are not clear and work through any potential misstatements or misunderstandings. • Give reassurance that the purpose of the interview is data collection and not oversight.

Ending
• End the interview properly by reviewing the main areas of discussion. • Confirm insights and observations you have recorded. • Summarize additional information to be received and the likely date of receipt. • Thank the interviewee/s for their time and information and let them know how they can contact you if further discussion is required. • When back at your desk, write or rewrite your notes promptly, highlighting any fresh leads and insights and recording any necessary follow-up (see example in exhibit 10-4). These notes become part of audit workpapers and may be used for evidential requirements at a later date.

Comprehending What Is Said

The way someone says something can be more revealing than what is actually said. For instance, the speaker's sincerity, emotions, attitudes, and intentions can be detected from the clues contained in the way the words are spoken. Listening alone is not always a sufficient means of two-way communication. Sometimes comprehension requires you to put yourself in the other person's shoes.

This is highlighted in the following exchange between a four-year-old (Zachary) and his grandfather:

GF: "You've been such a good boy, Zachary, here's a $5 bill to put in your piggy bank."
Z: "But how can I?"
GF: "Not now, Zachary, when you get home."
Z: "But I'm not sure what you mean."
GF: "Give the money to mom. When you get home, she'll give it back so you can put it in the piggy bank."
Z: (*getting exasperated*) "So you want me to cut it into small pieces to fit it into the piggy bank?"
GF: "Hmmm … you mean how do you fit it through the coin slot?"

Interview Practices to Avoid

The anticipated outcomes of interviews can be diminished if an auditor does not avoid common problems such as those listed below.

- Avoid going into an interview without an internal frame of reference (when something is found to be confusing, our brain can refuse to actually even see it).
- Avoid using language your audience does not know or use.
- Avoid being inflexible during the interview, as other issues may emerge that can be useful in achieving the audit objectives (beyond the preplanned questions).
- Avoid missing the big picture by being control- and evidence-oriented (the psychological phenomenon of inattentional blindness reflects an overreliance on a micro-level understanding of systems, policies, and procedures that prevent auditors from seeing the big picture).
- Avoid focusing too much on being right or for the interview to be just about us (be aware that for many people, their work is close to their hearts and they have a great deal of emotion invested in it).
- Avoid letting your emotions go unchecked; you risk tainting the message.
- Avoid turning an audit interview into an interrogation.
- Avoid the temptation to fill in the silence when a client is considering their answer.
- Avoid missing facial expressions and body language that do not align with the message.
- Avoid missing the opportunity to seek clarification to ensure you understood the message.
- Avoid engaging in disruptive habits such as finger drumming or pencil tapping.
- Avoid asking multiple questions at once.
- Avoid making inappropriate and personal comments during the interview and in the record of interview unless they are material to the audit.
- Avoid emotional or uncomfortable situations as they can detract from your ability to focus and listen.

Barriers to Effective Communication

Despite an auditor's best efforts, problems can still occur during interviews due to commonplace barriers, some of which are listed below. An awareness of these barriers can help the auditor keep the interview on track to achieve its objectives.

- Body language can be problematic if it contradicts what we're saying.
- Charging on with judgments or opinions when not all of the information has been considered.
- Defensiveness occurs when people feel they are under attack, and they don't always hear what's being said.
- Emotions are experienced by someone when they impart or receive information.
- Information overload occurs when too much information is presented, making it difficult to process it.
- Filtering is a conscious manipulation of meaning to make it benefit either party.

- Influence of different cultures can cause communication difficulties.
- Language can be problematic when our experiences, background, gender, age, and culture cause us to have different meanings for words or phrases.
- Stereotyping can cause us to shortcut the process of understanding others by identifying attributes of a group of people and making sweeping judgments about individuals.

Practices for Documenting the Interview

It is not enough for auditors to have highly tuned technical knowledge and experience. They need personal influencing skills to gain cooperation and buy-in from management and staff. Persuading people to impart information, meet at suitable times, provide documentation, confide concerns, and accept recommendations for improvement is crucial to carrying out the audit.

All interviews conducted as part of the audit must be carefully and completely documented and a formal record of interview document must be included in the workpaper file. An example format is included in **exhibit 10-4**.

Interview records are important documents. They should never just be prepared and left statically in the workpaper file. They should be used during the different stages of the audit to inform the work and (before wrapping up the audit) be reread to ensure that all observations and insights have been documented appropriately and all commitments given to management have been effectively fulfilled.

Exhibit 10-4: Example Format of a Record of Interview

Record of Interview (Use Bullet Points for Multiple Points)			
Audit Name:		Reference Number:	
Date:			
Location:			
Participants:			
Purpose/objective of Interview:			
Main discussion points (including fresh leads and insights):			
Documentation obtained and/or to be sought:			
Other follow-up:			
Conclusion:			

Perspectives on Interviewing

Matilda had completed the company's graduate recruitment program that involved rotations through a range of different business areas, including three months with the internal audit activity. Because of her accounting degree, she had been appointed to a trust account administration role and was meeting her new supervisor, Tasneem, who had been in the role for a short time.

As part of her induction to the new role, Tasneem asked Matilda to interview existing employees to find out how robust the checks and balances were over trust account administration. Tasneem had completed some initial legwork to understand key elements of the control framework, which included code of ethics, delegations of authority, system validation functionality, reconciliations, segregation of duties, mandatory leave policy, and employee engagement survey results.

Matilda enthusiastically applied the interviewing techniques she learned during her graduate rotation in internal audit. In particular, she found it helpful to understand body language, ask follow-up questions, and seek evidence of the controls operating in practice.

Matilda reported back to Tasneem later in the week and informed her that she had some shortcomings to address, in particular:

- Employee turnover had been high over the last year (more than 50%). The new employees did not receive an induction into the company and were not aware of the code of ethics or corporate values.
- Excessive levels of coding errors are slowing the processing work considerably.
- The delegations validation functionality of the accounting software is not turned on, and there are no compensating checks for transactions authorization.
- Reconciliations are completed monthly but include many high-value, long-outstanding reconciling items that have never been actioned because employees don't have enough time.
- Segregation arrangements do not operate for many weeks of the year when employees take leave.
- Nobody monitors the mandatory leave policy, and longer-term employees have not been able to take any leave for more than two years because they need to train new employees.
- The employee engagement survey was last completed three years ago, and her impression is that morale is low and employees have little understanding of the corporate values or strategic direction.

Tasneem was interested when Matilda spoke with her. When they discussed Matilda's interviewing approach, Tasneem was impressed, realizing that she had not thought to verify information and facts supplied to her. She asked Matilda to help her prepare an action plan to strengthen the control framework. Matilda was delighted to do so and looked back appreciatively on her experience with the internal audit activity, particularly the advanced interviewing and validation skills she had acquired.

What Practitioners Love About Internal Audit

"You obtain a helicopter view across the organization and, from time to time, undertake deep dives into specific areas. With this in mind, the focus (or value add) tends to be strategic in nature."			
Audit Manager	Generation X	Over 20 years' auditing experience	Accounting

The Broader Context

Communicating with Effect Within the Business

One of the CBOK reports reflected on internal audit career path characteristics, including: [2]

- **Understanding of Business and Risks:** A deep knowledge of the business and the ability to evaluate risks faced by the entity.
- **Leadership and Ethics:** Always conducting oneself at the highest levels of ethical standards.
- **Critical Thinking:** Ability to analyze critical and complex issues objectively to ensure that subsequent decisions are sound, practical, and effective.
- **Breadth of Knowledge:** An understanding of all aspects of the business.
- **Executive Presence:** Be similar in approach, tone, manner, and communication style to the top executives of the organization.
- **Excellent Communication:** Provide the link between the internal audit activity and top management and be able to communicate effectively with all stakeholders.

The development of these characteristics will help all internal auditors undertake more effective interviews as part of their audits.

Tips for New Auditors

- Become as knowledgeable as possible about an organization or process before interviewing a client to show genuine interest in their business. It's difficult to change a first impression.
- Listen, listen, listen. Ask questions, but learn to ask the right questions. It's easy to go down a certain path and lose your way. This will take some time to master, but it makes for an interesting and rewarding journey.

- Develop an ability to synthesize what you have observed into short messages that are easy to convey in a minute or two, and also have a five-minute explanation. When preparing interview notes, prepare them as normal but, at the end, set out key messages taken from the interview. During team meetings where team/executives are in attendance, take good notes on how they organize the information discussed.
- Ask all of those questions that are in your head and learn to ask them the right way. You're not expected to be an expert in every part of the business, and sometimes asking questions that challenge the status quo can help you collaboratively make recommendations to improve the business.
- Learn to listen carefully and to confirm what you think you heard. Use the six wise questions: what, why, how, who, where, and when.

Related Standards

Standard 2310 – Identifying Information

Internal auditors must identify sufficient, reliable, relevant, and useful information to achieve the engagement's objectives.

Chapter 11
Audit Risk Assessments, Internal Controls, and Walkthroughs

Audit risk assessments allow internal auditors to focus on areas posing the highest risk to an organization. This chapter covers the process for assessing risk, identifying internal controls to respond to the risk, and performing walkthroughs of internal controls.

Understanding the Basics

Risk-Based Methodology

Risk-based auditing is the most common form of contemporary internal audit practice (see exhibit 6-2 and exhibit 6-3 earlier). It involves three key steps: assessing risks, identifying controls, then verifying that the controls have been correctly captured through a walkthrough (or confirmation) of the controls operating in practice. The connections between these steps are illustrated in **exhibit 11-1**.

Exhibit 11-1: Overview of the Process for Assessing and Confirming Risks and Controls

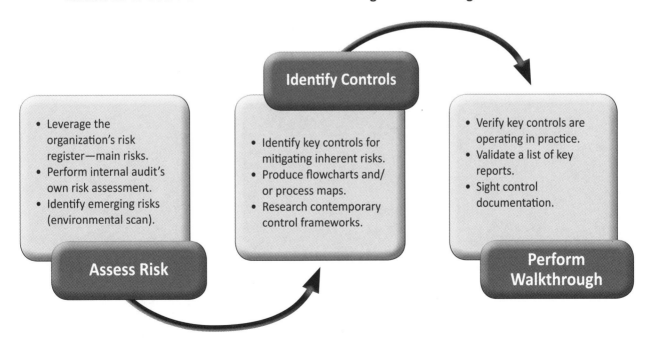

Process for Assessing Risk

The organization's risk register (which is explained in chapter 5) is the starting point for an auditor to assess risk. If there is no risk register available, the auditor will need to undertake a risk assessment, perhaps using the international standard ISO 31000:2018 (see chapters 5 and 6). If there is a risk register, the auditor needs to establish whether it is complete and updated. A systematic approach is used to assess each risk to establish whether the related control objectives are adequately addressing the inherent risks, taking into consideration the related business objective.

Identifying Internal Controls to Respond to the Risk

Auditors are encouraged to leverage insights gained in chapters 5 and 7 when completing this phase of the audit, notably by:

- Using an appropriate system of control model as the basis for identifying internal controls
- Embracing both soft and hard controls
- Considering control of corruption, misappropriation, and fraud depicted in the fraud tree

The identification and assessment of internal controls should provide reasonable, but not absolute, assurance that the fundamental elements of the system of internal control are sufficient to accomplish their intended purpose—the reduction of inherent risks to within the organization's risk appetite. The identification and assessment process should be adequately supported by well-constructed documentation.

Internal controls are identified through one or more of the collaborative techniques illustrated in **exhibit 11-2**. All key controls identified through this process should be evaluated and tested (guided by the audit program as outlined in chapter 12). Internal control weaknesses do not need to be tested, but they will need to be brought to the attention of management (i.e., reported) after validation of the weakness.

Exhibit 11-2: Common Collaborative Techniques for Identifying Controls

Facilitated Workshops	• Enables in-depth probing of issues to deliver realistic insights. • Leverages the expertise and open dialog of participants who often bounce ideas off each other (see further information on control self-assessment). • Provides learning opportunity for participants, enhancing their holistic awareness of the control framework and risk management beyond their work area.
Surveys	• An efficient approach for gathering information from a large sample of the population. • Responses are readily quantified and analyzed. • Confidentiality encourages respondents to be candid.
Structured Interviews	• Enables in-depth probing. • Follow-up questions should be asked where the body language of the interviewee suggests more probing is necessary. • Further information on conducting an interview can be found in chapter 10.

Auditors should also consider the efficiency, effectiveness, economy, and ethics of the process, taking into account the risk appetite of the organization. Use of a business process improvement methodology can help to streamline business processes through recommendations on better ways of working, including stripping obsolete or ineffective controls from a process.

Control Self-Assessment (CSA)

Control self-assessment (also called risk and control self-assessment) is a structured process where management and the work team collaboratively assess the effectiveness of controls, the level of residual risk, and the achievability of business objectives. These typically involve facilitated workshops and surveys and can be conducted during the planning stage of an audit or during the evaluation and walkthrough phase of risks and internal controls.

Where an organization has a robust risk management function as part of the second line of defense (the Three Lines of Defense model was mentioned in chapter 7), it might collaborate with management and the work team to identify, document, and assess their systems of internal control for specific functions and activities. Alternatively, the internal audit activity might facilitate the process by guiding participants through the self-assessment. The outcome of the self-assessment will be confirmation of the adequacy of internal controls and/or recognition of control weaknesses, which require action to remediate, and/or the identification of opportunities for improvement where existing controls are excessive and inefficient.

Auditors can use the outcomes of a control self-assessment as part of their risk and control assessment to inform the development of the audit program (chapter 12). Should the control self-assessment reveal any significant governance, risk management, or control issues, the auditor has a responsibility to report them to the CAE who, in turn, will appropriately advise the audit committee and senior management.

List of Key Reports

A common audit objective is to review the reliability and integrity of financial, operational, and decision-support information. Auditors are encouraged to use a systematic approach in determining and ranking key reports by identifying each report relied upon by management or distributed by management to other areas of the business, then capturing details of the report illustrated in **exhibit 11-3** into a list of key reports.

Exhibit 11-3: Common Elements of a List of Key Reports

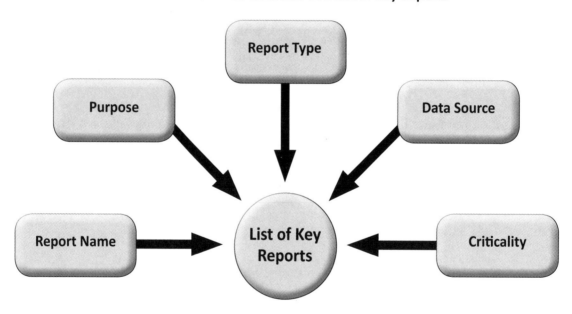

For each meaningful financial, operational, and decision-support report identified, the auditor will document the following in the list of key reports:

- Report name: What is the official name of the report and the colloquial name?
- Purpose: What is the nature and primary use of the report?
- Report type: Is the report used for financial, operational, or decision support?
- Data source: Is the data from a well-controlled and credible application, or a spreadsheet (see the perspectives on work programs story in chapter 12) or another source?
- Criticality: How important is the report to management in achieving business objectives?

Business-critical reports in less controlled data environments should be included in the audit program, requiring control over content integrity to be reviewed as part of the audit. The auditor should also determine if there is a single source of truth for reporting content and assess whether reasonable reconciliation controls are in place.

Performing Walkthroughs of Internal Controls

A walkthrough leverages the risk assessment and control identification phases of the audit outlined in the preceding sections. The auditor uses the walkthrough to determine whether or not established controls are as described and whether they are actually operating in practice.

An abridged example of a walkthrough is included in **exhibit 11-4**, which illustrated the different steps for the risk and control assessment and validation. The example is intended to demonstrate how each phase connects with the other. Please note that, for reasons of simplicity, the example is not intended to capture all risk elements, controls, walkthrough steps, or phases of the audit recommendation, and does not include root cause analysis or cultural assessment. The example continues the chapter's storytelling theme focusing on passenger rail services.

Exhibit 11-4: Example: Assessing and Confirming Risks and Controls of On-Time Running Statistics

Audit Phase	Auditor's Assessment
Strategic Priority	Deliver reliable railway services (part of a social charter with the government).
Risk Assessment	Failure to maintain the integrity of on-time running statistics published daily on the internet (critical key performance indicator [KPI] for train reliability).
Control Identification	The list of key reports highlights the importance of daily reporting of on-time running statistics.
Key Control	• Train arrival times are captured manually by station workers each time a train arrives, and these times are immediately recorded into a standard database. • The station manager reviews the captured times for reasonableness at hourly intervals throughout the day. The daily database is printed and signed by both the station workers and the station manager as evidence of these checks. • The database is uploaded to a central record at head office at 9 p.m. each evening. An analyst checks that the information has been received from a valid source, then prints the coversheet and signs it as evidence. • All database information is consolidated and checked for reasonableness. On-time running statistics are calculated using a standard formula and checked by an independent senior analyst who evidences the check. • The higher-level manager provides evidence of all of these checks to the general manager. The general manager must approve and sign off the upload of the on-time running statistics to the organization's website and provide a hardcopy schedule to an appointed government official. ***Preliminary conclusion:*** Effective controls have been established.

Exhibit 11-4: Example: Assessing and Confirming Risks and Controls of On-Time Running Statistics (cont.)

Walkthrough *(see chapter 14 for further discussion of the audit processes for observations and recommendations)*	The auditor attended several railway stations to validate the established controls. He formed the view that it was common practice for the station workers to leave it to the end of the day to record all of the train arrival and departure times, and station workers make most of them up on a best-guess basis. They used this approach because it is a tedious and boring process, management abuses staff if the statistics look bad, and poor indicators are not well received by the government. ***Observation***: Established controls are not operating as designed. The manual system for maintaining on-time running statistics is seriously flawed and inefficient.
Draft Recommendation	Automate on-time running data capture through electronic tags on trains that communicate to electronic capture points at stations, with a direct interface to the mainframe computer system.

Perspectives on Risk, Control, and Walkthroughs

Christine was general manager of the passenger services division of state railways. She had heard whispers that station workers at the City West station were not regularly checking that passengers had valid tickets for their completed journeys.

She wanted to maximize the recovery of running costs through the sale of tickets, as any seepage in fare collection affected profitability and affordability of pricing. Passenger travel statistics were used to identify passenger usage trends and the number of train services needed on each line; if the statistics were flawed, then train cars would potentially become congested.

Christine contacted the station manager several times and was assured tickets were being checked. She was reminded of established controls, including electronic ticket barriers monitored by station workers and passengers needing a valid ticket to proceed through electronic ticket barriers.

Christine was still not fully satisfied, and asked one of her trusted advisors, Mike, to spend the morning at the City West station to see firsthand what was happening. Mike took a digital camera with him, and not wanting to breach civil liberties or privacy laws, confirmed he had the authority under the digital surveillance policy to take still shots of crowds. Mike arrived early, about 7 a.m., and found a seat at the nearby cafe that had a clear view of the electronic ticket barriers. He felt a bit like an undercover boss.

City West was one of the busiest stations. The first half hour was uneventful. By 7:45, the peak period was underway, with crowds lined up to enter the station through the electronic ticket barriers. Then a strange thing happened. Station workers opened the large entrance gates and turned all electronic ticket barriers to an open state. Mike took a series of still shots. The crowd slowly dissipated and the station workers eventually reversed the process two hours later.

Mike made his way to the city-bound platform wondering how many passengers who were familiar with the process were traveling for free. He found a station worker having morning tea and struck up a casual conversation, confirming that the local practice he witnessed was a daily occurrence as a crowd control measure.

After Mike contacted Christine, she spoke with her station manager. Following further evaluation, she ultimately authorized the installation of additional electronic ticket barriers.

Scenarios like this highlight the importance for internal auditors to assess the risks themselves, then determine the existence and validate the operation of key internal controls. Walkthroughs are an essential step to validate that controls are actually operating in practice.

What Practitioners Love About Internal Audit

"The variety in our work. The different types of audits, different risks, different stakeholder expectations, different departments, and different countries and locations that you visit."			
CAE	Generation X	10 to 20 years' auditing experience	Business

The Broader Context

Transitioning from Hindsight, to Insight, to Foresight

In his *Chambers on the Profession* blogs, IIA President and CEO Richard Chambers has reflected on the journey of internal auditors shifting from solely a hindsight perspective (assessing what happened in the past to provide control assurance), to delivering fresh insights to management (perspectives on risks facing the organization and control assurance in the here and now), and increasingly to providing foresight (helping organizations prepare for the future).[1]

Explanation of Foresight for Internal Auditors

According to Richard Chambers, "Foresight is the ability to contemplate key risks and challenges that our organizations could conceivably face, so that we can share those perspectives with management and the board. This way we help our clients prepare for challenges or opportunities before they materialize. Foresight enables us to warn of pending disasters that may befall our organizations in the event management is ignoring strategic or business risks."[2]

Chambers has also reflected in his book *Lessons Learned on the Audit Trail* that, "Foresight can mean the difference between an engagement resulting in another routine audit—or a major success story."[3]

Auditors need to understand the changing environment if they are to provide foresight. For instance, radical digital transformation is significantly impacting the risk landscape, with media reports painting a challenging picture. For example[4]:

- Artificial Intelligence (AI): AI augmentation will boost worker capability to soon recover 6.2 billion hours of productivity globally.
- Big Data Analytics: The planet's data collection will soon top a trillion gigabytes (44 zettabytes), which would be sufficient to store every word ever spoken by humans.
- Biometrics: An individual will be able to be identified by a range of characteristics, including face, voice, iris, fingerprint, or vein pattern.
- Blockchain: The technology behind the cryptocurrencies provides a distributed ledger, a means of sharing and authenticating information, and a way of transferring value.
- Conversational Commerce: Demand for voice-triggered action is taking off, with the demand for smart speakers growing by 600% a year, much faster than the rate at which smartphones took off.
- Dark Web: Provides an unregulated and unpoliced environment where stolen business data can be sold, or where it can be dumped if it is found to be of little value.
- Internet of Things: IoT provides a key to linking IT and operational technology to enhance efficiency by enabling organizations to sense, source, and share data at a granular level.
- Robotic Process Automation: RPA can be 65% cheaper than hiring humans to perform the same task, so automation may become more favored than outsourcing and off-shoring of activities.

Note: ©2018 Australian Institute of Company Directors, Australia. Reprinted with modifications from Company Director, May 2018, with permission of the Australian Institute of Company Directors, Australia. Any changes to the original material are the sole responsibility of the author and have not been reviewed or endorsed by the Australian Institute of Company Directors, Australia.

While the world is quickly changing, many risk registers remain static. Auditors need to periodically conduct an environmental scan to determine the type of risks that are coming over the horizon that might significantly impact the business and the areas they are auditing. Their foresight will be well received.

Wisdom of a Global Luminary

"Aspiring internal auditors must be able to look beyond today's concerns to what future demands and changes might be. This includes the provision of high-end consulting advice. Organisations continue to demand more value from internal audit, more insight into the affairs of the business and an improved level of assistance around control optimisation. Internal auditors now need to ensure they are capable to meet this demand, have the necessary industry experience, have the business acumen to gather company knowledge and deliver high-value advisory services. Internal auditors need to think critically about whether their stakeholders are getting the right information on each key control and risk area and that internal audit is devoting the time it needs to discuss these key risks and controls and their view on the best method of mitigation. Internal audit should be aligned with sustainable longer-term organisational growth and stakeholder interest."

—Anton van Wyk
Partner Big 4 Firm, South Africa
Past Chairman of IIA Global Board of Directors 2014–15

Tips for New Auditors

- Understand the whole and the context, and make it a key objective to always provide value.
- Most people are trying to do a good job; it is systems, processes, and circumstances that inhibit them. It is our job to empower them to do the best they can, and we do this by providing information to them and their managers.
- Enjoy the role of trusted advisor both within and outside the organization. Collaborate and connect with different people who always have something different to offer.
- Even in the age of artificial intelligence, thinkers and problem solvers will be needed. Experience is a positive force toward developing a sustainable career.
- Be resilient. Use your analytical skills wherever possible. Communication is extremely important, both written and oral. Present yourself in a professional manner and always listen to what you are being told before you analyze the information.

Related Standards

Standard 2320 – Analysis and Evaluation

Internal auditors must base conclusions and engagement results on appropriate analyses and evaluations.

Chapter 12
Audit Program Development

Evaluating internal controls guides internal audit in the final stages of engagement planning, which includes creating a test plan and a work program. The work done to create audit programs is completed in the planning stage of the audit model. This chapter discusses the process of preparing a value-added audit program and tailoring audit programs to specific types of audits.

Shaping the Detailed Audit Work

Understanding the Basics

The audit program builds on the approved audit planning memorandum and contains detailed information on how step-by-step audit procedures will be performed. A sampling and testing strategy is often included.

A well-developed audit program is vital to completing the audit engagement in an efficient manner that ensures audit objectives are achieved and a value-added outcome is delivered. It helps the auditor determine whether the system of internal control is in existence and working as designed. Where gaps are identified, they are recorded in the workpapers as observations. The observations will ultimately be assessed against the organization's risk appetite, and, where warranted, appropriate recommendations will be considered as part of the reporting phase (see chapter 15).

Audit programs may look slightly different depending on whether the internal audit activity uses automated audit software or manual workpapers. A value-added audit program provides:

- Detailed audit steps for identifying, analyzing, evaluating, and documenting information during the audit
- A systematic plan for the audit that provides the basis for allocating distinct segments of work to the auditors and for communicating the overall activity to the audit team
- A firm basis for the team leader to review and compare performance of the audit to the approved audit planning memorandum
- Support for inexperienced (new) auditors by acquainting them with the objectives, scope, criteria, and audit steps, and making clear connections to the risk and control assessment
- Summarizing audit work actually performed
- Assistance to successive auditors on the nature of work carried out previously

The content of an audit program generally includes the features shown in **exhibit 12-1**. The first six rows flow horizontally; the remainder flow vertically.

Exhibit 12-1: Example of Audit Program Content

	Prepared by:	Reviewed by:	WP:
PROGRAM NAME: *<Primary business area>*			
SECTION OF AUDIT: *<Subset of the business area or activity>*			
RISK: *<Description based on risk assessment>*	CROSS-REF: *<To risk/control assessment>*		
AUDIT OBJECTIVE:	*<Based on audit planning memorandum>*		
AUDIT CRITERIA:	*<Shows the criteria the steps are assessing>*		
CONTROLS FOR TESTING:	**DETAILED AUDIT STEPS:**		**CROSS-REF:**
<Based on control assessment>	*<Determined by auditor and approved by team leader>*		*<To fieldwork>*

Building the Audit Program

The audit program is developed based on the results of the risk and control assessment (see chapter 11) and guides the audit fieldwork and testing (see chapter 13) carried out by the auditors. The audit program outlines the steps and tests that are required to ensure audit objectives are achieved. Evidence of the tests will be documented in the workpapers (see chapter 13). The audit program is a living document and may be updated throughout the audit as necessary.

The following example (using the audit program content in exhibit 12-1) illustrates how an auditor might build an audit program for human resources management (program name) that is focusing on recruitment (section of audit).

Following an environmental scan, the auditor established that industrywide[1]:

- Employment application fraud is a form of corrupt conduct.
- Between 20% and 30% of job applications contain falsehoods.
- Employment application fraud includes claiming a false qualification, adding an incorrect employment history or false reference, or creating a false identity.
- People who submit false résumés often engage in further corruption once they are employed.
- For public sector agencies, employment application fraud can undermine the integrity of the public sector and impair confidence in public administration.

Based on the results of the risk and control assessment, the auditor recognized the potential consequences of employment application fraud (*risk*). The auditor reflected on the related objective contained in the audit planning memorandum, which was to determine the design adequacy and operating effectiveness of controls in recruitment (*audit objective*). To achieve the audit objective, the auditor considered employment laws, policies, procedures, and best practice guides (*criteria*).

The auditor then determined the steps that would guide the audit fieldwork and testing (*controls for testing*). Some of these steps associated with employment screening are illustrated below (not a full list); the steps were informed by organizational policies and best practice guidance. [2]

CONTROLS FOR TESTING:	DETAILED AUDIT STEPS:
Risk-based approach applied to employment screening. Qualifications are verified.	1. Select a representative sample of new hires (including contingent hiring/non-permanents) and assess whether: a. The comprehensiveness of screening corresponded to the risk of the role based on its position description. b. The justification for the extent of screening checks was documented. c. Original documentation (degree, certificate, etc.) was sighted and certified copies were obtained and held on file. d. Qualifications were separately verified directly with the issuing institution as evidenced by a suitable file note or communiqué.
Periodic rescreening (including police checks) is completed when substantial role changes occur.	2. Select a representative sample of upgraded positions where substantial changes to the role objectives and/or conditions (including remuneration) occurred and assess: a. Requisite approvals are held. b. Employee rescreening occurred with satisfactory results.

Tailoring Audit Programs to Specific Types of Audits

A generation ago, auditors typically provided a hindsight perspective. At that time, the audit universe was relatively shallow and focused substantially on financial risks. As a consequence, the audit plan covered a three- to five-year cycle, and there were very few new topics added to what was a substantially static plan. Cyclical audits focused on topics like the revenue cycle, accounts payable, and payroll, with standard audit programs for these topics changing very little from year to year.

In the twenty-first century, the risk landscape is continually changing, stakeholder expectations are forever expanding, auditors are expected to be agile, and the audit plan is dynamic and more flexible. Most audits are new topics, or where they are repeat audits, the objectives and scope are often broader.

As an example of changing expectations, the story in chapter 15 provides perspectives on reporting and highlights a situation where recruitment had become a slow and tedious process; there was therefore a need to consider the risks through the separate lenses of compliance and performance. That example reflected a broader scope (i.e., not just a compliance focus but insights on recruitment performance), but if an auditor was preparing the audit program now, he or she would conduct a further environmental scan and probably include an assessment of employment screening (see previous example).

Assessing Soft Controls

A study of internal auditors conducted in the Netherlands in 2015 established that[3]:

- 40% of respondents said they already perform soft control audits, and a large majority of the remainder said they planned to perform soft control audits in the future (on this basis, it is expected that 75% of Dutch internal audit activities will be performing soft control functions in the near future).
- Around half of the internal audit activities performing soft control audits examine behavior and culture as an integral part of audits, with 11% performing specific soft control audits and a quarter performing both integrated and specific soft control audits.

In developing the audit program, auditors need to consider the best options for including an assessment of soft controls, which include implicit attitudes like culture, tone at the top, living shared values, morale, integrity, trust, and empowerment. **Exhibit 12-2** illustrates the steps that an auditor undertook to determine the scope of an audit of a client contact function where soft controls were to be assessed.

Exhibit 12-2: Example – Performing an Integrated Audit of Hard and Soft Controls[4]

Context	
Function audited	An area with virtually continuous client contact.
Aim	Gain insight into the hard and soft controls that contribute to client trust.

Potential Success Factors to Be Factored into Audit Program Development	
Hard Control Success Factors	**Soft Control Success Factors**
<ul><li>Clear, supported case for change</li><li>Sticking to agreements</li><li>Clear priorities and objectives</li><li>Well-trained personnel</li><li>High rate of first time right</li><li>Focusing on responsible approach to client</li><li>High client satisfaction</li><li>Product meets client requirements</li></ul>	<ul><li>Demonstrating expertise and professionalism</li><li>Showing empathy, integrity, trust, and loyalty</li><li>Communication (open, honest, personal)</li><li>Visibly acting in interest of client</li><li>Living up to expectations</li><li>Taking responsibility for the client</li><li>Client satisfaction</li><li>Learning from experience</li></ul>

Soft Controls Identified for Inclusion in Audit Scope of Audit Program (Fine-Tuned Following a Workshop)	
<ul><li>Appreciation</li><li>Sense of responsibility</li><li>Cooperation</li><li>Involvement and loyalty</li></ul>	<ul><li>Accountability</li><li>Clarity</li><li>Respect for each other</li><li>Feasibility</li></ul>

Better Ways of Working

A key focus for the internal auditor should be to look for better ways of doing things. This is achieved by developing an audit program with some operational auditing coverage of efficiency, effectiveness, economy, and ethics of the topic being audited, rather than just compliance or financial correctness. These elements are described in **exhibit 12-3** and were illustrated in exhibit 1-4.

Exhibit 12-3: The Four E's - Efficiency, Effectiveness, Economy, Ethical

Term	Meaning	Example
Efficiency	Using resources well. Producing the maximum output from inputs.	Where cost has been reduced over time.
Effectiveness	Using resources wisely. Achieving objectives as intended.	Where wastage has been reduced over time.
Economy	Using resources economically but still maintaining quality. Minimizing the cost of resources used.	Where supplies of a specific quality are purchased at the best price.
Ethical	Applying resources ethically. Living the corporate values of honesty and integrity (or similar).	Where integrity and ethical behavior is evident throughout all phases of the process.

Note: Author's creation based on research.

Perspectives on Work Programs

Therese worked in the middle office of the treasury function of a mid-size bank. The head of the bank's risk management activity, Danny, had asked her to review the integrity of information used by and provided by the dealers. He said he had heard the head of another function of the bank was in strife because of serious errors in a spreadsheet used to provide decision-support information to senior management.

As part of her environmental scan, Therese determined[5]:

- In one organization, 75% of spreadsheets (of a large number) were assessed as "business critical" and a significant proportion of the remainder were identified as significant for business management.
- In a recent flash poll, 70% of participants confirmed that their entities rely heavily on spreadsheets for critical portions of the business; with 43% having little or no specific processes to confirm that the spreadsheets are functioning in accordance with management's intentions.

- Organizations across the world had suffered major reputational damage when errors occurred and remained undetected; these included adverse financial impacts (e.g., profit overstated by $A10 million; income expectation overstated by $US15 million; underestimation of profit by 3.5%); democratic outcomes compromised (e.g., false election result); and serious privacy breaches.

Therese compiled a list of key reports used within the treasury activity, then systematically worked her way through each report to determine the source of data being used to populate the reports. She informed the head of risk management there was overreliance on uncontrolled spreadsheets for business critical functions in many parts of the treasury activity. Therese emphasized these spreadsheets were relied upon for critical decision support.

Danny asked Therese to establish a program of work over spreadsheets to provide assurance of their accuracy, completeness, and integrity until they could be replaced by well-controlled computer systems. Therese convinced Danny he first needed to establish a treasury-wide framework for controlling spreadsheet risks until computer systems could be implemented. A framework was established to guide spreadsheet development, usage, and control; there was also a review requirement to ensure spreadsheets remained current and fit for purpose. Employees were trained and the framework was introduced into practice. Therese acquired suitable analytical software for spreadsheet checking with a view to introducing a rolling program of spreadsheet reviews.

A common objective for internal auditors is to evaluate the reliability and integrity of financial and nonfinancial operational information. It is helpful to use a list of key reports (see chapter 11) as a first step in any audit work program to determine what reporting is being relied upon or is delivered to other areas of the business. From a broader risk management perspective, it is useful to determine whether there is widespread utilization of spreadsheets for business critical functions, in which case a broader program of work may need to be recommended.[6]

What Practitioners Love About Internal Audit

"It is a job where you can influence change for the better. It is the one of few roles, besides the CEO and legal, you are exposed to the whole organization and get to make recommendations for improvement. Every audit you do, you learn about the business. You get to communicate with all levels of the business, not just people at the same level or only within your own business area."			
Other: Lawyer	Generation X	5 to 10 years' auditing experience	Law

The Broader Context

Right-to-Audit Clauses

Many organizations now outsource to third-party providers all or part of their routine processing activities and activities requiring specialist expertise. While these processes are typically non-core and may be low-value/high-volume, they do represent operational risks and require effective controls. When auditors are developing their audit program, they need to be cognizant of any activities within the scope of their audit that are undertaken outside their organization. In these cases, they should confer with their team leader on the optimal approach for assessing the effectiveness of controls. This could well involve invoking a right to audit as part of their audit fieldwork and testing, building it into the audit program.

Explanation of Right-to-Audit Clauses

A right-to-audit clause is often included in significant tenders and critical contracts, based on the overall contracting risks (e.g., value, duration, and industry-specific). It follows the age-old concept of trust but verify. The clause provides internal and external auditors access to information, books, records, and assets held by contractors (and subcontractors) for purposes of auditing, including a right to make copies.

The right to audit relates to the specific contract and typically covers operational practices and procedures; security arrangements; accuracy of invoices and reports; compliance with confidentiality, privacy, and security obligations; books, records, and accounts; and any other matters determined as being relevant to the contract. There are usually provisions requiring the records and information to be in a data format and storage medium accessible by the customer who, in turn, must provide reasonable notice of the audit. A suitable onsite space for the auditor to work is also a common feature in these clauses.

A right-to-audit clause does not establish any obligation to undertake an audit—it merely reserves the right for auditors to conduct an audit where they determine a need. It will usually have survival provisions to enable it to be used for seven to 10 years after the termination of the contract.

Note: This is intended to provide an example of typical content. It is not intended to represent legal advice. The Association of Certified Fraud Examiners website has a Sample Right-to-Audit Clause.

Even outsourced processes at reputable service organizations need to be independently verified periodically, as illustrated in the case study in **exhibit 12-4**. (See also Spotting a Significant Shortfall in Services in chapter 20, "Stories from the Frontline," that involved a significant dollar value; the auditor leveraged a right-to-audit clause in the service contract to prove that the security service supplier never had the resource levels to deliver the services that it had charged in the service schedule.)

Exhibit 12-4: Case Study – Invoking Right-to-Audit Clauses to Great Effect

The audit program required a deep dive of selected higher-risk contracts. While the audit steps completed within the organization had established there was a strong security culture internally, the team leader arranged for the auditor to review selected outsourced security arrangements to provide a complete picture.

A third-party provider was selected for review as it was contracted to destroy hardware in a highly secure environment; the hardware had contained sensitive corporate and personal information. The auditor activated the right-to-audit clause and went into the provider's premises to verify the destruction process.

It was the first time the provider had been audited under a right-to-audit clause. Despite the contractor being of good repute, the auditor identified and raised myriad serious breaches of critical contractual conditions, including lax custodianship, absence of security clearances for contractor's staff, poor timeliness of destruction, and deficiencies of separation of hardware from other non-secure items. Security bins were left open, which allowed people to just take the hardware; the risk was exacerbated as the contractor employed many casual staff who were regularly coming and going but had no security clearances.

The auditor reported to senior management the escalated reputational and compliance risks should the organization's highly sensitive information make its way into the public domain. They were paying for a premium service and receiving something less.

Tips for New Auditors

- The audit program needs to be thoughtfully crafted to ensure that you are looking at the right things at the right time using the most appropriate techniques. Thinkers and problem solvers will be needed, even in the age of artificial intelligence.
- In developing the audit program, recognize how the pieces of the organization fit together to produce the whole, and recognize the ability of the internal audit activity to influence the organization.
- Any audit by its nature is disruptive to regular work practices, so the flow of the audit and the engagement with clients need to be considered in the construct of the audit program.
- Execution of a thoughtfully crafted audit program assumes the auditor has an analytical, questioning, and open mind.
- You will stay focused during the engagement if you always start with the question you are seeking to answer for the section of the audit program you are undertaking.

Related Standards

Standard 2240 – Engagement Work Program

Internal auditors must develop and document work programs that achieve the engagement objectives.

PART 4 – THE *WHEN* OF INTERNAL AUDITING

Chapters 13 through 17 leverage the preparatory work of the preceding chapters and explore the audit processes once "the rubber hits the road" from fieldwork through to reporting and ultimately follow-up. It captures the critical lead-up to the audit product that is most visible to clients—the audit report.

Fieldwork → Observations → Reporting → Quality → Follow-Up

Wisdom of a Global Luminary

"Be always a benchmark in ethics and transparency. Your clients have to know where you stand. This will foster trust, the fuel for your success as an internal auditor. And before you judge, think about this: how would you behave if you were the client. Internal audit exists, in part, because there are humans who make mistakes."

—Oliver Dieterle
Chief Audit Executive, Germany
Past Member of IIA Global Board of Directors 2012–2016

Chapter 13
Audit Fieldwork and Testing

Performing the engagement involves applying specific audit procedures to conduct tests and gather evidence. The evidence is then evaluated to form conclusions about whether controls are designed accurately and operating effectively to develop observations (also referred to as findings) and provide recommendations. This chapter covers audit evidence, data analysis in fieldwork, sampling and testing, and documentation of results into reviewable workpapers.

Performing the Engagement

Foundations of Fieldwork

Fieldwork is the result of considerable effort in planning and developing the program of work for the audit engagement. Development of an audit planning memorandum is discussed in chapter 9, as is the opening conference. Meaningful fieldwork is underpinned by interviewing skills (chapter 10) and development of the audit program (chapter 12). Fieldwork helps to determine audit observations (chapter 14), some of which form the audit report (chapter 15).

When the audit begins, the internal auditor will use the step-by-step audit program and update it throughout the audit as necessary. The audit program builds on the approved audit planning memorandum and contains detailed information on how the step-by-step audit procedures will be performed. The flow is illustrated in **exhibit 13-1** and features of fieldwork are discussed in the following pages.

Exhibit 13-1: The Flow from Planning and Program Development to Fieldwork

Audit Planning Memorandum				
Audit Objectives	Audit Scope	Audit Criteria	Audit Approach	Sampling Strategy

Audit Program

Features of Fieldwork			
Audit Evidence	Data Analysis	Sampling and Testing	Documentation of Results

Audit Evidence

To support their conclusions, auditors will gather evidence, which may be physical, testimonial, documentary, analytical, and/or photographic (see **exhibit 13-2**). Auditor's evidence will be documented in the internal auditor's workpapers.

> **Explanation of Audit Evidence**
>
> Audit evidence is information that auditors obtain through observing conditions, research, benchmarking, interviewing people, and examining records. It should provide a factual basis for audit opinions, conclusions against audit objectives, and recommendations. Audit evidence should reflect four attributes: it should be relevant, useful, sufficient, and reliable (competent).

Exhibit 13-2: Common Types of Audit Evidence

Physical	Testimonial	Documentary	Analytical	Photographic
Obtained through observing people, property, and events. Can include CCTV, tapes, videos, maps, charts, graphs, and other pictorial representations.	Takes the form of statements in response to inquiries or interviews. Not conclusive in themselves and should be supported by documentation.	Most common form of physical and electronic evidence. Includes letters, memoranda, accounting records, reports, and copies of outgoing correspondence.	Comes from analyzing and verifying data, including computation and analysis of ratios, trends, and patterns. Benchmarking information can also provide useful context.	Another form of physical evidence through pictures of people and property.

Data Analysis in Fieldwork

Data Mining

Data mining is an efficient, relatively low cost, and innovative way of analyzing large amounts of data with a significant population. It uses analytical software products such as ACL or Idea, or Microsoft products such as Excel. There are a number of data manipulation techniques that can be used, including filtering, sorting, pivot tables, and formulas.

Data analysis helps auditors to see the bigger picture, make sense of large amounts of data, pinpoint areas requiring additional focus throughout the audit, and identify trends or abnormalities for detailed testing. Before obtaining relevant data, they should first consider what it is they have to understand about the data in the context of their audit objectives and/or inherent risks. For instance:

- What would we normally expect to see from this type of data?
- What would be considered unusual in this data?
- Where could errors potentially occur in this business activity or process?
- Where would potential fraud be likely to occur, and what would the red flags look like in the data?

Once the auditors understand how the data can best be used to achieve the audit objectives, they need to retrieve data that is relevant, reliable, complete, and accurate. They also need to be able to properly format the data to facilitate their analysis.

Trend Analysis

Trend analysis is an analytical review procedure that can be used to determine the reasonableness of recorded data and assess operational results. It is a flexible procedure that can be used in both planning and fieldwork. Advantages include:

- Reveals both expected and unexpected trends
- Results in savings in audit resources by giving direction to the audit effort
- Highlights potential problems and key areas of risk
- Relatively easy to perform

Trend analysis is performed by comparing account balances or examining other metrics over time, such as performance data, key performance indicators (KPIs), or consumption data (e.g., fuel for trucks; see also Finding Unusual Activity Through Data Analytics in chapter 20, "Stories from the Frontline"). The results are analyzed by reviewing the resulting trend and highlighting significant fluctuations, trends that differ from those expected, and assessing how past performance has led to the present position. It is best suited to analyzing items of income and expense.

Examples of trends that might be analyzed as part of specific tests in the audit program:

- Monthly payroll costs: month-on-month comparison
- Broker commission costs: compared to trend in foreign exchange transactions
- Movements in property valuations: compared to other indices of property price movements
- Monthly loan interest costs or investment interest: compared to trend in interest rates

Sampling

The purpose of audit sampling is to apply an audit procedure to fewer than 100% of the items being audited to draw an inference about a characteristic of the population. It is useful for testing systems and processes. Statistical sampling is efficient in achieving a particular audit objective, allows conclusions to be reached about an entire population by drawing on analysis of a portion of it, and provides a justifiable basis for conclusions and opinions without the need to review all transactions or balances.

> **Explanation of Population**
>
> The population within the internal audit activity refers to the entire set of data from which an auditor selects a sample in order to arrive at a conclusion against a specified audit objective.

There are several stages to the sampling process:

- Identify the population: Determine the population and ensure it is a complete and valid dataset.
- Select an initial sample: Estimate an appropriate sample size based on the population and the precision/confidence they require.
- Test the sample: Test the selected sample according to the predetermined test criteria and calculate the sample result.
- Project the results: Project the implications for the testing results across the whole population to determine a statistically valid estimate.
- Verify the outcome: Establish whether the result reflects sufficient precision/confidence for the auditor's purposes. If not, further testing may be necessary.
- A sampling strategy involves consideration of each audit objective against the composition and location of a population to establish the most appropriate sample selection techniques.

The sampling strategy considers each audit objective against the composition and location of a population and determines the most appropriate sampling technique to achieve the audit objective. The sampling strategy is documented and retained with audit workpapers. Five common techniques are:

- Judgment: Selects examples to support an auditor's contention that the system of controls is weak.
- Attribute: To estimate, with a specified degree of reliability, the characteristics of a population to arrive at an estimate of a rate or percentage of occurrence or non-occurrence (e.g., error rate).
- Variables: To estimate, with a specified degree of reliability, the value of a population of one of the characteristics (e.g., dollar value of slow-moving inventories) and to determine how much (with an allowance for sampling risk, such as achieved precision).
- Stop-or-Go: To obtain reasonable information from a sample about the characteristics (such as maximum error rates) of a population by selecting the lowest sample size. If there are no errors in the sample, the auditor will stop. If there are errors, the auditor will select a larger sample, then go again.
- Discovery: To find evidence of at least one improper transaction in the population.
- There are four common approaches for selecting samples statistically:
    - Random—selecting items in no particular order using automated techniques or random number generator software
    - Interval—selecting items at predetermined intervals (e.g., every 100th item)

- Stratification—breaking the population down into distinct groups of comparable or similar items (e.g., all items over $1 million; every 10th item between $100,000 and $1 million; and every 100th item below $100,000)
- Cluster (or multistage)—typically selecting samples from different populations (using one of the approaches above) on a geographic or other basis where it would be burdensome to select randomly from the entire population

An example of a sample selection form is included in **exhibit 13-3**.

Exhibit 13-3: Example of a Sample Selection Form

Description (e.g., transactions/account/activity)		
Period sampled		
Transactions selected (number and value)		
Total population (number and value)		
Percentage of population sampled (number and value)		
Type of sampling		
Justification for sample method		
Evaluation of results		

Testing

Auditors will determine a testing strategy based on the audit objectives, which will usually involve either compliance or substantive testing, or a combination of both.

Compliance testing is an approach to determine whether prescribed controls actually exist and are being complied with in practice.

Substantive testing is an approach for determining whether data includes a material amount of dollar errors. This is typically completed through statistical and non-statistical sampling of transactions, accounts, or activities.

Once the test strategy has been determined, the testing will be completed as part of the fieldwork phase of the audit. The results of testing will determine the outcome of the audit. The audit outcome will usually be a combination of assurance (that controls are operating as intended) and observations (on areas of noncompliance, errors, or improvement). The audit report will then reflect the audit outcome. The flow through these steps is illustrated in **exhibit 13-4**.

Exhibit 13-4: Illustrating How the Outcome of Testing Flows into the Audit Report

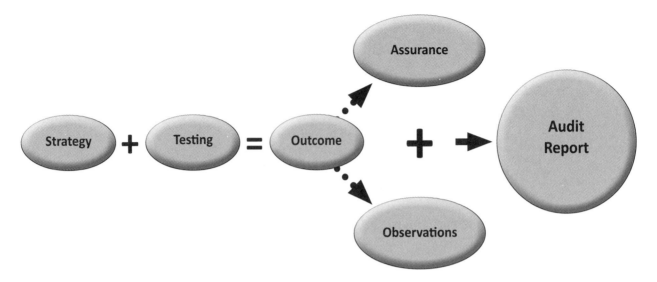

Documentation of Results (Workpapers)

Workpapers are prepared by the internal auditor to document the work performed in the planning and performance of audits. Workpapers should clearly document how the auditor has identified, analyzed, and evaluated sufficient information to achieve the engagement's objectives by providing:

- Clear flow of the workpaper files, linking back to audit objectives
- Evidence of integrity for any data analyzed (i.e., source of data used for computer assisted audit techniques [CAATS])
- Clear evidence of like-for-like comparisons when using research, reports, and benchmarks
- Clearly constructed conclusions

This form of workpaper documentation is necessary to:

- Provide the principal support for audit results.
- Evidence whether audit objectives were achieved.
- Demonstrate the auditor's basis for conclusions about the achievement of the overall objective.
- Support the accuracy and completeness of the audit work performed.
- Provide evidence the audit was planned and performed in accordance with the standards.
- Provide a sufficient and appropriate record to support the internal audit report.
- Serve as a line of defense when observations, recommendations, and conclusions are challenged.
- Enable team leaders to monitor the audit's progress and quality on an ongoing basis.
- Provide a basis for the quality of the audit to be assessed.
- Contribute to continuous improvement.
- Facilitate reviews by third parties such as the external auditor and other independent scrutineers.
- Provide a basis for measuring the performance of the auditors.

Insights on quality assurance arrangements are covered in chapter 16, "Audit Quality Review and Wrap-Up," and chapter 18, "Quality Assurance and Improvement Program." Quality assurance arrangements need to be well supported by auditors, as they help to ensure that the right evidential processes have been maintained to support the conclusions of the audits. Where quality is maintained through all stages of the audit methodology, all audits should be able to withstand independent scrutiny at a corruption, coronial, or parliamentary inquiry, a federal or state prosecution investigation, a royal commission, or an external quality assessment.

Perspectives on Fieldwork

Jack was the chief operating officer for a mid-size energy company. He was on the first day of a tour of operational sites when he arrived at a remote rural town located several hundred miles from the capital city head office. It was late afternoon when he arrived at the town, and he decided to visit the facility to introduce himself. Jack was impressed with the bright and colorful garden that greeted him at the entrance to the facility, coupled with the friendly and enthusiastic welcome he received.

It was a bustling site that was used to store wooden power poles (among other things). There were many movements of cranes and trucks as several hundred power poles had to be transported to a worksite where old and deteriorated poles were being replaced the next day. The facility had designated painted safe walkways that employees had to use to minimize harm through accidents; vehicles were prohibited from using these areas. Aware of onsite safety protocols, Jack put on his personal protective equipment, including a high-visibility fluorescent safety vest, steel-capped boots, and a helmet.

The manager and local employees offered Jack a fresh cup of tea. While chatting with the locals, Jack noticed one of the employees using the emergency fire hose to water the garden. He thought this was odd as the use of the fire hose was restricted by government regulations to emergency situations.

Sipping his tea, Jack watched employees ambling across the worksite paying little attention to the designated walkways, sometimes across the path of moving vehicles. Nobody wore approved safety vests; they had superseded versions that did not meet current safety standards as the material was highly flammable. Very few employees wore helmets. Jack remembered that nobody had given him the standard safety induction to the site. He was alarmed when he spotted several obvious fire and environmental risks (discussed in chapter 14).

When he arrived the next day, Jack spoke to the manager and reflected on his observations from visiting the facility the previous day. He mentioned that under new workplace health and safety laws, the manager was personally accountable and liable for safety at the facility, and could face fines or imprisonment if there was an incident. The manager was embarrassed, and confessed he was new to the role and had never been trained in workplace health and safety. He said it was really helpful to have Jack visit the facility with a keen set of eyes, a fresh mindset, an inquisitive nature, current knowledge, and time to observe and ponder.

Internal auditors undertaking fieldwork are similarly expected to observe onsite operations to determine whether employees are following the company's established policies, procedures, and protocols. Their fieldwork involves interviewing clients, observing onsite activities, scanning the way the site is organized and maintained, and conducting walkthroughs to evaluate onsite risks and how they are controlled. Auditors need current knowledge and technical capabilities (discussed in chapter 3), and they need appropriate experience, training, and credentials to conduct specialist onsite audits (e.g., health and safety, which is different than a financial audit).

What Practitioners Love About Internal Audit

"There are so many things I like about internal audit. But if I can only choose one it would definitely be the profession brings me to meet people from different parts of the organization, and through this you will be able to see how internal audits are applicable in different levels of the organization."			
Senior Auditor	Millennial	1 to 5 years' auditing experience	Accounting

The Broader Context

Public Scrutiny

It is never an ideal situation when the internal audit activity is drawn into court action. While these situations occur infrequently, they do draw media attention.

To avoid adverse public scrutiny, auditors have a responsibility to protect the reputation of the internal audit activity and the organization it serves. This can be achieved where internal auditors:

1. Compile well-prepared workpapers to document the results of audits (discussed earlier in this chapter).
2. Write balanced and credible audit reports that the world can see (see chapter 15).
3. Support effective quality assurance (see chapters 16 and 18).
4. Maintain effective follow-up of audit recommendations when tasked to do so (see chapter 17).

Tips for New Auditors

- Don't be afraid to ask questions. We cannot be experts in every part of an organization, so it is important to understand the subject matter as much as possible and ask questions of your colleagues regarding the audit process. There are no silly questions, and the more you ask, the more you learn.
- You need to remain resilient and use judgment. Focus on key areas that will make a difference.
- As auditors we do not usually have all the answers: we have the questions. By asking questions we can help individuals and organizations articulate their problems and find solutions for them. Regardless of the outcome, we do not own the solution: the result belongs to management.
- Always approach your work with the mindset that you are there to help. This way you will get positive engagement with business areas and the best outcomes from your work.
- When you raise an observation, anticipate the next question (so what?). If you struggle to answer the "so what" question, then it either isn't a meaningful observation or you haven't really linked the issue back to how it may impact on business objectives.

Related Standards

Standard 2300 – Performing the Engagement

Internal auditors must identify, analyze, evaluate, and document sufficient information to achieve the engagement's objectives.

Chapter 14
Audit Observations and Recommendations

Communication is a critical element of the audit and occurs throughout the engagement process, not just at the end of the audit. The results of the audit can be communicated in various ways, including memos, outlines, discussions, and draft workpapers. The final audit communication is typically provided in a formal audit report. This chapter covers communicating audit observations, sample write-ups, approaches to audit write-ups, developing recommendations, and guidelines for rating audit recommendations.

Communicating Audit Observations

Raising Observations

Determining meaningful audit observations is the result of painstaking effort through all phases of the audit process, from planning (including defining audit objectives, scope, approach, and resourcing capability); client interviews; risk and control assessments; audit program development; and audit fieldwork and testing. Flaws in any of these early phases of the audit are likely to diminish the auditor's ability to identify observations that add value to the client.

The concepts outlined in this chapter are illustrated in a high-level example illustrated in **exhibit 14-5**.

> **Explanation of Audit Observations**
>
> An observation is a term used by internal auditors to describe the connection between the audit criteria and the audit evidence collected. Observations can reflect conformity (usually a good result) or nonconformity with the audit criteria (gaps between the audit criteria and audit evidence that require corrective action) or opportunities for improvement. Observations may also be referred to as findings.

Shaping Observations for a Higher Audience

Audit observations will ultimately flow through to the audit report. Significant observations will be reported to the audit committee, with criteria established to determine the degree of risk exposures, control weaknesses, and fraud risks that require escalation to this level. The audit committee and senior management are typically interested in observations that:

- Result in residual risks that are beyond the organization's risk appetite
- Reflect on management's failure to report an inability to achieve organizational objectives
- Relate to organizational integrity and values such as fraud, ethical behavior, social responsibility, and significant noncompliance with legislative and regulatory obligations

To broach observations with senior management in a language they understand, it is helpful to translate observations into business risks. **Exhibit 14-1** contains 13 generic business risks.

Exhibit 14-1: Example of Generic Business Risks

BR1	Inability to withstand unanticipated events such as natural disasters
BR2	Interruption to continuity of operations
BR3	Unnecessary costs
BR4	Revenue not maximized
BR5	Internal and external information unreliable and/or irrelevant
BR6	Inefficient use of resources
BR7	Inability to take advantage of opportunities
BR8	Loss of licenses, penalties, and other sanctions (noncompliance with laws and regulations)
BR9	Failure to develop people
BR10	Loss of reputation/credibility
BR11	Quality of service or product not at acceptable standard
BR12	Misappropriation, theft, misuse, or damage to assets (assets not safeguarded)
BR13	Environmental harm or people hurt, resulting in death or injury (lack of safety of employees, customers, or the environment)

Source: ©2018 CPA Canada. Adapted from Guidance on Control, 1995, with permission Chartered Professional Accountants of Canada, Toronto, Canada. Any changes to the original material are the sole responsibility of the author and have not been reviewed or endorsed by the Chartered Professional Accountants of Canada. The original descriptions for BR8, BR12, and BR13 are shown in brackets.

The mindset of the auditors and their approach to communicating effectively will ultimately determine the value that management gains from the insights they deliver. This is illustrated in **exhibit 14-2** where the pendulum shifts between punitive and educative.

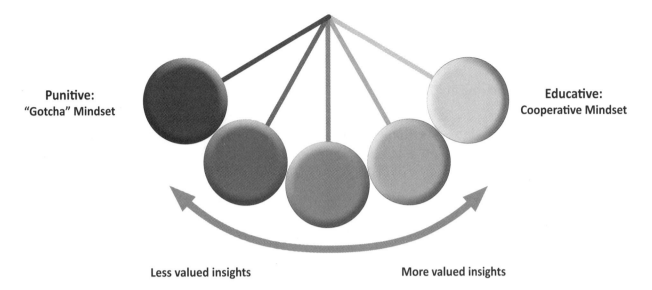

Exhibit 14-2: Shaping Observations that Add Value

Punitive:
"Gotcha" Mindset

Educative:
Cooperative Mindset

Less valued insights

More valued insights

Ongoing Communication

Client communications are a normal part of an internal auditor's work (in the context of internal auditing, a client is internal to the organization). Clients will often prefer advice on any significant observations on an ongoing basis throughout the audit. This can be done as part of informal "corridor conversations" or as part of interim meetings.

Where audits are longer in duration (taking weeks or months), it is useful to arrange periodic interim meetings with management as a means of regular coordination. Planning and preparation is essential for interim meetings, and the following steps have been modified from a top tips publication from the Chartered Institute of Internal Auditors United Kingdom and Ireland[1]:

- Send meeting invitations well in advance.
- Make sure adequate time has been allocated for the meeting.
- Be clear about the purpose of the meeting (write down the goals and do your research).
- Draw up a summary of fresh observations and a list of questions (be clear about what you want to say and ensure your summary is structured in a series of linked and progressive points).
- Have information printed or copied if you want to discuss or refer to specific documents during the meeting (including mind mapping and root cause analysis).

Getting to know the clients will help the auditors understand their preferred method and frequency for receiving advice on observations. A meeting with the main client (or audit sponsor) before the closing meeting can also provide an opportunity to clarify observations and recommendations before the exit conference is held (see chapter 15) and the draft report is prepared and delivered.

Where auditors consistently maintain the doctrine of no surprises throughout an audit, there is a lower likelihood of observations being disputed when the audit reaches its conclusion and the draft report is being prepared. Clients are also more likely to have tested the reasonableness of potential solutions so the articulation of recommendations can proceed more smoothly. Collaboration and co-design of recommendations with clients usually result in stronger recommendations that are practical and workable.

Explanation of Doctrine of No Surprises

Internal auditors apply the doctrine of no surprises when they maintain effective communication with clients throughout their audit. By doing so, their clients are not surprised or caught off guard by significant observations raised during the wrap-up and reporting stage of the audit; they will have been informed when the observation was initially made and have an opportunity to pursue rectification action while the audit is still in progress. The auditor also benefits from this approach as management will sometimes be able to provide additional information to help the auditor reach a balanced conclusion.

Sample Write-Ups

Observations can be determined during different phases of the audit engagement, but mostly through either (i) audit risk assessment, internal controls, and walkthrough, or (ii) audit fieldwork and testing. Once an observation has been identified, it should be recorded and cross-referenced in the workpapers and documented in a summary-of-observations document (or equivalent). A summary of observations will typically record the observation, the associated risk and impact, the root cause, a potential solution, and the results of discussions with management. The summary-of-observations document will be the main source for populating the draft audit report and ultimately the final audit report (discussed in chapter 15). This process is illustrated in **exhibit 14-3**.

Exhibit 14-3: Indicative Process for Audit Observations Flowing into the Audit Report

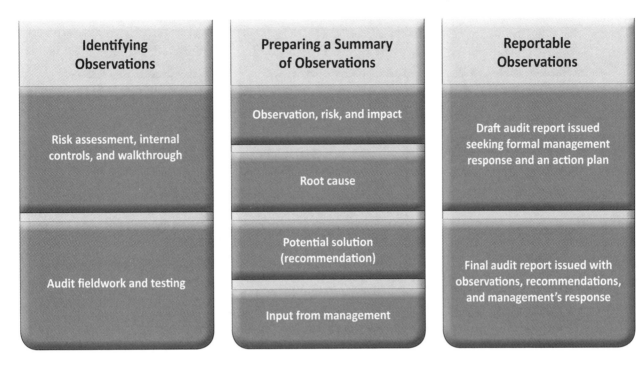

Identifying Observations	Preparing a Summary of Observations	Reportable Observations
Risk assessment, internal controls, and walkthrough	Observation, risk, and impact	Draft audit report issued seeking formal management response and an action plan
	Root cause	
Audit fieldwork and testing	Potential solution (recommendation)	Final audit report issued with observations, recommendations, and management's response
	Input from management	

Observations represent the facts produced as a result of the auditor's efforts, and are the product of their assessment and/or fieldwork. They are the source from which recommendations and opinions ultimately flow. Depending on the severity and importance of observations, they can be communicated through discussions, semi-formal methods like mind maps, summary-of-observations documents, or more formally through memos.

Approaches to Audit Write-Ups

Through every stage of the audit engagement, write with the reader in mind. Well-written workpapers are easier to discuss with the client, more meaningful for the team leader to review, and can be more seamlessly exported to an audit report. Start with the end in mind so that observations can be readily converted into a well-constructed narrative that informs practical, useful, and actionable recommendations.

From the first phase of your involvement in an audit, understand the style of reporting that your team leader will be delivering to communicate the audit results. What you write should be clear, concise, and constructive. Reporting styles can vary widely, as illustrated by the examples in **exhibit 14-4**.

Exhibit 14-4: Styles of Audit Reporting

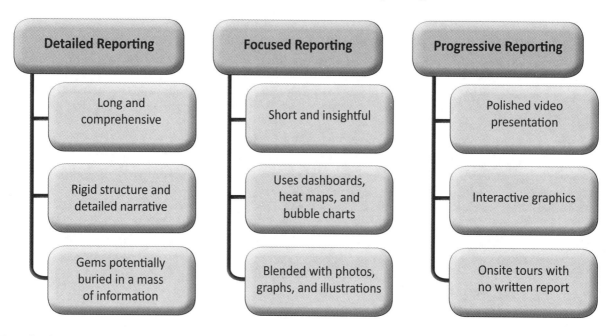

Detailed Reporting
- Long and comprehensive
- Rigid structure and detailed narrative
- Gems potentially buried in a mass of information

Focused Reporting
- Short and insightful
- Uses dashboards, heat maps, and bubble charts
- Blended with photos, graphs, and illustrations

Progressive Reporting
- Polished video presentation
- Interactive graphics
- Onsite tours with no written report

Developing Recommendations

Audit recommendations will typically have five main elements:

1. Observation: What was wrong?
2. Criteria: What standard was used?
3. Effect: What happened or could happen because the condition differed from the criteria?
4. Cause: Why did it happen?
5. Recommendation: What should be done to rectify the situation?

When raising recommendations, the relationship to the underlying cause of the condition should be clear, logical, and unambiguous. Recommendations will usually be meaningful to the client where there is a demonstrable relationship between the proposed action and the condition.

Well-developed audit recommendations will usually involve close consultation with the client, and should be relevant, practical, and reflect a proper understanding of the organization's business. Management's agreement to a recommendation needs to be obtained (or reasons for not accepting it) with management's formal response included in the final audit report together with an implementation or action plan (clarity over what needs to be done, by whom, by when, and periodic progress reporting arrangements).

Guidelines for Rating Audit Recommendations

Each audit recommendation needs to be prioritized through a risk rating process to:

- Clearly show the severity of the associated audit observation.
- Focus management's attention on high risks that need prompt attention.
- Allow resources to be first applied to high risks rather than lower risks.

The features of a rating system for the reporting of audit observations are summarized in exhibit 15-3. The ratings fit into one of four levels: Good Practice; Satisfactory; Improvement Opportunity; Unsatisfactory.

Perspectives on Observations

Jack returned to his company's remote facility the next day (continuing the story from chapter 13). He was given a tour of the facility by the manager.

He was puzzled by the absence of safety signage throughout the facility, though there were plenty of notice boards filled with posters of well-humored jokes and social outings. He asked what he should do in the event of an evacuation and where the designated evacuation point was, and the manager looked at him blankly.

Jack walked to the facility's southern boundary, noticing wooden power poles stacked close to the wire fence, with a dense forest a few yards away. The power poles could provide fuel for a wildfire, exacerbating damage and jeopardizing people's lives. Jack had listened to the news while traveling to the facility where he heard of the current extreme risk of wildfires. This was a result of thick, dry undergrowth following several years of drought, coupled with hot, dry, and very windy weather conditions predicted for the week. He wondered why there was no clearing between the forest and the power poles, and why the power poles that were removed yesterday were from an area of the facility that was reasonably well protected from fires.

Along the northern boundary of the facility, Jack noticed dozens of used power transformers covered by dust and cobwebs. The manager said that they would eventually be dismantled for spare parts or the copper content sold as scrap metal once they removed the gallons of oil within each transformer (the oil helped to cool them when operational). Jack saw that the transformers had been stored haphazardly, and climbed to the back of them for a closer look. He then noticed oil leaking from many of the transformers; the oil was running down a slight slope towards a creek that, in turn, flowed into the river that supplied the town water. As it was flammable, it provided another potential fuel for wildfires.

Jack informed the manager of his observations and emphasized the immediate fire risks posed by the power poles along the southern boundary, and the environmental catastrophe likely to result from the leaking transformer oil on the northern side. He stressed the need to promptly address the range of safety shortcomings and the poor safety culture. The manager baulked, commenting that he did not have the authority to address the problems because of budgetary constraints, and would escalate them as soon as the regional manager returned from leave in two weeks.

Jack was astonished that the manager had little grasp of how to put into practice the company's values concerning safety and environmental care. He took a few photos and sent them to the chief executive, highlighting the more immediate serious issues; the chief executive exploded into action and the deficiencies were rectified later that day.

Through their audit fieldwork, internal auditors identify observations that need to be addressed by the business. The auditors will apply a commonsense approach to determining solutions and priorities and timely reporting. They will be guided by their organization's values, mission, strategic priorities, and risk appetite. Auditors can also be creative in how they document, showcase, and report an issue, with photographs providing compelling evidence in some situations (like this).

What Practitioners Love About Internal Audit

"Working with different stakeholders and auditing different functional areas/projects means that I get to constantly learn and acquire knowledge fast to be able to come up with meaningful insights for the stakeholders – so there is never a dull moment!"			
Audit Manager	Generation X	10 to 20 years' auditing experience	Engineering

The Broader Context

Mind Mapping

When considered together, the individual audit observations will help to shape the overall conclusion of the audit engagement. Auditors need to shift their thinking from the detail of individual observations to the headline opinion. This can be aided by mind mapping.

Mind mapping is a way to visually organize information. Major observations are connected to a central concept (such as an audit objective or business goal) and associated ideas can branch out from there. It can be used to complement root cause analysis. For instance, there may be many observations of varying degrees of importance, and mind mapping can help to identify commonalities.

A mind map will help to maintain meaningful discussions with clients throughout the audit and aid in structuring the audit report and deciding on an overall opinion. An example is included in exhibit 14-6.

Root Cause Analysis

Informing management of individual observations arising from the audit without analysis of the reasons that a problem occurred may miss the underlying reasons and restrict the insights to a narrow operational perspective. Auditors have an opportunity to raise the focus of their insights to a strategic level where they conduct root cause analysis to determine why the problem occurred in the first place.

Root cause analysis would typically involve a series of five "why?" questions. As an example:

Observation: The filing of manufacturing paperwork had lapsed. Why? The responsible worker had injured his arm when he slipped and fell. Why? Because oil was on the floor. Why? Because a part was leaking. Why? Because the parts keep failing. Why? Because the quality standards for suppliers are insufficient.

Auditors who focus on the backlog of filing might raise a recommendation reminding staff that filing is to be undertaken before finishing work for the day (a weak recommendation, adding little value to management). In doing so, they miss the more beneficial recommendation of improving the supply chain.

According to the Chartered Institute of Internal Auditors United Kingdom and Ireland, root cause analysis can be applied at different points in the audit process, such as[3]:

- If you're undertaking an audit carried out previously and the same issues are cropping up.
- Where an assignment is to formally investigate an incident.
- At the scoping meeting, the manager may raise issues of ongoing problems that require attention or risks that are not being managed.
- During one-on-one supervisory meetings between the auditor and team leader, or team meetings.
- Through audit testing, you identify a large number of actions/recommendations that are linked in terms of root causes, allowing for combined observations.
- At the debriefing stage of the audit, prior to the drafting of the audit report, it may be determined that a follow-up audit be carried out using root cause analysis techniques.
- The CAE or team leader may find a pattern developing over a range of completed audits that warrants an audit on a particular topic or area.
- When reporting to the audit committee, analyze the overall trend of observations that internal audit is reporting on.

Exhibit 14-5: High-Level Example of Translating Observations into a Broader Context

Chapter 12 cited an example of an audit program under development, where the auditor was evaluating employment screening as part of an audit of recruitment. Using statistical sampling techniques (described in chapter 13), the auditor followed the established sampling strategy and randomly selected 30 sample items of new hires using random number generator software.

As a result of testing the controls (i.e., evidence on respective recruitment files), the auditor determined that:

A risk-based approach was not being consistently applied to employment screening. In 15 instances of recruitments to high-risk cash handling roles (50%), there was no employment screening conducted, even though the organization's policy required satisfactory police checks and reference checks with past employers.

In 10 cases (33%), there was no evidence of a check of qualifications even though the position description required an undergraduate degree and the selection criteria weighted this highly. Given these observations, the auditor extended the testing (under advice from the team leader) by verifying the qualifications for each of the noncompliant recruitments directly with the issuing institution. In three instances (10% of whole sample), the university had no record of the successful completion of the course.

The auditor undertook root cause analysis to establish that significant changes to the organization's recruitment processes had been made the previous year, but the changes had not, as yet, been incorporated into training courses because the number of course development staff had been cut during an organizational restructure, resulting in a serious backlog of updates to training materials. Using mind mapping, the auditor drew together the respective observation to determine a headline opinion and practical recommendations for discussion with the team leader and client. The primary recommendations did not center on the noncompliances but rather on the availability of sufficient training resources to maintain updated course materials. The three employees who lied about their qualifications were referred for internal disciplinary action (subsequently dismissed) and reported to the police for criminal action.

The mind map associated with the above example might include thoughts like those illustrated in the truncated example in **exhibit 14-6**.

Exhibit 14-6: High-Level Example of Mind Mapping Used to Organize Recruitment Failings

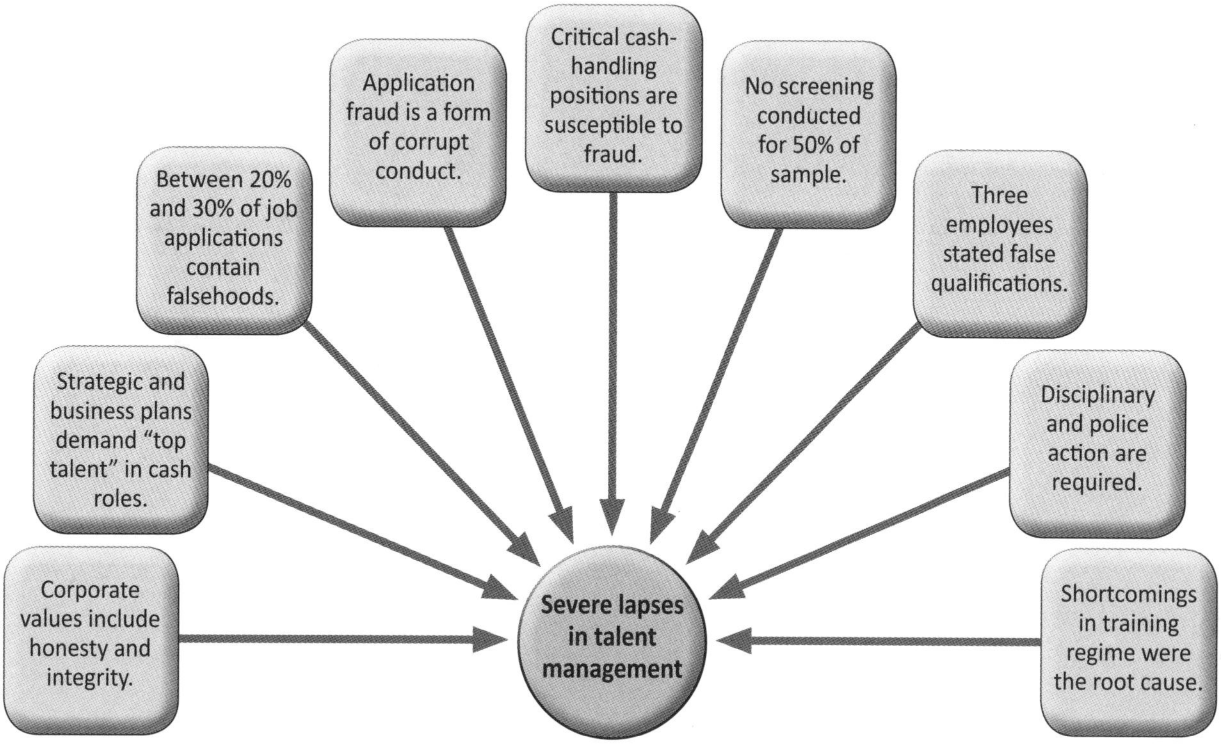

Tips for New Auditors

- Share early on what looks like it might be a reportable observation to discuss the situation with the appropriate stakeholders, giving upper management a signal that you are looking at something.
- Always keep asking "why?" Too many times, the answer will be because we have always done it that way. Challenge the status quo.
- Strive to be educative rather than punitive, as this is the key to getting cooperation, achieving real corrective action, producing better outcomes, and getting some thanks.
- Establish relationships with stakeholders where they see the internal auditor as a friend who can help them figure out how to fix what they're most worried about.
- Constantly expose yourself to different ideas and what others are doing. For example, (i) make a habit of looking at the reports of leading organizations like the U.K. National Audit Office, Australian National Audit Office, and U.S. Government Accountability Office. Their reports are always good and provide a different perspective; (ii) look at the work of think tanks, such as Canada West Foundation; and (iii) gain exposure with keynote speakers at conferences who come from a different background.

Chapter 15
Audit Reporting and Exit Conference

Internal auditors must communicate the results of audits. This chapter covers the applicable standards, planning the audit report content, developing the audit report, things not to say in an audit report, guideline for overall audit rating, and conducting an effective audit exit conference.

Audit Reporting

Planning the Audit Report Content

The audit report is typically the primary means of communicating the outcomes of an audit, reflecting the auditor's observations, opinions, and recommendations arising from the audit. Above all, reports need to be clear and concise, and address agreed audit objectives. Stakeholders are becoming more discerning in their expectations of audit reporting and are looking for greater value-add from audits. They want audit reports that are easy to read, get to the point, tell a story, and provide a conclusion or opinion.

The starting point for preparing the audit report is the determination of reportable observations and recommendations (discussed in chapter 14). The audit report is like a melting pot (as illustrated in **exhibit 15-1**) where content will be provided by different sources. Reportable observations may be delivered from several different auditors (depending on the size of the audit team) and then the team might collectively analyze the overall root cause. The team leader usually collates the summary of recommendations and develops an action plan in consultation with management before the team collaborates on the overall opinion. At that point, the team leader incorporates the audit objectives and scope that was determined up front.

Exhibit 15-1: Overview of Common Inputs to an Audit Report

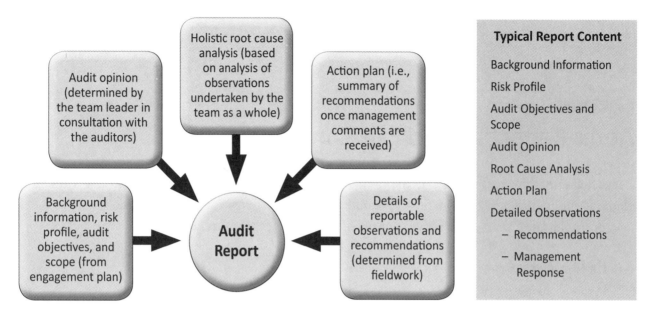

The different styles of audit reporting are illustrated in exhibit 14-4. A new auditor would usually be expected to contribute details of reportable observations based on the fieldwork they completed. They would draft this part of the audit report, and it would be reviewed and edited by the team leader. Under Standard 2420 – Quality of Communications, internal auditors are required to ensure "communications are accurate, objective, clear, concise, constructive, complete, and timely."

The CBOK report *Driving Success in a Changing World: 10 Imperatives for Internal Audit* provided insights on the broader communication expectations of audit committees[1]:

• Communicate risks in the context of the business's goals and objectives.
• Provide an overall opinion on how the business is managing itself.
• Eliminate non-value-adding controls and activities to streamline costs.
• Advise the audit committee of the issues it should be most concerned about on a regular basis.
• Give an overview of the control environment and report whether it is improving or getting worse.

The Role of a New Auditor in Preparing an Audit Report

Because the audit report is the most visible part of any audit, it usually has a high level of involvement of the team leader and ultimately the CAE. For new auditors, their involvement in audit reporting will start by writing up their observations and recommendations (in line with the organization's style guide and standard reporting format) and inserting them in the report under the guidance of the team leader. Some audits do not make recommendations, but they develop action plans jointly with management, and these are included in the audit reports. Chapter 14 discussed the development of audit observations, recommendations, and ratings, and the use of mind mapping and root cause analysis techniques. The new auditor's role in report preparation will expand with experience.

Developing the Audit Report

A well-written audit report is a highly valued instrument for senior management. The effectiveness of the internal audit activity is often judged on the quality of the final audit report, including its analysis, findings, conclusions, and recommendations. While audit reports are usually prepared in Word, a reporting style prepared in PowerPoint can also be used.

A reporting template will usually be made available by the CAE. The template will reflect the common structure and features expected in the audit report, including the layout, orientation, font type and size, language, and spacing.

The internal audit manual will typically include a style guide to help an auditor develop the content of the audit report. The style guide ensures there is a consistent look and feel for audit reports to help build the brand and enhance the credibility of the internal audit activity. Typically, the CAE is required to sign and clear all audit reports (relying on the effectiveness of quality review and wrap-up arrangements discussed in chapter 16).

Draft reports provide the basis for discussing observations and potential recommendations with appropriate levels of management before the final audit report is issued. Significant observations should have been discussed previously. If management disagrees with any facts or the proposed solution in their formal response, the draft report should be corrected (if agreed) or further discussions held. In most situations, agreement will be reached, otherwise significant differences are escalated to the CAE and ultimately senior management and/or the audit committee. In undertaking their work and establishing solutions, auditors should avoid taking on management responsibilities and should not audit controls they designed (or helped to design).

The typical process for audit reporting is illustrated in **exhibit 15-2**. This is complemented by exhibits 14-2, 14-3, and 14-4.

Exhibit 15-2: Typical Internal Audit Reporting Process

Observations	Draft Audit Report	Exit Interview	Revised Draft Audit Report	Management Response	Final Audit Report

In some cases, the team leader might opt to issue progress or interim reports periodically, incorporating suggestions from auditors. For instance, where the duration of an audit is longer than normal (perhaps due to complexities or for systems under development); there are significant observations that require prompt action by senior management; to communicate changes to the audit objectives or scope; and to keep management apprised of audit progress. The content of interim reports is usually then incorporated into a single final report upon conclusion of the audit.

All audit reports should be subject to rigorous review prior to release to ensure clarity, conciseness, accuracy, timeliness, spelling, and grammar. The executive summary is intended to give senior management and the audit committee a broad overview of the audit outcome, including an overall opinion, significant observations, awareness of residual risks, and an agreed action plan to strengthen internal controls.

Busy audit committee members and senior management dread the prospect of reading long and wordy audit reports. Every extra word means there is more potential for disagreement and lengthier time to agree and finalize a report. A leading practice audit report reflects the following features:

- Is in a format that invites the reader to read the report.
- Relates to broader organizational objectives.
- Communicates effectively to reflect IPPF core principles: aligned to strategies, objectives, and risks; risk-based assurance; insightful, proactive, and future-focused; and promotes organizational improvement.
- Crafted carefully for the world to see, especially in regions where transparency is delivered through freedom of information laws that might result in reports being accessed by the media, citizens, or others.
- Uses as few words as possible so it's easier to digest.
- Tailors the message for the audience and applies a neutral tone.
- Uses the most appropriate communication medium.
- Answers a typical focusing question, why did we do this audit?
- Provides clear conclusions for each objective.
- Uses tabular formats where suitable, especially for detailed observations and agreed actions.
- Includes tables, graphs, diagrams, and photographs.
- Includes a table of contents and a glossary of terms and acronyms.
- Includes positive commentary on satisfactory performance and what is being done well.
- Includes a statement of assurance.
- Includes a statement on the audit's value proposition to show what value was added (not just "we provided assurance"; identify the real value to enhancing business operations or reducing cost).

Things Not to Say in an Audit Report

- Never make comments that cannot be substantiated by the audit work.
- Avoid as much as possible telling senior management what they already know.
- Do not make an observation sound worse than it is.
- Avoid throwaway recommendations that serve little purpose.
- Avoid reporting that focuses on the negative; recognize good work also.
- Do not make reports too long or too wordy.
- Avoid audit-style terms and jargon.
- Do not deliver a report without including an overall conclusion or opinion.
- Avoid vague conclusions (for instance, there is little value in general statements like: (i) "This activity is operating satisfactorily, with opportunity for improvement" or (ii) "The audit objective was partially achieved.")
- Don't inflate risk ratings (risk ratings applied to audit observations should align with the organization's risk management framework, including its risk appetite statement, rather than representing a subjective evaluation by the internal auditor).
- Do not ignore politically correct trends in the broader community and environment (be sensitive to embracing changes in the vocabulary; for instance, when speaking generally, use neutral terms like "they" rather than gender specific "he," or "chair" rather than "chairman").
- Avoid adjectives and adverbs. Instead, express your analysis and commentary in clear, unemotional language that can be shown to be based very carefully on your work.

Guideline for Overall Audit Rating

Not all observations and recommendations are equally important. The internal audit activity should have a rating system that is consistently applied to the overall results of the audit. The goal is to help senior management focus on higher priority observations and recommendations.

Internal audit's rating system should be explicitly based on the risk table (impact/likelihood) and the risk appetite statement that form part of the organization's risk management framework. There are different rating systems and rating levels used, so it is appropriate to check on the approach used for your organization. As an example, a rating system could reflect the features illustrated in **exhibit 15-3**.

Exhibit 15-3: Example of an Audit Report Rating System

	Overall Conclusion Reflects	Overall Rating
Defined by Risk Factors – Based on Organization's Risk Management Framework – Likelihood/Impact and Risk Appetite Statement	• Overall control environment reflects leading practice and is well designed, efficient, effective, economical, ethical, and functioning as designed. • No improvement opportunities identified.	Good Practice
	• Well-designed control environment is generally operating properly. • Small number of lower-level risk improvement opportunities reported and requiring action at a management level.	Satisfactory
	• Reasonably adequate control environment for most activities. • Moderate level of risk improvement opportunities reported and requiring action with senior management oversight.	Improvement Opportunity
	• Some key controls do not exist or are not functioning as required, and there are high-level risk improvement opportunities reported. • The control environment is impaired with significant actions requiring oversight by the executive team and the audit committee.	Unsatisfactory

The systematic definition of audit objectives up front as part of the engagement planning process is crucial to providing measurable audit criteria upon which to provide an overall conclusion. The use of a recognized control framework can be helpful.

Conducting an Effective Exit Conference

The primary goals of the exit conference are to inform management of the outcomes of the audit and reporting process, and to get their acceptance of recommendations and agreement to implement them. The exit conference will usually be held in a nonconfrontational, low-key, and relatively informal manner.

Ongoing communications throughout the audit should ensure a situation of no surprises at the exit meeting. Prior to the exit conference, a meeting strategy should be developed and roles allocated. It is essential that the level of management present at the exit conference is high enough to enable prompt resolution and finalization of the draft audit report. When management disagrees with the facts, it is up to the auditor to prove the facts. This is where a well-structured and complete set of workpapers is essential (see chapter 13). Where the outcome is contentious and/or there are significant observations, the CAE should be invited to attend. Qualities of an effective exit conference are illustrated in **exhibit 15-4**.

While the team leader will usually control the exit conference, auditors may be called upon to assist by:

• Outlining the objectives and scope of the audit and discussing the overall opinion
• Acknowledging good practices
• Concentrating the conversation on major points of disagreement (if there are any)

- Concluding the meeting by advising management that changes discussed and mutually agreed upon will be included in the final audit report, which will be shown to them prior to formal release

Exhibit 15-4: Qualities of an Effective Exit Conference

Balanced	Conversation should provide a balanced view and perspective with discussion of both effective and ineffective practices.
Calm	If the discussion gets heated, stay calm. Avoid getting provoked into an emotional outburst, even if your personal credibility is challenged.
Clear	The conversation should be logical, easily understood, unambiguous, and informative.
Concise	The conversation should not be rambling. It should avoid duplication and unnecessary detail, express thoughts completely and succinctly as possible, and emphasize the observations of greatest significance.
Constructive	There should be credit given for management's accomplishments.
Convincing	The auditors need to do their homework prior to the exit conference so they know the subject matter and have attempted to predict any points of disagreement or contention. They should be well versed in the observations and associated risks, and be aware of how they relate to the strategic objectives and key business drivers.
Determined	Where management disagrees with a proposed recommendation, they should be asked to provide an acceptable alternative solution. If management acknowledges an observation and risk but does not propose taking corrective action, then the auditor will explain that the matter will be escalated to senior management and the audit committee.
Inviting	The conversation should be conducted professionally, in a friendly manner, and with the right tone. Emotive words should be avoided.
Objective	The conversation should be based on fact, unbiased and free from distortion.
Prioritized	Observations should be prioritized in advance, reflecting the top, middle, and bottom concerns. The top concerns should be considered as a minimum.
Recommendations workshopped and/or agreed	Recommendations should be practical, action-oriented, specific, measurable, and cost-effective with meaningful discussion of alternative options. Where management has already taken corrective action, this should be acknowledged.

Management typically has 14 to 21 working days to formally respond to the draft audit report, which is delivered at or just after the exit conference. Management's formal response should articulate their plan of action to address audit recommendations, including acceptance, agreed action, accountable manager, and targeted completion date.

Perspectives on Reporting

The chief operations officer, Howard, was worried that several strategic objectives were being jeopardized by the absence of approved levels of resourcing. He asked the human resources manager, Emma, to evaluate the reasonableness of current recruitment arrangements, as there seemed to be a blockage.

Emma had her technical leaders undertake the evaluation and reported the results to Howard, concluding the company's policies and procedures were operating well with strong compliance. The results were counterintuitive to Howard, so he asked Emma to complete a further evaluation, looking through a performance lens rather than a conformance lens.

Emma met with Howard a few days later and provided an updated report. She confirmed her previous opinion on conformance but sheepishly admitted that performance was well below expectations. None of the key performance indicators (KPIs) were being met. And there were serious shortcomings in the KPIs for measures like time to recruit, candidate care, and attracting quality candidates externally.

Recruitment had become a slow and tedious process following automation, which required online processing of applications. Sluggish technology and frequent dropouts meant potential candidates became frustrated and often did not complete online applications. Those applicants who persevered then waited months (rather than days or weeks) before the company acknowledged the application and arranged interviews. By then, many applicants had already found other jobs elsewhere through their competitor's slick recruitment processes. That necessitated positions to be re-advertised using the same tardy processes. In the meantime, the positions remained vacant.

Through consultation, collaboration, and co-design, Howard and Emma determined technical and operational solutions to address the poor recruitment processes. With the support of the executive team, more effective recruitment outcomes were achieved quickly that consistently met established recruitment KPIs.

Internal auditors also need to critically evaluate the outcomes of their audits before they proceed to the reporting stage. Well-founded reporting will result when meaningful audit objectives and scope are established up front and the reasonableness of outcomes is challenged by the team leader at the quality review stage and by clients during the exit conference.

What Practitioners Love About Internal Audit

"Understanding the business and providing valuable advice is making a positive difference for the business."			
Audit Committee Chair	Baby Boomer	Over 20 years' auditing experience	Accounting

The Broader Context

High-Quality, Effective Communications

According to the CBOK report *Six Audit Committee Imperatives: Enabling Internal Audit to Make a Difference,* it is important to prioritize high-quality, effective communications, with a strong majority of board members giving high scores for the quality (83%) and frequency (81%) of internal audit's communications with them.[2]

Stakeholders who are time constrained find words "by themselves" to be boring and uninspiring. Auditors can use individual creativity to deliver effective communications through visual representation of observations. For example:

- Photos and illustrations grab the attention of stakeholders, especially for observations that relate to the organization's broader strategic objectives. The fictional stories in the perspectives section of several chapters highlight opportunities for internal auditors to use photographs to pitch their messages. These include the environment where David stole cash (chapter 6), the building where Bjorn circumvented security arrangements (chapter 7), the station where Christine was curious about ticket sales (chapter 11), and the observations of Jack who was touring his energy company's sites (chapters 13 and 14).
- Graphs, tables, and comparative statistics also help to pitch the message and to complement the narrative with fewer words; for instance, the fictional story in chapter 12 where Therese highlighted the risk associated with spreadsheets being used for business-critical functions.
- In some cases, videos help to provide an on-the-ground perspective; for instance, the railway station where Mike informed Christine that ticket barriers were not operational during peak hours (chapter 11).

Tips for New Auditors

- Learn, understand, and apply the dynamics of people's decision-making behavior at work, including the dynamics that underpin the needs and expectations of your stakeholders.
- Effective communication skills are just as important as technical auditing skills. This is not taught enough in university, so you need to ensure this is a priority in your development plan.
- Understand the business, management's objectives, and challenges from the stakeholder's perspective, not yours. Don't let theory get in the way of the right outcome.

- Concise reporting (both verbal and written) is important. Management generally wants to know about the key issues that need fixing. I like to provide the following scenario to new starters. Assume you bump into the audit sponsor in the elevator and they ask how the audit is going. What will you say in the 20 seconds of time you have? If you take longer, you probably haven't been succinct enough.
- Most people are trying to do a good job; it is systems, processes, and circumstances that inhibit them. Our job is to empower them to do the best they can by providing insights to them and to their managers.

Related Standards

Standard 2400 – Communicating Results

Internal auditors must communicate the results of engagements.

This is supplemented by related standards, notably:

- Communications must include the engagement's objectives, scope, and results (Standard 2410).
- Final communication of engagement results must include applicable conclusions, as well as applicable recommendations and/or action plans. Where appropriate, the internal auditors' opinion should be provided. An opinion must take into account the expectations of senior management, the board, and other stakeholders and must be supported by sufficient, reliable, relevant, and useful information (Standard 2410.A1).
- Internal auditors are encouraged to acknowledge satisfactory performance in engagement communications (Standard 2410.A2).

Chapter 16
Audit Quality Review and Wrap-Up

At the end of the audit, there are many tasks that need to be performed to fully bring an audit to closure. This chapter covers the process to ensure all phases of the audit, including workpapers, are fully reviewed, and the steps for wrapping up miscellaneous items related to the audit.

Understanding the Basics

Ongoing Monitoring of Quality

The ongoing monitoring of quality represents one of the main elements of a quality assurance and improvement program for the internal audit activity, as discussed in chapter 18. The other elements include internal assessments, external assessments, incident monitoring, qualitative measures, and quality assertions. An important precursor for any audit is that the internal auditor has the necessary knowledge, skills, and other competencies to perform the audit.

It is important for the new auditor to recognize and support the team leader's focus on quality (often through the use of "coaching notes"), which begins with engagement planning and continues throughout the audit process through to reporting, as illustrated in **exhibit 16-1**.

Exhibit 16-1: Ongoing Quality Assessments Span All Phases of the Audit

Quality of Planning   Quality of Fieldwork   Quality of Reporting

Explanation of Coaching Notes

Coaching notes are used as part of the supervision of an audit, with the team leader typically raising coaching notes as part of his or her ongoing monitoring of quality. The purpose of coaching notes is to clarify any parts of workpapers that appear unclear, are incomplete, or do not support the conclusions. They can also be used to challenge points that appear judgmental or subjective.

Five key purposes of coaching notes include: reminding auditors of work that needs to be completed; seeking clarification of work completed; identifying other potential areas of review and analysis; delivering helpful insights for future audits; and providing positive feedback for good work. In many cases, the experienced team leader may pick up on potential weaknesses or improvement opportunities overlooked by a less experienced auditor.

Coaching notes may also be referred to as review notes and, for all auditors (but particularly the new auditor), aid in their continued professional development. They should never be regarded as criticism; their intent is to be constructive and instructive.

The benefits to the auditor of the team leader's ongoing supervision and monitoring include:

- Providing auditors with real-time feedback on the reasonableness of their output
- Determining whether conclusions are reasonable, defensible, and have a firm basis
- Assessing whether recommendations are reasonable, practical, actionable, and useful
- Confirming conformance with the code of ethics and auditing standards
- Avoiding reworking of audit steps and potential delays at the conclusion of the audit

As a result of the above, there is a greater likelihood of key performance indicators (see chapter 19, particularly exhibit 19-4) reflecting favorable audit outcomes (e.g., value added, usefulness of recommendations, cycle time, budget to actual times, compliance with standards, and use of resources).

Supervision of the Audit

The primary objectives of audit supervision (including detailed workpaper reviews) are threefold:

- Provide assurance as to the overall quality of the audit.
- Enhance the value of the audit report.
- Ensure employees are professionally developed.

In line with the requirements of the internal audit policies and procedures manual, it is likely that all audit workpapers should carry evidence of review by the team leader. In a manual set of workpapers, this will be through initialing and dating each workpaper, whereas there is usually an automated signoff facility in electronic workpaper software. A shared folder is another electronic repository, though providing evidence of a reviewer's signoff can be problematic.

Given the possibility of external scrutineers reviewing the audit workpapers (see exhibit 16-3), they must be able to stand on their own merits even if the auditors involved are not available. The detailed workpaper review will consider the work documented by each auditor and cover completeness and reasonableness checks over the following elements for each audit phase:

Planning
- Confirm the availability of an audit planning memorandum (sometimes called an audit engagement plan, or the terms of reference) that has been prepared, agreed with stakeholders, and approved by the CAE (or delegate).
- Confirm that the audit objectives and scope (detailed in the audit engagement planning phase) have been fully met, the risk assessment is adequate, and there is audit evidence supporting the audit conclusions.

Fieldwork
- Assess compliance with professional auditing standards and the internal audit activity's defined methodology.
- Determine the reasonableness of the sampling and testing strategy, and whether it aligns with the audit objective.
- Ensure the audit work has been performed in a thorough manner and workpapers are logically arranged.
- Determine whether audit workpapers are complete, concise, relevant, and meaningful to support the conclusions.
- Challenge any points of view of the auditor/s that may have been judgmental or subjective.
- Assess whether all potential weaknesses have been properly analyzed to determine the effect on controls.
- Determine whether workpapers adequately support the audit observations and recommendations.
- Confirm all of the coaching (or review) notes raised by the team leaders have been adequately addressed and cleared.

Reporting
- Confirm that all reportable observations have been raised in the audit report and the root cause has been sufficiently analyzed.
- Confirm that the observations (findings or weaknesses) and potential solutions (recommendations or agreed actions) have been socialized with management throughout the audit.
- Ensure version control has been maintained over the various iterations of the report, and that copies have been maintained in the workpaper file together with management responses.
- Ensure the internal audit report is accurate, objective, clear, concise, constructive, and timely.

Audit Closeout Memorandum

The audit planning memorandum is prepared at the start of the audit (see chapter 9). It is good practice to prepare an audit closeout memorandum (see **exhibit 16-2**) at the conclusion of the audit to reconcile actual audit effort against what was planned in the audit planning memorandum, and to articulate the value proposition from a senior management perspective (which is included in some audit reports). The team leader may call on an auditor to compile this.

Exhibit 16-2: Example Format of an Audit Closeout Memorandum

	Prepared by:	Reviewed by:	WP:

PROGRAM NAME: *<Primary business area>*			
AUDIT TEAM: *<List names>*		DATE APM APPROVED:	
PLANNED COMMENCEMENT DATE: *<Per APM>*	ACTUAL COMMENCEMENT DATE:	REASON FOR VARIANCE:	
TARGET COMMENCEMENT DATE: *<Per APM>*	ACTUAL COMMENCEMENT DATE:	REASON FOR VARIANCE:	
DURATION TARGET: *<Per APM>*	ACTUAL DURATION: *<KPI of the number of weeks from start to finish of audit>*	REASON FOR VARIANCE:	

TIME BUDGETED/ACTUAL PER SEGMENT:			
SEGMENT	TIME BUDGETED (DAYS)	ACTUAL TIME (DAYS)	REASON FOR VARIANCE
<All segments listed from APM>			
TOTALS:			

TIME BUDGETED/ACTUAL PER PERSON:			
SEGMENT	TIME BUDGETED (DAYS)	ACTUAL TIME (DAYS)	REASON FOR VARIANCE
<All names listed from APM>			
TOTALS:			

CHANGES TO AUDIT OBJECTIVES OR SCOPE:		
ORIGINAL OBJECTIVE OR SCOPE	AMENDED OBJECTIVE OR SCOPE	REASON AND IMPACT

Exhibit 16-2: Example Format of an Audit Closeout Memorandum (cont.)

VALUE PROPOSITION:	*<Audit team collectively articulates the value the audit has provided to management>*	
I confirm that the audit engagement has been completed in line with the approved Audit Planning Memorandum; any variations are noted herein with reasons.	**TEAM LEADER:** **DATE:**	

Wrapping Up the Audit

The final wrap-up phase will consider whether all the loose ends of the audit have been tied up neatly. Considerable effort is invested in every audit. Before an audit is closed out, there are important steps that need to be taken to ensure that the workpapers are complete and represent reasonable evidence of the work undertaken. While most aspects of an audit are completed prior to the issuance of the final audit report, the wrap-up stage occurs after all stages of the audit (including reporting) have been completed.

In the final wrap-up, the team leader (often with the assistance of an auditor) will typically:

- Confirm all coaching notes have been adequately addressed and cleared.
- Ensure appropriate evidence of audit supervision is documented and retained.
- Confirm availability of performance evaluations for in-house and service provider engagements.
- Monitor the analysis of actual versus budgeted times using the audit closeout memorandum (see exhibit 16-2).
- Confirm client feedback surveys have been sought.
- Determine appropriate retention arrangements for workpapers in line with the policy of the internal audit activity (i.e., period of retention, secure storage, restricted access to only those authorized).

Perspectives on Quality

Ahmed was excited to have his parents visiting for a couple of weeks. They were arriving the next morning after a 16-hour flight. He was running behind schedule as he had spent the morning at the motor vehicle repair shop. His new car had an emergency recall because of faulty airbags, which required the inflators to be replaced as they were prone to more frequent rupturing. He pondered how lapses in quality control had resulted in a worldwide safety recall and the damaging effect it had on the brand of motor vehicle.

On the way home, Ahmed visited the multinational furniture store that sold ready-to-assemble furniture. He purchased a double bed for his parents to use during their visit, and made his way home to assemble it. His first step was to check the detailed instructions to ensure all the parts were there. He noticed that a 12-pack of bolts was missing. They were critical to the integrity of the construction and were specially manufactured for this bed.

Ahmed rushed back to the store, making it just before the store was closing for two days because of a public holiday. After working on the assembly for more than an hour, Ahmed discovered that both of the distinct bed sides were for the left-hand side of the bed. They were pre-drilled, so he could not continue with the construction. He was annoyed at the poor quality control that had failed to identify the missing bolts and the problem with the bedsides; he had lost so much time and would not have the bed ready for his parents.

Ahmed was delighted to pick his parents up from the airport. He found that they had become quite ill while in transit because they had consumed contaminated water from the water fountain during a mid-flight stopover. A subsequent inquiry found that quality tests had not been completed consistently to detect coliform bacteria in the water.

Quality control safeguards are essential to the many goods and services people use in their daily lives. Likewise, effective quality control arrangements are fundamental to professional internal auditing.

What Practitioners Love About Internal Audit

"The most satisfying element of having an internal audit career is the vast array of work that you have exposure to. Essentially, every audit is like a new job: new stakeholders; fresh objectives; a different set of risks; new processes and controls. It's hard to get bored!"			
Principal Auditor	Millennial	Almost 5 years' auditing experience	Accounting

The Broader Context of Audit Quality and Wrap-Up

Systematic and Disciplined Approach

The CBOK 2015 Global Internal Audit Practitioner study reflected that one of internal audit's major assets is its credibility with stakeholders, with this being protected through ongoing monitoring of quality that was happening in some ways.[1]

The definition of internal audit (see chapter 8) reflects, in part, the need for internal auditors to embrace a *systematic and disciplined* approach, and that is the impetus for audit quality and the proper wrap-up of audits. There will be occasions when the workpapers for audits may be the subject of review by scrutineers from outside the organization.

Explanation of External Scrutineers

A scrutineer in the context of this book is a person or entity from outside the organization that has the power to scrutinize any process or activity that requires rigorous oversight. Their focus is on preventing or detecting noncompliances, corruption, and genuine errors.

Organizations can be subject to scrutiny from a range of independent regulatory authorities. Most commonly this includes the organization's external auditors.

Within the public, private, and not-for-profit sectors, there will also be industry-related scrutineers that have the authority to independently assess an organization's compliance to laws, regulations, standards, licences, policies, plans, procedures, contracts, guidelines, specifications, or other requirements relevant to their business. Taxation collection authorities also have wide powers.

To maintain the credibility of the internal audit activity, all audit workpapers need to be prepared in such a way that they can withstand intense external scrutiny. The purpose and intensity of independent reviews undertaken by external scrutineers can be quite diverse. Some of these reviews can represent a relatively high risk to the brand of the organization and the reputation of its senior management. Examples of scrutineer reviews are illustrated in **exhibit 16-3**.

Exhibit 16-3: Examples of External Scrutineers that Could Require Access to Audit Workpapers

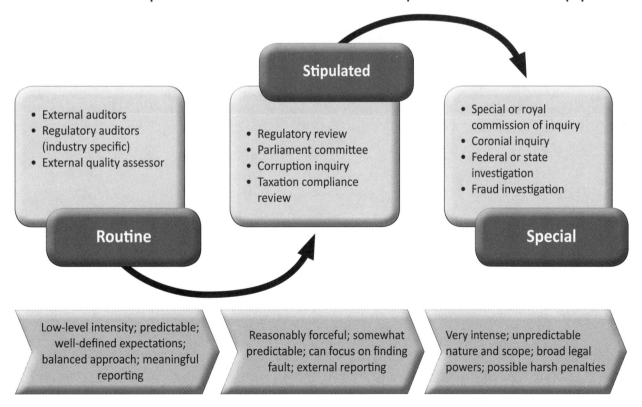

Tips for New Auditors

- Embed the pursuit of knowledge and excellence into your work routines.
- Continue learning and asking questions.
- The business environment is constantly changing, so auditors continually need to diversify.
- Your observations and recommendations will be challenged. You need to have courage. Your ethics, quality, and actions need to be credible if you expect others to follow your proposed actions.
- Approach everything with an open mind. Internal audit activities can range from strategic discussions with senior management to counting cows at a remote farm. No matter what project or task at hand, you should aim to excel at it and even think of a more efficient way to complete it or increase its value.

Related Standards

Standard 1311 - Internal Assessments

Internal quality assessments must include:

- Ongoing monitoring of the performance of the internal audit activity.
- Periodic self-assessments or assessments by other persons within the organization with sufficient knowledge of internal audit practices.

This standard reflects the overarching requirements of Standard 1300 - Quality Assurance and Improvement Program, which is discussed in more detail in chapter 18. That standard requires the CAE to develop and maintain a quality assurance and improvement program that covers all aspects of the internal audit activity.

Chapter 17
Audit Observations: Follow-Up, Validation, and Resolution

Value is added to an organization when audit recommendations are implemented. This chapter covers the process for following up on audit recommendations to ensure proper corrective action has been taken and the various methods to perform an audit follow-up.

Understanding the Basics

Action Plans

Once internal auditors have communicated the results of their audits, management will formally respond to the recommendations by establishing an action plan (or equivalent) where they agree with the recommendations. The nature of audit reporting and the coordination with management is discussed further in chapter 15. The action plan provides the basis of following up the implementation of recommendations.

Internal auditors may be tasked with:

- Recording and monitoring audit recommendations
- Undertaking audit follow-ups through:
    - A desktop review of high-priority recommendations
    - Follow-up audits to specifically focus on prior recommendations
    - Incorporating the follow-up of recommendations in the next scheduled audit
- Preparing a report for the audit committee and management on the status of recommendations

Recording and Monitoring Audit Recommendations

The internal audit activity uses a follow-up process to evaluate the adequacy, effectiveness, and timeliness of actions taken by management on reported observations and recommendations. It also determines whether management has assumed the risk of not taking corrective action on reported observations.

> **Chapter Focus Is on Recording, Monitoring, and Reporting of Recommendations**
>
> The most valuable audit recommendations are typically derived from well-planned audits that are executed by capable audit professionals. Effective stakeholder engagement strategies help to ensure audit recommendations reflect the key business drivers and strategies, and are developed in the context of wider organizational changes and policy directives. This chapter focuses on the recording, monitoring, and reporting of recommendations and assumes appropriate steps were taken to ensure the recommendations are appropriate, practical, and of value.

A typical process for monitoring audit recommendations is illustrated in **exhibit 17-1**. While developing the process is the responsibility of the CAE, the various steps are typically undertaken by an auditor (or auditors) under the direction of a team leader.

Exhibit 17-1: Overview of a Typical Process for Monitoring Audit Recommendations

Raise	Log	Update	Summarize	Report
• Issue initially raised • Best solution agreed with management to remedy the issue • Recommendation formally raised • Action and time frame agreed with local management	• Audit report and management action plan formally issued • Senior management agreement obtained to recommendations and action plan • Recommendations logged in internal audit's database	• Periodic (usually quarterly) update sought on status of audit recommendations • Database updated with status provided by management • Situation flagged where management or audit committee assumed the risk of not taking corrective action	• Produce summary of all "open" audit recommendations • Analyze data for trends	• Compile status report for the audit committee • Different reporting styles are illustrated in exhibit 17-3

Note: See exhibit 17-2 for database content.

Internal audit activities use a range of mechanisms for systematically logging, tracking, and monitoring the implementation of audit recommendations. The approach depends on the size of the internal audit activity, the extent of the internal audit program, and the number of recommendations being tracked. This ranges from basic approaches that log and track recommendations using Excel or simple databases through to more sophisticated integrated audit software solutions that have client interfaces and/or email functions.

The design of the database will be informed by the needs of the audit committee and management. For instance, it would be expected to show:

- **Open recommendations.** Audit recommendations that have not yet been implemented. Includes recommendations that are not yet due, as well as overdue recommendations.
- **Overdue recommendations.** Audit recommendations that have passed the implementation date originally proposed by management.
- **Ageing of periods overdue.** Aged overdue recommendations will need to be identified, tracked, and reported in accordance with the time frames agreed with the audit committee. Typically these are grouped into recommendations that are overdue less than three months; between three and six months; between six and 12 months; and more than 12 months.
- **"At-risk" recommendations.** These include both higher-risk recommendations that are overdue and medium- and low-risk recommendations that are overdue for longer than a certain period (such as six or 12 months).

The integrity of reporting on audit recommendations relies on the processes for capturing details of recommendations into the database when they are initially raised (see dark gray tabs in **exhibit 17-2**) and ongoing capture of updates received periodically from management (see light gray tabs in exhibit 17-2). The design of the database is the responsibility of the CAE, who would typically be informed by the auditors who undertake the follow-up process and the team leaders who supervise the work.

Exhibit 17-2: Example of Information Commonly Held in a Recommendations Database (or Excel)

Task	• Shows the name of the audit report and date issued (and audit reference number, if used) • Summary or full narrative of recommendation and agreed action with unique reference number • Flags recommendations where management assumed risk of not taking corrective action
Assign	• Indicates the responsible business unit (area responsible for implementing recommendation) • Identifies the person primarily responsible for implementation
Risk	• Shows risk rating and/or priority of the recommendation (e.g., high, medium, low) • Identifies the risk category (if used)
Target	• Identifies the original target implementation date agreed with management • Identifies dates of key milestones (where relevant) for complex and/or technology solutions
Change	• Shows the current status of corrective actions and whether the status has been confirmed • Shows the revised implementation date (where advised by management) • Provides comments from management on reason/s for change/s to target dates
Status	• Indicates current status of recommendations (e.g., complete, in progress, deferred, identified) • Flags outcome where CAE has completed formal follow-up options and concurred to closure • Flags any at-risk recommendations

> **Meaning of Follow-Up**
>
> According to the International Professional Practices Framework, Practice Advisory 2500.A1-1:
>
> *Follow-up is a process by which internal auditors evaluate the adequacy, effectiveness and timeliness of actions taken by management on reported observations and recommendations, including those by external auditors and others. This process also includes determining whether senior management and/or the board have assumed the risk of not taking corrective action on reported observations.*

Validation

The CAE will typically have a process documented in the internal audit policies and procedures manual for following up and obtaining evidence that higher-risk recommendations have been implemented by management before recommending closure of audit recommendations to the audit committee. This validation is usually undertaken by auditors by one of four means:

1. Assessment of comments received from management on the status of recommendations. This can be in the form of correspondence, email, or the direct update of the recommendations database where sophisticated software is available with management access (usually medium to large internal audit activities). The auditor will undertake a reasonableness check to determine whether management's comments reflect the appropriate closeout of the recommendations.
2. Desktop review of evidence that high-priority recommendations have been implemented. For instance, if management is required to update delegations or introduce a policy, the auditor will seek copies and assess whether the document/s fully address the recommended solution.
3. An onsite review in consultation with management to assess evidence the recommendations have been implemented. These reviews are typically undertaken at the instigation of the audit committee, management, or the CAE where there were many audit recommendations, residual risks were high, or there was a divergence between the organization's values and the culture of the area.
4. Incorporation of the follow-up of recommendations in the next scheduled audit. This usually applies where there is confidence in management's commitment to implement the recommendations, and the activity is reviewed periodically, such as accounts payable, payroll, and the revenue cycle.

Resolution

Past practice saw the delivery to the audit committee of a long and detailed list of audit recommendations together with the current status. The listing was often in sequential order with little attention given to prioritizing high-risk and/or long overdue at-risk recommendations or closing out implemented recommendations. Absence of meaningful analysis meant that the real story was buried in a mass of data.

Delivering a list of audit recommendations does little to assist the audit committee to discharge its responsibilities in respect to the resolution of closed recommendations or the reasonableness of progress of open recommendations. **Exhibit 17-3** illustrates the difference between two contrasting reporting styles.

Exhibit 17-3: Overview of Reporting Styles for Follow-Up of Audit Recommendations[1]

Report style	List of all audit recommendations
Approach	Obtain updates from management and update the recommendations database. Print list of: • All audit recommendations with their status, or; • All open recommendations with their status.
Content	Short covering paper; essentially we are required to follow up on recommendations under auditing standards; here is a list of all the audit recommendations. List of recommendations with their status.
Value	Low. Barely meets the basic requirements of the audit committee.
Report style	A report on open recommendations that contains analysis that tells the story
Approach	Obtain updates from management and update the recommendations database. Download and analyze the data for trends and prepare relevant graphs. Discern the story of how well recommendations are being addressed by management and prepare appropriate narrative.

Content	• Opinion on management's overall level of commitment to addressing agreed audit recommendations, and insights on the positive improvement from implementation.
	• Validation of the implementation of higher-risk recommendations for closure by the audit committee.
	• Commentary on at-risk recommendations, including their original and revised targeted completion dates and comments on action in train.
	• Trends (3 to 5 years) of actions opened, closed, on track, completed on time, overdue, and total number of actions currently open.
	• Trends and/or graphs on recommendations being raised applied against different business risk categories (see exhibit 14-1).
	• Graphs illustrating through different lenses overdue recommendations, for instance:
	  – Risk ratings (high, medium, and low).
	  – Ageing of periods overdue.
	  – Business area.
	• List of open recommendations (in full or part) as an attachment.

Value	High. In addition to meeting the basic requirements of the audit committee, this reporting type helps to provide risk-based and objective assurance, advice, and insights (i.e., "value proposition" as discussed in chapter 1).

Note: This table is intended as a simplified overview, recognizing that variations can and do occur.

Perspectives on Implementing Recommendations

If you were buying your first home, you would be excited by the prospect of getting your foot into the property market. Given your likely apprehension of the risks involved, you would assess the options for mitigating the risks by carefully considering the recommendations of property experts. As an example, when buying an existing property, you would:

- Establish the value and ownership of the property through an accredited appraiser.
- Assess the building integrity through pre-purchase inspections from experts in the field (e.g., building, power, pest, and termite inspections).
- Arrange a loan through a bank or other lender and ensure you could service the debt.
- Establish insurance coverage with a reputable insurer.
- Undertake legal requirements to transfer ownership under advisement of your lawyer or conveyance expert.

In some of these cases, you will assess and adopt recommendations through stages along the way without the need for recommendations in a written report (e.g., valuation, loan, insurance, and legals).

Pre-purchase inspection reports usually contain many recommendations of varying significance. Each recommendation needs to be carefully assessed against the exposure (risk likelihood and consequence), remediation cost, effort, and benefit. You will accept the risk of some recommendations, seek compensation or repair by vendors in some cases, and in other cases will commit to making the repairs when you own the property.

You will preserve the value of your investment in the property when you implement the higher-priority recommendations of the pre-purchase inspections. For instance, repairing water leaks will avoid subsidence; replacing worn electricity cables will prevent shock and potential harm to people; installation of smoke detectors reduces the risk of smoke inhalation from a fire; strengthening the capping of floor pillars will minimize the risk of termite damage; and replacing damaged gutters and roofing will prevent damage caused by water leaks.

The value of the pre-inspection recommendations is only derived when the recommendations are actually implemented. Where you have used contractors to complete the work, you will follow up implementation until the work is completed and seek validation (e.g., certificate of compliance) to confirm absolute resolution of the underlying problems.

Similarly, organizational value is protected when management implements internal audit recommendations. The internal audit activity maintains a rigorous process to follow up implementation, seek validation, and confirm resolution.

What Practitioners Love About Internal Audit

"Enjoy the role of trusted advisor both within and outside the organization."			
CAE	Baby Boomer	Over 20 years' auditing experience	Accounting

The Broader Context of Follow-Ups

Documented Approach

The approach for monitoring the status of audit recommendations should be documented in the internal audit activity's policies and procedures. This will guide the process and ensure consistency and completeness.

The policies and procedures will cover key aspects of the monitoring arrangements, such as:

- Type of information and level of detail the audit committee and senior management expect
- Breadth of coverage; whether it is just internal audit recommendations, or also recommendations raised by external auditors, regulators, and other scrutineers
- Operating arrangements for the database/tools used for logging recommendations and their status (see exhibits 17-1 and 17-2)
- Extent of monitoring (e.g., all recommendations or just the higher-risk recommendations)
- Frequency of initial capture of information and updates
- Frequency, style, breadth, and nature of reporting, and the analysis required
- Approach for validating the closure of recommendations

Tips for New Auditors

- Recognize the strategic benefit of audit recommendations that collectively enhance and protect organizational value.
- If you have an opportunity to be involved in the follow-up of internal audit recommendations, do so, as it:
  - Shapes your thinking on crafting meaningful recommendations that are clear and unambiguous and can be practically implemented
  - Provides a rich opportunity to learn about and engage with different parts of the business
  - Requires a range of skills from recording data and analyzing trends through to high-level reporting
- Review and understand the internal audit activity's policies and procedures covering the monitoring arrangements. Offer suggestions on leading practices that may warrant adoption (guided by the practices described in this chapter).
- Aim to deliver powerful insights to the audit committee and management by shaping a report on the status of audit recommendations that tells the story.

Related Standards

Standard 2500 – Monitoring Progress

The chief audit executive must establish and maintain a system to monitor the disposition of results communicated to management.

This is elaborated upon further as 2500.A1: The chief audit executive must establish a follow-up process to monitor and ensure that management actions have been effectively implemented or that senior management has accepted the risk of not taking action.

PART 5
THE *WHAT* OF INTERNAL AUDITING

Chapters 18 through 20 reflect on the outcomes the internal audit activity has delivered. These chapters highlight that internal audit is expected to undertake work that helps the organization deliver its business strategies and objectives. The concluding chapter showcases some of the amazing outcomes that a selection of expert practitioners has delivered.

QAIP	Performance	Stories

Wisdom of a Global Luminary

"New auditors must not be afraid to challenge the status quo. Just because something's been done a certain way before doesn't mean it's fit for purpose in today's rapidly changing world. The best advice I can offer new auditors is to have an insatiable curiosity and not be afraid to ask questions. Rudyard Kipling said it best in his book *The Elephant's Child* – 'I keep six honest serving-men (They taught me all I knew); Their names are What and Why and When and How and Where and Who.'"

—Paul Sobel
Chief Audit Executive, U.S.
Past Chairman of IIA Global Board of Directors 2013–2014

Chapter 18
Quality Assurance and Improvement Program

A quality assurance and improvement program (QAIP) is designed to enable an evaluation of the internal audit activity's conformance with the *Standards* and an evaluation of whether internal auditors apply the Code of Ethics. This chapter covers the applicable QAIP standards and methods to ensure the internal audit activity is functioning at a high standard and adding value to the organization.

Understanding the Basics

Core Elements

As quality is so fundamental to the credibility of the work of internal auditors (as explained in chapter 16), it is crucial for them to understand the internal audit activity's overarching quality assurance and improvement program, even though they may have no direct involvement in it. This chapter aims to provide a high-level overview.

The CAE is required under Standard 1300 – Quality Assurance and Improvement Program to establish and maintain a quality assurance and improvement program and report the results to the audit committee and senior management periodically (usually at least annually). The purpose of the program is threefold: evaluate conformance with professional auditing standards, establish whether The IIA's Code of Ethics is being applied, and nurture improvements.

The five core elements are illustrated in **exhibit 18-1** and discussed more fully thereafter. An auditor will usually be most exposed to the ongoing monitoring arrangements for quality assurance (as described in chapter 16). The work of the auditor could also be selected for review as part of the internal and external assessments, so their work needs to stand up to the scrutiny of professionals outside the internal audit activity and organization (exhibit 16-3 contains examples of external scrutineers). It is also worthwhile to understand the lessons arising from the assessments as a basis for continuous improvement.

Exhibit 18-1: Five Core Elements of a Quality Assurance and Improvement Program

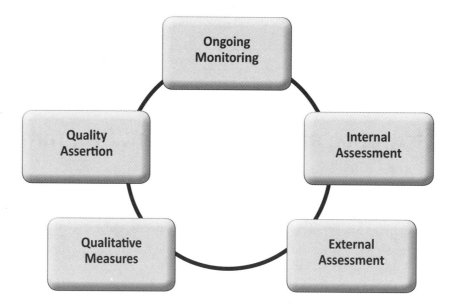

Ongoing Monitoring

Auditors will experience the monitoring of quality at every stage of an audit—from planning, to fieldwork, into reporting, and ultimately to the follow-up of audit recommendations. The ongoing monitoring is focused on ensuring:

- Output of internal auditors is reasonable, their conclusions are defensible and have a firm basis, and recommendations are reasonable, practical, actionable, and useful
- Conformance with the code of ethics and auditing standards
- Evidence of workpaper reviews and supervisor sign-off for in-house and service provider engagements
- Actual versus budgeted analysis (monitoring metrics; see audit closeout memorandum in exhibit 16-2)
- Performance evaluations for in-house and service provider engagements
- Client feedback surveys after each audit

The quality reviews are often undertaken on a daily basis for less experienced auditors. There are review features built into automated audit workpaper software to facilitate these reviews, otherwise the reviews are undertaken manually. The arrangements are discussed more fully in chapter 16.

Quality monitoring arrangements may extend beyond audits to other elements that underpin the quality of the internal audit activity, including ensuring:

- Internal audit employees have completed mandatory organizationwide training (e.g., corporate values, information security, privacy, anti-fraud and corruption, anti-bullying).
- Goal setting and performance evaluation are undertaken as required (as discussed in chapter 19).

Periodic Internal Assessments

Auditors might also experience holistic assessments of the internal audit activity that are undertaken periodically (at least annually, though they may be staggered throughout the year). The internal assessments may be completed on a self-assessment basis (e.g., by other auditors) or by someone from another area of the organization (e.g., risk management, compliance, legal, or finance). In either case, the internal assessment needs to be conducted by someone with a strong grasp of all elements of the International Professional Practices Framework.

The internal assessments will also consider the process and outcomes of the ongoing monitoring, and confirm whether the related sections of the internal audit policies and procedures manual remain current.

The periodic internal assessments may include:

- Review of the internal audit charter
- File reviews for in-house and service provider audits to assess conformance with the *Standards*
- Assertion on conformance with internal auditing standards
- Staff declarations (e.g., conflicts of interest or commitment to and compliance with The IIA's Code of Ethics)
- Performance measures (e.g., whether KPI counting rules are defined and whether calculations are complete, accurate, and supported)
- Annual audit committee and client feedback surveys (where they are being obtained)

The outcomes of the internal assessment are usually reported to the audit committee and senior management at least once each year. Where improvements have been identified, the audit committee will be apprised of the action plan.

External Assessment

It is a mandatory requirement under the *Standards* for an external assessment to be conducted at least once every five years by a qualified, independent assessor or assessment team from outside the organization. The focus is to assess the organization and operations of the internal audit activity against the *Standards* issued by The IIA. The scope would usually include an assessment of the internal audit activity's contribution to the achievement of business objectives.

A typical external assessment methodology will involve a phased approach, including:

- Providing an opinion as to whether the internal audit activity conforms to the *Standards* and Code of Ethics
- Assessing the efficiency and effectiveness of the internal audit activity
- Determining the expectations of the internal audit activity expressed by the audit committee, chief executive, and senior management, and whether these are being met

- Undertaking an assessment of skills, knowledge, and experience within the internal audit activity
- Reviewing the risk assessment and audit planning leading to the forward audit plan
- Evaluating the internal audit activity's structure and resources
- Examining internal audit techniques and methodology
- Identifying ways for improving internal audit methodology, policies, and practices

Where an external assessment confirms the internal audit activity conforms with the *Standards*, it may use the following words in its audit reports: *conforms with the International Standards for the Professional Practice of Internal Auditing* (in line with Standard 1321). This is a powerful statement that internal auditors should be proud to achieve and use as it enhances the credibility of the internal audit activity with stakeholders.

The outcomes of the external assessment will be reported to the audit committee and senior management. Where improvements have been identified, the audit committee will usually monitor the action plan.

Qualitative Measures

A key element of an internal audit activity's quality assurance and improvement program is the usage of satisfaction surveys for key stakeholders, most notably audit committee, senior management, and internal audit employees. The stakeholder feedback will often roll into specific qualitative-based key performance indicators, such as those illustrated later in the example balanced scorecard in exhibit 19-4.

Stakeholder surveys typically use measures that are qualitative in nature and reflect the perceptions of stakeholders. Exhibit 19-4 illustrates how the results of stakeholder surveys flow into the balanced scorecard and ultimately to an auditor's individual performance measures. The audit closeout memorandum (see exhibit 16-2) also provides important qualitative context.

Quality Assertion

It is a mandatory requirement under most internal audit charters approved by the audit committee for the internal audit activity to operate in a manner that is consistent with The IIA's *Standards* (or words to this effect).

Conformance to some standards may be evident from the reports and papers routinely delivered to the audit committee. But there are some requirements of the *Standards* that sit in the shadows unless they are brought to light.

An annual assertion provided by the CAE to the audit committee will provide explicit confirmation that these oblique standards are understood and have been applied appropriately. For instance, it will confirm the internal audit charter remains current; identify any restrictions on the scope of internal audit activities (independence); report on any real or perceived conflicts of interest and how they were managed; identify how any errors and omissions were (or would be) handled; disclose any nonconformance/s with the *Standards*; and confirm that auditors have adhered to The IIA's Code of Ethics.

Perspectives on Quality

The competitors of Fred's Flashy Floorings had well-established product lines, including carpet, tiles, linoleum, and polished wooden floor coverings. Fred had established a niche in the competitive floor-cover market as a manufacturer and supplier of a relatively innovative and hardy floor covering that combined the strength of floor tiles with the durability of linoleum and the softness of carpet.

After a decade of successful operation and an increasing market share, Fred wanted to test the robustness of the company's commitment to quality assurance and improvement. He organized a workshop and brought together the managers of all of his key divisions (including manufacturing, sales, supply, and installation) with external stakeholders representing key businesses in the supply chain.

The group initially explored two pillars of a quality improvement program on which the business had built its reputation and success, and these were:

- Quality across all facets of the operation; deliver optimum products and services for the least cost.
- Continuous improvement through innovation; ensuring customers were looked after obsessively.

While these pillars had served the business well, Fred and the workshop participants identified the opportunity to enhance them by adding a fresh qualitative measure:

- Finger on the pulse; knowing what the customers really think.

Fred continued to workshop the third pillar. He ultimately resolved to set service goals and targets; establish a record of customer feedback interactions (complaints and compliments); personally review and assess customer feedback; and personally make contact with customers who provided feedback or whose customer service ratings in the standard satisfaction surveys were outside the norm (better or worse).

There is a strong parallel in the quality assurance and improvement factors at the heart of a successful business like Fred's Flashy Floorings and those that result in a creditable internal audit activity. The stakeholder and performance factors are explored further in chapters 1 and 19. The quality assurance and improvement program should never become stale. It needs to be reviewed and reenergized periodically to remain relevant.

What Practitioners Love About Internal Audit

"The way that internal auditors are able to help in maintaining the integrity of an entity's activities and its governance."			
Audit Committee Chair	Traditionalist	Over 20 years' auditing experience	Law

The Broader Context of Quality and Improvement

External Pressures

External pressures can be brought to bear when organizational failures occur and the light is shone on the quality assurance and improvement program of an internal audit activity in the same business sector. This is illustrated by the media report below[1]:

> "The state-owned Industrial Development Bank of India is conducting a quality assurance audit to strengthen its internal audit function, ensure adherence to best practices, and determine whether its branches are complying with regulations. The move comes as India's public-sector banks face pressure to enhance their audit systems in the wake of recent fraud identified at Punjab National Bank."

Benefits of a Quality Assurance and Improvement Program

The CBOK 2015 global internal audit practitioner survey reflected that internal audit activities that conform with the *Standards* covering the quality assurance and improvement program seem to be different from other internal audit activities in many ways.[2] For instance, those reporting full conformance to the standard:

- Were more likely to have complete and unrestricted access to information as appropriate for the performance of audit activities
- Worked in organizations with more highly developed risk management processes, especially processes for enterprise risk management
- Used a wider variety of resources to develop audit plans
- Made more use of technology in internal audit processes
- Were more likely to have documented procedures in an internal audit manual
- Received more hours of training and were more likely to have formalized training programs
- Were more likely to report that funding for the internal audit activity was completely sufficient

Abiding by and Enforcing Quality Standards

The CBOK 2015 global internal audit practitioner survey also highlighted the risk of the internal audit profession failing to abide by and enforce its own quality standards, including[3]:

- Nonexistent or ineffective QAIPs may increase the risk that internal audits will fail to identify and address significant issues.
- They may lead to inefficient or ineffective use of resources, not just within the internal audit activity, but as a result of ineffective auditing throughout the organization.
- In some jurisdictions, boards of directors are starting to face increased liability if internal auditors do not conform to professional standards.
- Some people believe that internal auditing will not universally be considered a true profession until internal auditors not only have mandatory professional standards, but also begin to apply and follow those standards consistently.
- The IIA's *Quality Assessment Manual for the Internal Audit Activity* points out that one of internal audit's major assets is its credibility with stakeholders.

Actions for Auditors

There are many different actions for strengthening quality assurance and improvement arrangements in organizations, depending on the roles of those involved. Some examples for auditors are illustrated in **exhibit 18-2**.

Exhibit 18-2: Examples of Steps to Optimize Quality Assurance and Improvement Arrangements

Opportunities for Internal Auditors
Understand the mandate and provisions of the internal audit charter and how it affects your planning, fieldwork, reporting, and evidence of quality assurance.
Gain a comprehensive understanding of the International Professional Practices Framework (IPPF) through self-study or attendance at a suitable training course.
Become a member of The IIA in your region to maintain current IPPF knowledge and to derive further member value.
Maintain contemporary internal audit skillsets through ongoing professional development (which is a shared responsibility with employers).
Keep abreast of emerging risks, issues, and practices through professional outreach activities (e.g., attend complimentary IIA webinars and member meetings).
Consider completing an internal audit certification or achieve professional membership, if offered in your region.

Tips for New Auditors

- Start with gaining an understanding of the IPPF and guidance, then work out how you can apply them to yourself and your organization.
- You should always perform your work with honesty and act with integrity. That will foster trust—the fuel for your success as an internal auditor.
- Be open-minded, a lateral thinker, keep a good reserve of imagination, and be part of the solution.
- Don't sweat the small stuff. There will be many times when it is more effective to let go of small issues so that energy can be directed to what is more important for the business.
- Be flexible, stay firm on your principles, and be courageous. A good auditor never compromises his or her observations because of management pressure; you sleep better with a clear conscience.

> **Related Standards**
>
> **Standard 1300 – Quality Assurance and Improvement Program**
>
> The chief audit executive must develop and maintain a quality assurance and improvement program that covers all aspects of the internal audit activity.

Chapter 19
Measuring Performance

A firm foundation for measuring performance is provided when there is effective goal setting, so that the personal goals of individual internal auditors are aligned to the goals of the internal audit activity and the organization's strategies. This chapter explores the steps that are typically established for measuring the performance of internal auditors and how that process corresponds to an effective performance culture for the internal audit activity and the organization as a whole.

Goal Setting

Goal setting is a key part of a performance management process. The establishment of individual goals is an iterative process between the auditor and the team leader.

The main aim is to identify the specific results the individual auditor is required to achieve to help the internal audit activity (and ultimately the organization) achieve its objectives. Depending on the organization's human resources policies, the goals may well be a combination of work-specific outcomes and personal development needs.

Over a typical one-year cycle, the auditor's performance goals are discussed and agreed, the auditor takes action to achieve the goals, performance against the goals is evaluated (see the annual reviews outline following), and the goals are refreshed to incorporate performance improvements and development initiatives. This process is illustrated in **exhibit 19-1**.

Exhibit 19-1: Common Steps in Goal Setting

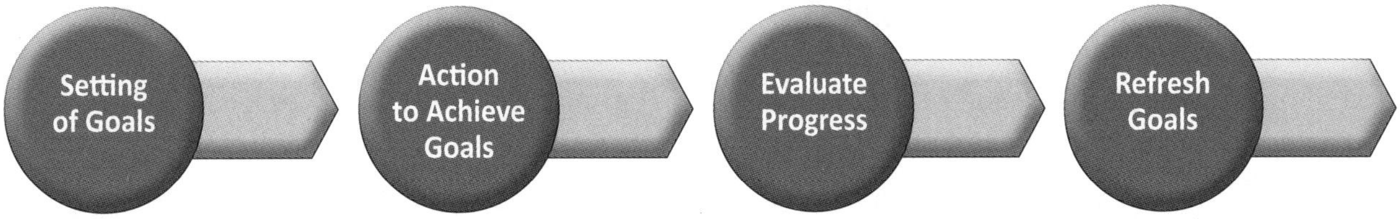

Setting of Goals → Action to Achieve Goals → Evaluate Progress → Refresh Goals

The outcomes achieved against the goals set at the start of the process are considered as part of the individual's performance evaluation. In turn, the evaluation contributes to the periodic refresh of the goals, including proposed professional development initiatives.

Internal auditors benefit when their team leader follows a structured goal-setting and evaluation process that:

- Provides sufficient time to develop and agree upon goals
- Establishes meaningful goals that are clear, measurable, and achievable
- Sets goals that are commensurate with an auditor's capability
- Aligns individual goals to those of the audit activity and organizational strategy
- Equips auditors with the necessary skills to meet goals (e.g., by providing training [internal or external resources] and/or professional development opportunities [attending conferences and IIA local chapter meetings; working with other business groups])
- Motivates auditors to meet their goals

Exhibit 19-2 provides an example of a specific outcome the team leader has assigned to the auditor (to complement auditing KPIs in exhibit 19-4). The auditor was seeking an activity aligned to the broader objectives of the internal audit activity, preferring something that would be challenging to achieve. The auditor had recently been tasked with the follow-up and reporting on audit recommendations (discussed in chapter 17), and had recently completed a better writing training course. The auditor liked a challenge and was motivated to do well. In assigning this goal, the team leader agreed to arrange an advanced training course on Excel graphics.

Exhibit 19-2: Example of an Auditor's Goals

Outcome Expected	Well-Developed Goal (clear, measurable, achievable)	Unclear Goal (unclear, not measurable, unclear if achieved)
A report on open recommendations that contains analysis that tells the story (see exhibit 17-3 for background).	Enhance the process to deliver well-rounded reporting of open audit recommendations by 31 December 20xx at a cost of $xx and achieve at least a "meets requirements" rating from the audit committee.	Better reporting on recommendations from audits.

Performance Evaluation

Internal auditors are expected to spend most of their time undertaking audits in line with the audit planning memorandum (see chapter 9). An auditor's work is typically subjected to close scrutiny, with the overall quality of their work assessed during the audit wrap-up and quality review stage (see chapter 16) that considers all stages of the audit process—planning, fieldwork, and reporting.

The common ways of evaluating an auditor's performance are illustrated in **exhibit 19-3** and discussed more fully afterwards. In essence, a constructive performance assessment will involve two lenses—the development of an auditor's skillsets and feedback on their performance. Some internal audit activities embrace self-assessment tools, whereas others are boosting the use of technology to automate performance assessment processes to increase the transparency and efficiency of the process.

Exhibit 19-3: Common Processes for Evaluating an Auditor's Performance

Developing an Auditor's Skillset

Professional Development

Annual Reviews

Engagement Feedback

Performance Insights

Probationary Reviews

Profiling

Coach or Mentor

Informal Feedback

Feedback on an Auditor's Performance

Annual Reviews

An annual review is one of the more common approaches for measuring an auditor's performance. Most organizations have structured formal performance evaluation processes typically involving three key face-to-face stages over a one-year span. The first stage involves goal setting followed by a formal mid-term review after six months and a further final formal review after another six months. Some regions embrace a two-step process rather than a three-step process (there is no mid-term review).

The formal performance evaluation process typically covers:

- The internal auditor's competencies (e.g., value-added, client-focused services; communication skills; technical competencies; knowledge of the business; outreach activities; and leadership characteristics)
- The delivery against performance goals
- Their continued professional development needs (e.g., on-the-job-training, specific training for specific needs, preparation for the Certified Internal Auditor [CIA] or other certification exams)

Some CAEs have introduced a blended approach to accommodate the different preferences of younger generations for recognition; for instance, Generation X has a preference for skill development opportunities, whereas millennials prefer constant and immediate feedback. The blended approach retains the well-established formal annual review process while establishing complementary processes that provide a more constant feedback and learning loop. There are many options for increasing the frequency of feedback to auditors, including informal feedback; professional development; skill profiling; and coaching and mentoring.

Engagement Feedback

A team leader will provide feedback immediately after an audit, usually after the draft audit report has been issued. The feedback covers the auditor's output/outcomes, overall results, behaviors, and suggestions on future training needs. The feedback can be delivered informally, and some medium to large internal audit activities use a standard feedback template to aid the consistency of feedback across its various team leaders.

Because auditors have distinct projects (i.e., audits) potentially under the direction of different team leaders, this style of feedback is a powerful, constructive, and timely development aid. Well-documented audit feedback can feed nicely into the annual review process.

Probationary Reviews

Team leaders are usually required to complete probationary reviews of a new auditor's performance at regular predetermined intervals in line with the organization's recruitment and onboarding policies. Regular feedback is provided throughout the probationary period, which can span periods of three, six, or 12 months. The feedback will align more closely to generic organizational measures (e.g., company values, attendance, and personal presentation) coupled with the defined position objectives in the auditor's position description. Even new employees recruited to senior executive positions (like the CAE) from outside the organization are often appointed with a probationary provision.

Informal Feedback

"Fireside chats" focus on the professional development of internal auditors and are held several times a year. These conversations are conducted for about 15 minutes by the CAE or team leader. The first chat typically focuses on the climate in which the auditor is operating (i.e., what is now, and what could be). The subsequent chats cover topics such as strength and talents; opportunities for growth; learning and development needs; and innovation and continuous improvement opportunities.

An alternative approach is an annual "skip-level conversation," which provides a sense of the pulse of the internal audit activity. It is conducted by the CAE or one of the senior leaders for all indirect reports. These conversations help the leadership cohort identify potential leadership talent across the activity and understand what drives the individuals.

Professional Development

Some CAEs establish a professional training target of five to 10 days each year where continuing professional education credits are awarded. For instance, guest facilitators are used from other areas of the business or externally (at little to no cost) to present a one-hour lunchtime seminar on relevant business areas (e.g., business strategy, emerging industry and audit hotspots, technical training, communications skills, new computer systems, data analytics).

Skill Profiling

Auditors can also gain value from understanding how their profile and/or skills compare to others. Three common examples include:

- An active career mapping conversation leveraging available resources. A useful resource is the *Mapping Your Career: Competencies Necessary for Internal Audit Excellence* publication. It helps new auditors understand the competencies of a successful internal auditor; compare their assessment to others; assess their strengths and weaknesses; choose skills they want to improve; and create a plan for investing in themselves.[1] This mapping can help with goal setting, as discussed earlier.
- Periodic 360° profiling involves the auditors' work being critiqued by their team leader, co-workers, subordinates (if any), and sometimes their recent clients. It typically uses automated software to produce a consolidated report for discussion. It is seen as a more well-rounded evaluation approach than feedback solely from the team leader.
- Completion of a personality type-finder evaluation (such as the Myer Briggs Type Indicator) helps individuals understand their strengths and weaknesses and how best to deal with other people. It uses an introspective self-assessment questionnaire to determine an individual's preferences on how they see the world around them and how they make their decisions.

Mentor or Coach

Auditors can benefit enormously when they have a mentor or coach who provides a self-evaluation approach and helps them deal with their personal performance challenges and development needs close to real-time through trusted advisors. Mentoring can be through either an informal arrangement or a structured mentoring program.

A good starting point for sourcing a mentor is through the local IIA chapter (where offered). Mentoring programs run by professional associations (including The IIA) typically commit to matching mentors and mentees and supporting them in their relationship during the term of the program (often six months). When new auditors have a strong relationship with their mentor, they gain valuable advice and insights.

Perspectives on Performance Measurement

George was responsible for selling souvenirs to retailers, and his focus on boomerangs this year made it his bestselling souvenir product. He had forward sales for the next six months that were 95% higher than the same period last year. He was looking forward to his performance appraisal discussion with his manager and excited at the prospect of a bonus. The organization's bonus scheme considers three facets: personal performance, the performance of the business area, and the performance of the company as a whole.

George met with his manager. She was downcast. The profitability of the business area had plummeted to a record low level. It had dragged the overall profitability of the whole company down.

The chief financial officer had pinpointed the root causes:

- Wholesale cost had increased to $100 for each boomerang, though they were still being sold to retail operators for $80 each (which was supposed to be a short-term, one-off stock clearance discount).
- Demand had outstripped supply by a significant level, creating serious (possibly irreparable) tensions between the company and its suppliers and retailers. In some cases, compensation had been paid to disgruntled retailers when their orders were not met.
- Boomerangs are traditionally made from a rare timber that is facing unrecoverable destruction. Supply is no longer sustainable, and the environmental impact is contrary to the company's brand.
- The rapid growth in sales, coupled with the other factors above, had compounded the company's losses. The company needs to unwind the high level of forward sales George generated because supply had stalled and would never recover.

George's performance was marked down. He thought that to be unfair because he did nothing wrong, and had simply focused on one of his performance goals. When he reread the performance goals he agreed with his manager last year, George reflected that one of his goals was very clearly related to the boomerang product line … *to discontinue the supply of boomerangs and exit the business without disrupting the relationship with the indigenous people who make and supply the boomerangs, or the retailers who stock them.* A simple misunderstanding!

This example reflects the importance of individual goals and performance outcomes of staff aligning with the goals of the business area—and ultimately the strategic objectives of the company. That approach is similarly important for internal auditors and reflects the need to fully grasp the goals and their intended outcomes.

What Practitioners Love About Internal Audit

> *"Being an internal auditor gives you the opportunity to look at all parts of the organization – not too many jobs can do that!"*

CAE	Baby Boomer	10 to 20 years' auditing experience	HR and IT

The Broader Context of Performance Measurement

Performance Culture

Culture is a key driver for an organization in achieving its stated purpose, objectives, and outcomes. A culture helps to guide the manner in which employees feel, think, and act. An effective performance culture reflects the systematic model for practically managing an organization, its business activities, and its employees.

An organization might have a well-structured and systematic performance management process that reflects the annual review arrangements discussed earlier—goal setting, mid-term review, and final review. However, if managers and supervisors do not embrace these arrangements and have meaningful conversations with their employees, then an effective performance culture will not blossom.

Balanced Scorecard Reporting

Internal auditors are more likely to help an organization accomplish its objectives when their personal performance goals and objectives align to the mission and objectives of the internal audit activity, which, in turn, should align with the strategic direction of the organization.

The individual performance measures on which an auditor's performance can be assessed should ideally correspond to their agreed performance goals and involve qualitative and quantitative factors. When the internal audit activity seeks client feedback after each audit in the form of a client satisfaction survey, the scores for the value added from the audit and the usefulness of audit recommendations are qualitative measures that are directly influenced by how well the auditors have completed their work.

Auditors need to have visibility between their personal goals and those of the internal audit activity. A good way to achieve a direct line of sight is through a balanced scorecard report where this approach is used by the internal audit activity, as illustrated in the example in **exhibit 19-4**.

The use of balanced scorecard reporting is continuing to increase across the world. According to one of the research reports from the latest Global Internal Audit Common Body of Knowledge (CBOK) practitioner study conducted in 2015[2]:

- The adoption of balanced scorecard reporting is a well-established tool for structuring quantitative and qualitative performance measures and reporting the results to the audit committee in a balanced way.
- Balanced scorecards were used by 26% of CAEs in 2015 (up from 4% in 2010).
- The KPIs in the balanced scorecard will almost always align to individual performance measures.

Definition of a Balanced Scorecard for Internal Audit[3]

The balanced scorecard performance management system is widely used by organizations and has become a leading management framework for strategy execution throughout the world. Balanced scorecards in internal auditing help translate strategy into action and manage and measure internal audit performance. They can also help to connect the internal audit activity's strategy with that of the organization.

Balanced scorecards often flow into the Annual Report on Internal Audit that showcases the contribution and achievements of the activity, demonstrates its value, and delivers consolidated insights to the audit committee and senior management.

Exhibit 19-4: Example of Balanced Scorecard KPIs Aligned to Individual Performance Measures

Balanced Scorecard Element	Example of Internal Audit Activity KPIs	Type of Measure	Individual Performance Measures	
			Team Leaders	Auditors
Partnering with the audit committee	Audit committee expectations met*	Qualitative	Yes	If directly relevant
	Percentage of audit plan complete	Quantitative	Yes for own team	Yes for personal allocation
Supporting executive and senior management	Client satisfaction goals - value added*	Qualitative	Yes for own team	Yes for own audits
	Client satisfaction goals - usefulness of recommendations*	Qualitative	Yes for own team	Yes for own audits
	Cycle times (duration period of audits)	Quantitative	Yes for own team	Yes for own audits

Exhibit 19-4: Example of Balanced Scorecard KPIs Aligned to Individual Performance Measures (cont.)

Managing internal audit processes	Performance against the internal audit financial budget	Quantitative	Applies to CAE	Not applicable
	Availability of current and relevant internal audit charter, intranet, audit manual	Qualitative	Applies to CAE	Not applicable
	Budget to actual audit times	Quantitative	Yes for own team	Yes for own audits
	Compliance with quality assurance and improvement standards (based on internal and external quality assessments)	Qualitative	Yes for own team	Yes for own audits
Managing internal auditors and their development	Internal auditor workforce satisfaction*	Qualitative	Yes for own team	Not applicable
	Completion of initiatives in professional development plan	Quantitative	Yes for own team	Yes personally
	Optimize use of internal audit resources (to conduct audits while minimizing "administration")	Quantitative	Yes for own team	Yes personally

Notes: 1) * Signifies that this is based on survey responses

           2) Specific KPI targets and measures are not included in this example

Tips for New Auditors

- Engage in a well-founded goal-setting and performance evaluation process, as it provides the basis for shaping a successful career.
- Don't listen to dinosaurs who tell you internal audit's only job is to make sure there is compliance and to point out errors; that is old school thinking.
- Find a great mentor; ask questions, listen, and try different types of audits.
- Understand how your personal performance goals align with the objectives of the internal audit activity and the strategic direction of the organization.
- How you and the internal audit activity are perceived in the organization and by particular individuals can sometimes be as a result of past experiences, so you have to work hard to make every experience count in a positive way.

Related Standards

Standard 2060 – Reporting to Senior Management and the Board

The chief audit executive must report periodically to senior management and the board on the internal audit activity's purpose, authority, responsibility, and performance relative to its plan and on its conformance with the Code of Ethics and the *Standards*. Reporting must also include significant risk and control issues, including fraud risks, governance issues, and other matters that require the attention of senior management and/or the board.

Chapter 20
Stories from the Frontline

While it is essential to recognize the what, why, and how of internal auditing outlined in earlier chapters, understanding stories from the frontline helps to inspire fresh, creative thinking. That, in turn, brings real life to the mission of *enhancing and protecting organizational value by providing risk-based and objective assurance, advice, and insight.*

Unleashing the Power of Storytelling

This chapter draws together a range of interesting stories from various contributors where they recalled their favorite audit ever. The six stories highlight the importance of an auditor's imagination and are followed by a series of short reflections on how the ABCs of auditing are applied in the business environment. They encourage a fresh approach to thinking outside the box, as this often contributes the greatest value to the business. These are all real-life stories that are intended to challenge auditors into thinking beyond the scope.

Meaning of Frontline

Frontline is an idiomatic term that refers to hands-on people who are responsible for producing and delivering services and goods directly to customers, clients, and stakeholders. They have to achieve targets and deadlines (like factory supervisors).

The term provides a distinction between these roles and senior management's broader leadership role, which is more involved in strategic planning, customer and public relations, and oversight rather than being directly involved in the operational aspects of the business.

The analogy is that internal auditors apply a hands-on approach, work to deadlines, and deal directly with clients.

Finding Unusual Activity Through Data Analytics

My first audit using data analytics way back in the late 1980s was one of my favorite audits. There was an unusually high volume of diesel usage at a center and, by analyzing industry and demographic data, I was able to prove it wasn't because of evaporation or leaking. I was able to run standard deviation on usage across several similar centers and identify unusual high-volume usage at the specific center.

All controls seemed to be in place with logging of usage and padlock with secure keying. I then ran an analysis of usage against staff at work and identified that very high usage occurred before and directly after an employee took vacation leave. Usage while that employee was absent on leave conformed to normal usage rates of the other centers surveyed.

With this information, the employee confessed and identified that he had been on duty when the overhead bulk tank was installed, took possession of the three security keys, and only handed two keys back to management. He was very surprised that he was found out without anyone from headquarters visiting the site. It was extremely satisfying to provide a solution using recently learned analytics skills from university, and it started my push for analytics in my audit teams.

Alerting Management to a Potential Multimillion Dollar Contractor Failure

My favorite audit was a very large one that reviewed how a critical contract was being managed for a program that was bringing about transformational change within the organization. The program had a high public profile and the scope of works was subject to constant change, resulting in more than 50 contract variations, which almost doubled the multimillion dollar contract value.

One of the key observations was that our organization was relying on a multimillion dollar contract that had significant safeguards built into it in the event of any failures to deliver. However, the contract was with a subsidiary company with very limited capital, and there was no parental support from the multinational parent company. In effect, if the subsidiary failed in any way, the parent company could walk away and our organization would have been heavily exposed—unable to transform the business to gain efficiencies, a huge investment that would not deliver improved technologies, a reputation that would be severely diminished, and a potential significant lawsuit.

The audit was challenging due to the technical nature of the program and the sense of ownership by key stakeholders involved in delivering the program. There were prolonged negotiations over the draft report, but I was very happy with the final product and it received attention at the highest levels within the organization. I had delivered a high-quality audit that really made a difference.

Identifying Poor Subsidy Arrangements to Save Millions

My favorite audits are those where you help to improve the business by pointing out to management something they hadn't thought of. For example, I remember a corporation that sold a product which was subsidized in the province (province A) where it was headquartered. The subsidy was based on the weighted average difference in selling price between the nonsubsidized province (province B) and province A.

Therefore, the higher the average selling price in province B the higher the subsidy. However, the sales people in province B were incentivized based only on the top line, and the average price was brought down as a result of their hard work to meet sales targets in province B. In effect, the sales team made several thousand dollars extra in commission while the corporation lost millions in subsidy opportunity cost.

Spotting a Significant Shortfall in Services

My favorite audit was one where I successfully applied my analytical skills to find major deficiencies within a system, which would never have been discovered through a traditional audit process. My projections accurately predicted a major shortfall of services from a third-party security supplier that were systematically charged but not provided by the supplier.

The service contract included a right-to-audit clause, which we leveraged. We compared the service schedule (attached to the invoice) with the supplier's employee and payroll records. We were able to prove that the supplier never had the resource levels to deliver the services that they had charged for in the service schedule. It gave me great pleasure that management expressed personal appreciation that my audit provided them with positive contributions in helping them to recover a large sum of money from the supplier, and also strengthened the system of internal controls.

Building Stronger Partnerships with Management

My favorite audit was for a technical service delivery area—parking services for a large urban local government authority. We started out with a skeptical and resistant manager, but ended up with him becoming a champion of internal auditing!

He wanted me to come back again to help him further improve not only his risk and controls, but enhanced performance and create enthusiasm for what could be improved in all areas under his leadership. We did a risk-based assessment of all his key areas, both financial and nonfinancial, so at the end of the audit he had a robust mechanism for justifying his business case for change and accompanying budget submission. I enjoyed learning about his technical area.

Taking the Extra Steps to Reshape the Control Environment

One of my favorite audits when I was a CAE was to observe one of my auditors undertaking what appeared to be a routine review of maintenance charges. It was a safety requirement for the rail organization to paint yellow stripes about two feet from the platform edge so customers would know not to cross the line into a dangerous area close to fast-moving trains. The yellow lines needed to be repainted every two to three years as passenger movements dulled the effect.

The organization had outsourced this work and paid a standard rate based on the total length of all the platforms at each station. The cost for each station was reasonably modest, but with hundreds of stations in the network and the ongoing nature of the work, the overall cost became much more significant.

The auditor was reviewing the accounts payable cycle when he identified several invoices for the yellow line-painting in his sample. It was relatively easy to check—the total length of the platforms in yards, multiplied by the dollar rate per yard, plus taxes, equaled the invoice.

With a reputation for thinking outside the box, the auditor hired a perambulator (surveyor's wheel or measuring wheel) and went onsite at several railway stations to independently calculate the length of the platforms. He found that, on average, the length of the platforms had been inflated by more than 20%. The organization had modified its platforms over the years but never updated its asset records. The contractor never highlighted the discrepancies. The auditor helped to reshape the organization's control environment, and his work resulted in a significant refund.

The ABCs of Auditing

An article published in the December 2013 edition of *Internal Auditor* magazine provided the context for auditors to apply the ABCs of auditing to their work by being attuned, balanced, and credible.[1] Excerpts from the article are included in **exhibit 20-1**.

Exhibit 20-1: The ABCs of Meeting Stakeholder Needs (Excerpt from an article in *Internal Auditor*)

In the eyes of an experienced audit committee chair, "Some internal auditors have good process developed into an art form where the process is perfect but nothing is ever discovered."

This situation was evident for a struggling internal audit activity where the audit committee's average satisfaction rating sat at a lowly 55%. Quite simply, the audit committee and senior management perceived that they were not getting value from their investment in internal audit. A new CAE was appointed. He articulated the vision and then established strategies to sharpen the team's focus and direction, enhance its contribution, and satisfy the needs of the audit committee and other stakeholders.

After three years, the audit team was discovering meaningful things and providing fresh insights. The activity was widely regarded as high-performing and was seen as mature. Its overall approach, processes, and reporting were representative of world class.

The article captured the essence of the transformation and reflected that delivering value is as simple as A-B-C—being attuned, balanced, and credible.

Attuned
Knows the business and what needs audit focus

Balanced
Applies a balanced approach to provide valued insights

Credible
Regarded as credible in the eyes of stakeholders

Value Added

Short Reflections on Their Favorite Audits Ever

Contributors to this chapter shared a range of reflections where they recalled their favorite audit ever. A selection is tabulated below and sorted into different categories by applying the ABCs.

Attuned - Knows the business and what needs audit focus	
Business Alignment	We engaged with the business, supported their goals and ambitions, and achieved a positive experience for all involved.
Catalyst for Change	We made a real difference and served as a valued catalyst for change.
Challenging	The irony is that my favorite audit was easily the most vexing but yielded good results. I was challenged and I couldn't wait to discover more.
Fixed Assets	I was involved in audits within a remote community. One of the interesting things about these audits was accounting for the fixed assets and those written off. City dwellers would not be familiar with unusual write-offs, such as when community vehicles had become stuck in a swamp.
Making Connections	One of my very first audits was an area that had been a bit neglected. There was a lot to find, and making the connections to where the organization could do better and where there were gaps was very satisfying. I would describe it as exciting and it's what set the standard for my future work. If I wasn't able to suggest ways to benefit the business, then I wasn't satisfied with my audit.
Operational Audits	Many internal auditors think their job is to make sure there is compliance and to point out errors, which is a lost opportunity. The best audits are those that adopt an operational auditing approach—efficiency, effectiveness, economy, and ethical. There is so much more value in these audits and potential to make a massive contribution to your organization. Turn every compliance audit into an operational audit—it's not that difficult.
Priceless Artifacts	I did an audit of a university library and inspected many old artifacts and books, including the *Philosophiæ Naturalis Principia Mathematica* by Isaac Newton, with his personal annotations. This is one of his best-known works containing basic laws of physics, and was first published in Latin in three volumes in July 1687.
Quick Fix	All our internal audit recommendations were accepted and implemented by management before the written internal audit report went to the audit committee.
Streamlined Practices	Internal auditing in a series of distribution warehouses—I learned a lot about the business operations, and the audit team made a huge difference to the organization by helping streamline work practices and closing out possibilities for theft and corruption. We really made a difference.

Strong Backing	It was an audit where we had commitment from the stakeholders, an energetic, enthusiastic team by my side, and the backing of the chief audit executive. From the beginning, we knew there was value in the work that we were doing and the audit team took pride in the final product. Recommendations were well received and agreed. However, we also knew that if we received any resistance, the chief audit executive would back the team. Stakeholders acknowledged the value of the audit and it was completed on time and within budget.
Balanced - Applies a balanced approach to provide valued insights	
Appreciation	It was challenging, but our observations were so significant they went straight to the head of the organization, external auditors, and the Government's Public Accounts Committee. It was rewarding to see the appreciation for the work we undertook.
Building Relationships	I have fond memories of building relationships with colleagues through traveling and working together under pressure to meet deadlines.
Changes Were Needed	We proceeded carefully in a sensitive but important area. Analysis and commentary were expressed in clear, unemotional language and were based very carefully on our work. We persuaded the organization that changes were needed.
Cooperation	The client was a government-owned corporation that embraced technology and had very modern facilities and an enthusiastic approach to continuous improvement. We were able to add substantial value through the availability of data and communication with highly cooperative team members.
Continuous Improvement	My favorite audit was one where the results were embraced by the business and were used to kick-start a cycle of continuous improvement. This happened in a new business area with a high potential exposure for corruption. The client was very happy to schedule follow-up audits and employ these as a key part of the assurance program for the new business area.
Cross-Border Challenges	My favorite internal audit ever involved lots of international travel, rolling out a whistleblowing hotline service throughout Asia and North America. The different cultures and different business expectations provided a great challenge to "sell" the process to the end users. It was an important consulting engagement, helping the business to bed down the whistleblower process. In short, travel, different cultures, variety, and cross-border considerations.
Great Civic Outcomes	Enriching and heartwarming. Working hand in hand with schools to improve budget outcomes, which in turn created favorable opportunities for school students. Better financial stewardship enabled the purchasing of new equipment for students and professional development training for teachers. This generated a real energy among schools and increased demand for internal audit services.
Learning About Yourself	Lots of favorite audits, but the ones that still come to mind are those where it was hard work, things went wrong, clients were upset, and there was lots of stress. But those are the ones we learn about ourselves and learn about resilience. In the end, you come out not only a better auditor but a better person.

Meeting New People	A month spent doing an IT audit with a team of six in a big mining company. It involved living in remote mining headquarters, reviewing complex IT systems that I was not familiar with, and seeing the mining operations first hand. The assignment also provided opportunity for seeing the countryside and meeting new people.
Process Improvement	It involved the detailed analysis of a compensation assessment and approval process with a view to identifying bottlenecks and potential failure points. The objective was to provide information about how both the speed and accuracy of processing may be improved.

Credible - Regarded as credible in the eyes of stakeholders	
Best Practice	We invented and tested a new approach for our operational audit. And the board used this as a "best practice" model for the whole organization.
Building Advocates	Politically sensitive, high profile, really tricky, and loads of fun—ended up with some strong advocates for internal audit.
Business Improvement	We gained the attention of the whole organization. Recommendations were implemented quickly and you could see an improvement in the way the business operated, with senior management recognizing the value that internal audit did, and can, provide to the organization.
Business Partner	An audit where opportunities for improvement were recognized and monies were then recovered by the business under review back to the organization. There was initial resistance from the client, but with good communication and the opportunities for improvement that we identified resulted in a change from the client, with the client viewing internal audit no longer as a compliance necessity but as a business partner. The change in the tone from the top made future reviews in the area so much smoother to finalize. A real win/win for the whole organization.
Engaging and Fun	With two words—engaging and fun: • Engaging with all the different people, both internal and external, and • Fun to be part of one of the best teams, working alongside the best talent within the industry.
Feeling Valued	Feeling valued—when you've told the business something they did not know and were invited to provide insights into their process after the audit.
Incredibly Energizing	When I was asked by the CEO to do a review focused on the biggest challenge facing the business, I knew I was being directed to answer a tough question which was central to the business strategy. I was trusted and valued. And it was a tough challenge to come up with the recommendations that could solve the challenge. The combination of these is incredibly energizing.
Making a Difference	The times I could come up with insights that surprised the business, and when they realized that you have added value to their function—so making a difference is what I strive for!

Positive Visibility	It began with an immediate request for audit's assistance based on previous positive dealings with a client. The size and extent of the problem was unknown and the solution was unclear. This required quick thinking and research using both consultative and technical audit skills. In the end, new relationships and positive visibility for internal audit was gained, which ultimately led to more meaningful and integrated use of audit in future projects.
Strategic Reviews	Post strategic decision reviews undertaken specifically for the chief executive: • Special requests • Reporting directly to chief executive • High degree of complexity • Large impact on organization • Outcomes were well received

Perspectives Through Stories

The perspectives sections of each of the preceding chapters translate a range of fictional stories into lessons related to the specific steps of internal auditing. Those fictional stories are overlaid in this chapter with stories from the frontline so new auditors can generate ideas from which to ultimately craft their own stories.

What Practitioners Love About Internal Audit

"I love the diverse, project-based nature of internal audit which means you are always doing something different. You can be auditing a high-profile, international project or program one day, cloud computing the next, and organizational culture the next. I love learning and internal audit provides a ready means for me to do this through researching new audit topics, learning about different areas of the organization, and keeping abreast of developments in my profession. I find it very satisfying that my work has a constructive impact in my organization."			
CAE	Generation X	10 to 20 years' auditing experience	Accounting

The Broader Context

Thinking Beyond the Scope

The stories from the frontline covered in this chapter are likely to breathe more life into the aspiration that auditors discover fresh insights, rather than merely apply a perfect audit process. This will be driven by auditors who think beyond the scope of the forward audit plan and move away from a check-the-box exercise. This change will help to inspire auditors to consider a big-picture perspective, strategic thinking, and a stronger focus on "connecting the dots." In turn, auditors will be well positioned to deliver stronger, more practical, and harder-hitting recommendations that reflect a business perspective and meet stakeholder expectations.

This aspiration (and others) are discussed in more detail in the 2015 CBOK Report *Six Audit Committee Imperatives: Enabling Internal Audit to Make a Difference.*[2]

There Has Never Been a Better Time to Be an Internal Auditor

Some practitioners recognize there has never been a better time to be an internal auditor. New auditors can prepare themselves by leveraging the following useful insights that were published in the 2015 CBOK report *Driving Success in a Changing World: 10 Imperatives for Internal Audit.*[3]

1. To play a leading role in the success of their organizations, internal auditors need to anticipate the requirements of their stakeholders.
2. Internal auditors must understand how the complex web of risks arising from geopolitical events, environmental change, and rapid advances in technology impact their businesses. They must assess the likely impact of possible future events—including their second- and third-order consequences—on their organizations' strategies and operations.
3. Advising the audit committee of the constantly changing compliance, regulatory, and risk environment is of great value to organizations because it helps them keep abreast of global developments.
4. Internal auditors must have the courage to tell stakeholders the truth, whether they want to hear it or not. This is easier said than done, but it is essential if internal audit is to gain credibility across the organization.
5. Internal auditors can close the expectations gap between themselves and key stakeholders by better aligning their work to the business's strategic objectives. Such alignment facilitates risk-based auditing and better anticipation of stakeholder needs.
6. Technology risks are extremely difficult to manage because they are constantly evolving. Internal auditors need to respond proactively by helping organizations identify, monitor, and deal with such emerging IT risks and advising their boards on how best to do so.
7. Internal auditors must continue to improve their data analysis skills and techniques to enhance their observations. In addition to being able to analyze complete data sets (rather than samples), such technologies enable auditors to improve efficiency and audit data-rich areas in more sophisticated ways.
8. The IIA's *Standards* provides internal auditors with guidance that enables them to successfully perform internal audit activities for the organizations they serve.
9. There has never been a better time to be an internal auditor. The skills shortage in the profession has triggered fierce competition for the best-qualified auditors. You can reap the full rewards by investing in your own development.
10. Internal audit departments need to cast their nets wider to attract, retain, and motivate team members who are able to understand and anticipate the rapidly changing business environment. This is crucial if internal auditors are to better understand the businesses and functions of the organizations they serve.

Tips for New Auditors

- Create a brag book. Audit achievements aren't always recognized publically as being a result of an audit, so create your own record. Develop and maintain your audit and business connections—you never know when they will be needed.
- Remain open to new approaches and ways of working—you'll eventually find what suits you best.
- Don't be afraid to audit a new and different area—use your previous skills and experience to ask good questions, research, and try new approaches.
- Treat the staff and management as friends, building relationships and being proactive in sharing information, while being careful not to compromise your independence.
- Never be afraid to ask people in the business hard questions or make difficult suggestions, but be diplomatic when doing so. Work hard to maintain your independence and objectivity because that, coupled with incisive and informed analysis, is how you can be most valuable.

PART 6
THE *WHERE* OTHER INFORMATION IS PLACED

This part of the book draws together information that helps to expand on the overall content.

Appendices   Glossary   Notes

Wisdom of a Global Luminary

"Master the fundamentals—the business, risk management (the way it should be, not the way it generally is), and internal control. Seek to understand why people do the things they do, the way they do them, and always think about what would be best for the organization as a whole."

—Norman Marks
Retired Chief Audit Executive, U.K. and U.S.
Author, Evangelist, and Mentor for Better-Run Organizations

Appendix A
Statistics for Expert Practitioner-Shared Insights to the Author's Questions

Insights were sought by the author from a representation of expert practitioners from across the world. Practitioners responded to the following five questions:

1. If you were to offer a new internal auditor one piece of constructive advice, what would it be?
2. If you were telling a new internal auditor what you love about internal audit, what would you say?
3. If you were recalling your favorite audit ever, how would you describe it?
4. If there are any other insights you would share with a new internal auditor, what would you say?
5. What pathway did you use to join internal audit originally?

The insights were provided from regions as diverse as Africa, Australia, Europe, Middle East, and North America through to Fiji and Tuvalu, which are smaller South Pacific nations. The insights were used as direct quotes (in some cases) to inform the tips for new auditors, to produce stories from the frontline (chapter 20), or to produce themes for inclusion in the narrative. The respondents were each acknowledged earlier.

Fifty (of the 53) respondents provided demographic information as summarized below

Current Internal Audit Role	9	16	13	12	50
	18%	32%	26%	24%	100%
	Audit Committee Chairs/Members	Chief Audit Executives	Team Leaders and Auditors	Others (Incl. Service Firms and Retired)	Total Responses

Base Qualification	25	5	4	4	12	50
	50%	10%	8%	8%	24%	100%
	Accounting	Economics	Business Administration	Law	Other*	Total Responses
*Other includes arts, education, engineering, finance, human resources, IT, mathematics, physics, project management, science.						

Years of Internal Audit Experience	25	14	7	2	2	50
	50%	28%	14%	4%	4%	100%
	More than 20 years	10 to 20 years	5 to 10 years	Between 1 and 5 years	Less than 12 Months	Total Responses
Generation	2	24	16	8	0	50
	4%	48%	32%	16%	-	100%
	Traditionalist Born 1927–1945	Baby Boomer Born 1946–1964	Generation X Born 1965–1980	Millennial Born 1981–2000	Generation Z Born after 2000	Total Responses

Gender	29	21	0	50
	58%	42%	-	100%
	Male	Female	Other or not disclosed	Total Responses

Appendix B
Statistics for Expert Practitioner "What I Love About Internal Audit" Insights

A representation of insights was selected from 20 expert practitioners who answered the question, "If you were telling a new internal auditor what you love about internal audit, what would you say?" The idea was to get insights from people in different internal audit roles with varying base qualifications, a spread of years of experience, across different generations, and between genders. Respondents had the opportunity to skip demographic information if they chose to do so.

Current Internal Audit Role	5	6	5	4	20
	25%	30%	25%	20%	100%
	Audit Committee	Chief Audit Executive	Auditors	Other	Total Responses

Base Qualification	10	3	2	2	3	20
	50%	15%	10%	10%	15%	100%
	Accounting	Economics	Business Administration	Law	Finance Engineering HR/IT (1 each)	Total Responses

Years of Internal Audit Experience	8	7	2	2	1	20
	40%	35%	10%	10%	5%	100%
	More than 20 years	10 to 20 years	5 to 10 years	Between 1 and 5 years	Less than 12 Months	Total Responses

Generation	1	7	8	4	0	20
	5%	35%	40%	20%	-	100%
	Traditionalist Born 1927–1945	Baby Boomer Born 1946–1964	Generation X Born 1965–1980	Millennial Born 1981–2000	Generation Z Born after 2000	Total Responses

Gender	11	9	0	20
	55%	45%	-	100%
	Male	Female	Other or not disclosed	Total Responses

Notes

Dedication

1. Motto for the author's alma mater, the Nepean Creative and Performing Arts High School in Emu Plains, part of the Greater Western Sydney, Australia.

Executive Summary

1. Text boxes on *What Practitioners Love About Internal Audit* within each chapter include the practitioner's insight, followed by several descriptors: current role; generation; years of auditing experience; and base qualifications. Appendix B includes related statistical information. "Generation" demographic descriptors are explained in the glossary.

Preface

1. "History Stories: DNA Study Finds Aboriginal Australians World's Oldest Civilization." Christopher Klein blog, www.history.com/news/dna-study-finds-aboriginal-australians-worlds-oldest-civilization (sourced July 4 2018). September 23, 2016.

Chapter 1
The Internal Audit Profession

1. Andrew Cox et al., *Internal Audit in Australia* (Sydney, Australia: The Institute of Internal Auditors Australia, 2016), 20.
2. James Rose, *Mapping Your Career: Competencies Necessary for Internal Audit Excellence* (Altamonte Springs, FL: The Institute of Internal Auditors Research Foundation, 2015), 15–18.
3. International Professional Practices Framework (IPPF) (Lake Mary, FL: The Institute of Internal Auditors, 2017).
4. The meaning of stakeholder has largely been sourced from the IIA–Australia white paper on *Stakeholder Relationship Management*. It also draws on content from a presentation on *Emerging Trends in the Public Sector: Stakeholder Relationship Management* delivered July 2014 at The IIA's International Conference in London.
5. "2018: Top Risks Faced by Chief Audit Executives," *Global Perspectives and Insights* (Lake Mary, FL: The Institute of Internal Auditors, 2018), 10.
6. Angela Witzany and Larry Harrington, *Voice of the Customer: Stakeholders' Messages for Internal Audit* (Altamonte Springs, FL: The Institute of Internal Auditors Research Foundation, 2016), 3.

Chapter 2
Pathways into Internal Auditing

1. James Rose, *Mapping Your Career: Competencies Necessary for Internal Audit Excellence* (Altamonte Springs: The Institute of Internal Auditors Research Foundation, 2015), 5–6, 8.
2. *Global Internal Audit Competency Framework* (Lake Mary, FL: The Institute of Internal Auditors, 2013), 2–3.

Chapter 3
Capabilities of Internal Auditors

1. J. Mike Jacka, "The Mind of Jacka: "Trust Me," Said the Smiling Auditor," *Internal Auditor* (June 2018): 59.

Chapter 4
Roles and Responsibilities

1. Naohiro Mouri and Douglas J. Anderson, *Stakeholders' Advice to the Chief Audit Executive* (Lake Mary, FL: The Institute of Internal Auditors Research Foundation, 2017), 4–5.
2. Bruce Turner and Jacqueline Turner, "Shaping Talented Audit Teams – The Top 10 Innovative Professional Development Programs for Internal Auditors," *Internal Auditor Middle East* (December 2014), 16–18.

Chapter 5
Governance, Risk Management, and Control

1. Australian Transaction Reports and Analysis Centre (AUSTRAC) Media Release June 5, 2018, "AUSTRAC and CBA agree $700 m penalty": 1–2.
2. "Prudential Inquiry into the Commonwealth Bank of Australia," April 2018, 3.
3. Ibid, 43.

Chapter 7
Understanding the Control Environment

1. The IIA's Practice Guide, Auditing the Control Environment (Lake Mary, FL: The Institute of Internal Auditors, 2011), 2.
2. The IIA's Position Paper, The Three Lines of Defense in Effective Risk Management and Control (Lake Mary, FL: The Institute of Internal Auditors, 2013), 2–6.
3. *Report to the Nations – 2018 Global Study on Occupational Fraud and Abuse* (Austin: Association of Certified Fraud Examiners, 2018), 4, 5, 8, 11.
4. Ibid, 11.

Chapter 8
International Professional Practices Framework

1. International Professional Practices Framework (IPPF) (Lake Mary, FL: The Institute of Internal Auditors, 2017), 34.

2. Jane Seago, "A New Framework for a New Age," *Internal Auditor* (August 2015): 53–57.
3. Dr. John Laker, *APRA Speech-Internal Audit and Prudential Regulation: the Common Link* (Sydney, Australia: Australian Prudential Regulation Authority, May 2006), 10.

Chapter 9
Audit Planning and Opening Conference

1. *Sawyer's Internal Auditing: Enhancing and Protecting Organizational Value*, 7th Edition (Lake Mary, FL: Internal Audit Foundation, 2019), 235.

Chapter 10
Conducting an Interview

1. Table created by the author leveraging insights from two primary sources. (1) IIA–Australia training materials: *Interview Skills for Internal Auditors – Participant Workbook*, 2014. (2) *Conducting an Interview: Top Tips.* Chartered Institute of Internal Auditors United Kingdom and Ireland, 2016.
2. Venkataraman Iyer, *CAE Career Paths Characteristics and Competencies of Today's Internal Audit Leaders* (Altamonte Springs, FL: The Institute of Internal Auditors Research Foundation, 2016), 15–16.

Chapter 11
Audit Risk Assessment, Internal Controls, and Walkthrough

1. "Internal Auditors Need Foresight to Provide Foresight." *Chambers on the Profession* blog, iaonline. theiia.org/blogs/chambers/2017. November 20, 2017.
2. Ibid.
3. Richard Chambers, *Lessons Learned on the Audit Trail* (Lake Mary, FL: Internal Audit Foundation, 2014), 273.
4. Beverley Head, "Tech Topics: A Director's Guide," *Company Director* (May 2018, Volume 34, Issue 04): 38–45.

Chapter 12
Audit Program Development

1. "Rèsumè Checks: No Time for Complacency says Independent Commission Against Corruption (ICAC) Report," *Corruption Matters* (May 2018, Issue 51): 1.
2. Ibid, 2–3.
3. *Discussion Paper-Soft Controls: What Are the Starting Points for the Internal Auditor?* (Amsterdam: The Institute of Internal Auditors Netherlands, 2015), 5–6.
4. Ibid, 13, 32.
5. Suzy Stamatonikolos and Bruce Turner, *White Paper-Controlling Spreadsheet Risks* (Sydney: The Institute of Internal Auditors Australia, 2017), 2.
6. Ibid, 3–7.

Chapter 14
Audit Observations and Recommendations

1. *Conducting an Interview-Top Tips* (London: Chartered Institute of Internal Auditors United Kingdom and Ireland, 2016), 1.
2. Implementation Guide 2320-Analysis and Evaluation (Lake Mary, FL: The Institute of Internal Auditors, 2017), 4.
3. *Root Cause Analysis* (London: Chartered Institute of Internal Auditors United Kingdom and Ireland, 2016), 3.

Chapter 15
Audit Reporting and Exit Conference

1. Larry Harrington and Arthur Piper, *Driving Success in a Changing World: 10 Imperatives for Internal Audit* (Altamonte Springs, FL: The Institute of Internal Auditors Research Foundation, 2015), 10.
2. Jim DeLoach and Charlotta LöfstrandHjelm, *Six Audit Committee Imperatives: Enabling Internal Audit to Make a Difference* (Altamonte Springs, FL: The Institute of Internal Auditors Research Foundation, 2015), 6.

Chapter 16
Audit Quality Review and Wrap-Up

1. Christie J. O'Loughlin and Jodi Swauger, *Internal Audit Quality Assurance and Improvement: A Call to Action* (Altamonte Springs, FL: The Institute of Internal Auditors Research Foundation, 2016), 7, 10–11.

Chapter 17
Audit Observations: Follow-Up, Validation, and Resolution

1. Bruce Turner, *White Paper: Reporting on the Status of Audit Recommendations* (Sydney, Australia: The Institute of Internal Auditors Australia, 2017), 3.

Chapter 18
Quality Assurance and Improvement Program

1. "Internal Audit Watch-India Owned Bank Undertakes Quality Assurance Audit Programme," *IIA Global SmartBrief* (17 April 2018): 1.
2. Christie J. O'Loughlin and Jodi Swauger, *Internal Audit Quality Assurance and Improvement: A Call to Action* (Altamonte Springs, FL: The Institute of Internal Auditors Research Foundation, 2016), 14.
3. Ibid, 7.

Chapter 19
Measuring Performance

1. James Rose, *Mapping Your Career: Competencies Necessary for Internal Audit Excellence* (Altamonte Springs, FL: The Institute of Internal Auditors Research Foundation, 2015), 4–25.
2. Bruce Turner, *GREAT Ways to Motivate Your Staff: Shaping an Audit Team that Adds Value and Inspires Business Improvement* (Altamonte Springs, FL: The Institute of Internal Auditors Research Foundation, 2016), 25.
3. Mark L. Frigo, *The Balanced Scorecard: Applications in Internal Auditing and Risk Management* (Lake Mary, FL: Internal Audit Foundation, 2014), vii.

Chapter 20
Stories from the Frontline

1. Bruce Turner, "The ABCs of Adding Value," *Internal Auditor* (December 2013): 48–53.
2. Jim DeLoach and Charlotta LöfstrandHjelm, *Six Audit Committee Imperatives: Enabling Internal Audit to Make a Difference* (Altamonte Springs, FL: The Institute of Internal Auditors Research Foundation, 2015), 4–5.
3. Larry Harrington and Arthur Piper, *Driving Success in a Changing World: 10 Imperatives for Internal Audit* (Altamonte Springs, FL: The Institute of Internal Auditors Research Foundation, 2015), 4–26.

Glossary

Term	Meaning	For Further Information, See Chapter:
ABCs of Auditing	Concepts of being attuned, balanced, credible.	20
ACFE	Association of Certified Fraud Examiners – professional body.	1
Action Plan	A document that stipulates the steps required to achieve a specific goal (in this case, implementation of audit recommendations). It identifies the resources needed, allocates responsibility, and reflects the agreed timeline.	17
Add Value	Providing objective and relevant assurance, and contributing to the effectiveness and efficiency of governance, risk management, and control processes.	1
Administrative Reporting	The chief audit executive will typically have an administrative reporting line to the chief executive or their delegate. In this context, administrative responsibilities include human resource administration and budgets. *See also* Functional Reporting.	7
Annual Audit Plan	*See* Forward Audit Plan.	9
Annual Report on Internal Audit	A formal report that showcases the contribution and achievements of the internal audit activity over the past year, demonstrates its value, and delivers consolidated insights to the audit committee.	19
Approach	*See* Audit Approach.	9
Assurance	Outcome of an independent assessment of governance, risk management, and control processes for an organization that is based on an objective examination of evidence.	1
Assurance Map	A high-level document that identifies the holistic risk coverage across the organization by a range of assurance providers. Helps to identify gaps and duplication of assurance coverage.	5

Audit Approach	Reflects the way that the auditors conduct their work (e.g., risk workshop; control self-assessment; use of technology; collaboration with others).	9
Audit Closeout Memorandum	Compiled at the conclusion of the audit to reconcile the actual audit effort against what was planned in the Audit Planning Memorandum.	16
Audit Committee	A committee of the governing body (such as a board of directors, if the organization has one) with its objectives clearly defined and documented in its charter, and its efficiency and effectiveness measured by reference to its objectives. An independent audit committee is fundamental to good governance. An audit committee typically (i) focuses on financial reporting integrity; (ii) oversees risk and assurance activities, including external audit, internal audit, risk management, internal control, and compliance; and (iii) liaises with the governing body, internal and external auditors, and management. The internal audit activity (through the chief audit executive) will typically report functionally to the audit committee.	All
Audit Evidence	Relevant, useful, sufficient and reliable information that auditors obtain in the conduct of their audits through observing conditions, research, benchmarking, interviewing people, and examining records.	13
Audit Objectives	Broad statements determined through a systematic and disciplined approach that define *what* the intended accomplishments of the audit engagement will be.	9
Audit Observations	Describes the connection between the audit criteria and the audit evidence to reflect conformity, nonconformity, or opportunities for improvement.	14
Audit Planning Memorandum (APM)	Consolidated single document that reflects the planning efforts for the audit engagement. It includes background and risk information; defines the audit objectives, scope, and approach; highlights known problems; articulates the budget and schedule; contains the requisite approvals; and documents conflicts of interests and how they will be managed.	9

Audit Program	Contains detailed information on how the step-by-step audit procedures will be performed during an approved audit engagement.	12
Audit Report	The primary means of communicating the outcomes of an audit, reflecting the auditor's observations, opinions, and recommendations arising from the audit.	15
Audit Report Rating System	Not all observations and recommendations are equally important, so a consistent, well-understood rating system based on the organization's risk table (impact/likelihood) and risk appetite statement helps management to focus on higher priority observations and recommendations.	15
Audit Scope	Identifies *where* the audit will be directed to achieve the audit objectives, such as places, activities, and time frames.	9
Audit Universe	The range of business activities, programs, functions, and entities that collectively contribute to the achievement of strategic objectives and could potentially be the subject of an audit.	12
Auditor	Someone whose job it is to independently undertake internal auditing, aimed at adding value and improving an organization's operations and helping to achieve its objectives.	4
Balanced Scorecard Reporting	A well-established approach to structuring qualitative and quantitative performance measures and reporting the results to the audit committee in a balanced way.	19
Body Language	The physical movements (rather than words) that communicate a person's attitudes and feelings, either consciously or unconsciously (e.g., hand gestures, facial expressions, eye movement, voice tone and volume, and posture).	10
Budget	The number of working days or hours allocated to the audit (for in-house resources) or the monetary budget (in the case of a service provider firm). Usually broken down into the distinct phases of the audit and as a resource allocation by auditor.	9
Business Risk Categories	Thirteen common generic business risks based on the Canadian control framework (CoCo).	14
CAE	*See* Chief Audit Executive.	4

Capability Model	Mechanism for identifying and assessing the fundamentals for effective internal auditing. The published Internal Audit Capability Model is a proven model where aspiring auditors can progressively focus on developing defined capabilities.	1
CBOK	*See* Common Body of Knowledge.	10
Certifications	The result of an action or process to achieve a recognized professional status or level of achievement (e.g., CIA, CISA, CFE).	1
CFE	Certified Fraud Examiner – certification issued by ACFE.	1
Charter	Formal document (in the form of a mandate) that defines the purpose, authority, and responsibility (in this case, of internal audit).	8
Chief Audit Executive (CAE)	The head of internal audit—a person in a senior position responsible for effectively managing the internal audit activity in accordance with the internal audit charter and the mandatory elements of the IPPF.	4
CIA	Certified Internal Auditor – certification issued by The IIA.	1
CISA	Certified Information Systems Auditor – certification issued by ISACA.	1
Coaching Notes	Used by the team leader as part of the audit quality review process to seek clarification of any parts of the workpapers that appear unclear and incomplete, or do not support the conclusions. May also be referred to as "review notes."	16
CoCo	Canadian-developed control framework that provides a way for management to evaluate the reasonableness of controls that minimize risk and ensure the reliability of financial and other reporting (acronym derived from <u>C</u>riteria <u>o</u>f <u>C</u>ontrol).	7
Code of Ethics	Principles relevant (in this case) to the profession and practice of internal auditing, and Rules of Conduct that describe the behavior expected of internal auditors.	4, 8
Common Body of Knowledge (CBOK)	A living reference that represents the collective knowledge of the internal audit profession. CBOK is the world's largest ongoing study of the internal audit profession, including studies of internal audit practitioners and their stakeholders.	10

Competency Framework	A framework that illustrates the connectivity between the Core Competencies.	2
Compliance Framework	A structured approach to managing compliance obligations (arising from policies, plans, procedures, laws, regulations, contracts, and other requirements) and mitigating compliance risk in order to achieve an organization's compliance objectives.	5
Compliance Testing	An approach to determine whether prescribed controls actually exist and are being complied with in practice.	13
Consulting	Advisory and related client services.	1
Control	Any action taken by management, the board, and other parties to manage risk and increase the likelihood that established objectives and goals will be achieved. *See also* Hard Controls and Soft Controls.	5
Control Environment	The attitude and actions of the board and management regarding the importance of control within the organization. It provides the discipline and structure for the achievement of the primary objectives of the system of internal control.	7
Control Self-Assessment	Structured process where management and the work team collaboratively assess the effectiveness of controls, the level of residual risk, and achievability of business objectives. Typically involves facilitated workshops and surveys.	9, 11
Core Competencies	The 10 core competencies for internal auditors recognized in a CBOK report for mapping your career to achieve excellence.	2
Core Principles	Highlight what effective internal audit looks like in practice, as it relates to the individual auditor, the internal audit activity, and internal audit outcomes. Part of the IPPF.	3, 8
COSO	U.S.-developed control framework structured on the basis that a direct relationship exists between *objectives*, which are what an entity strives to achieve, *components*, which represents what is required to achieve the objectives, and the *organizational structure* of the entity (acronym is derived from the Committee of Sponsoring Organizations of the Treadway Commission).	7
CSA	*See* Control Self-Assessment.	9, 11

Culture	A system of shared assumptions, values, and beliefs that reflects the way people behave. The lived culture across an organization dictates what internal control practices are actually applied in practice.	5
Data Mining	An efficient way for analyzing large amounts of data through data manipulation techniques (e.g., filtering, sorting, pivot tables, and formulas) to pinpoint areas requiring additional audit focus and identifying trends and abnormalities for detailed testing.	13
Definition of Internal Auditing (in IPPF)	An independent, objective assurance and consulting activity designed to add value and improve an organization's operations. It helps an organization accomplish its objectives by bringing a systematic, disciplined approach to evaluate and improve the effectiveness of risk management, control, and governance processes.	1, 8
Doctrine of No Surprises	An approach where auditors maintain effective communication with clients throughout their audit so that clients are not surprised and caught off guard by significant observations raised during the wrap-up and reporting stage of the audit.	14
Efficiency, Effectiveness, Economy, and Ethical	Efficiency is doing things right. Effectiveness is doing the right things. Economy is doing the right things at the least cost. Ethical is doing the right things the right way. Collectively these help to deliver value for money.	1, 12
Environmental Scan	A systematic process for identifying and interpreting external threats and opportunities.	9
Exceptions	*See* Audit Observations.	14
Exit Conference	A nonconfrontational, low-key, and informal meeting between internal audit and management at the conclusion of audit fieldwork to inform management of the outcomes of the audit, inform them of the reporting process, get their acceptance of recommendations, and agreement to implement them.	15
External Audit	An audit of financial statements undertaken in accordance with laws and external auditing standards by an external auditor who is independent of the organization being audited.	2

Facilitation Payments	Payments made to public or government officials to incentivize them to complete an action or process that is beneficial to the party making the payment. They are illegal in most countries and are tantamount to bribes.	7
Fieldwork	The process of completing the audit engagement to achieve audit objectives through testing, data analysis, and other techniques pursuant to an approved audit program.	13
Follow-Up (of Recommendations)	A process by which auditors evaluate the adequacy, effectiveness, and timeliness of actions taken by management on reported observations and recommendations, including those by external auditors and others. Includes determining whether senior management and/or the board have assumed the risk of not taking corrective action on reported observations.	17
Foresight	The ability to contemplate key risks and challenges that organizations could conceivably face so that perspective can be shared with management and the board to help them prepare for challenges or opportunities before they arise.	11
Forward Audit Plan	A high-level, risk-based internal audit plan that identifies the areas of the organization to be independently reviewed, together with the related business strategies, objectives and risks, with indicative objectives, scope, timing, and resourcing levels (budget).	9
Four E's	Efficiency, effectiveness, economy, and ethical.	1, 12
Fraud Tree	An occupational fraud and abuse classification system developed by the ACFE that illustrates the three primary categories of occupational fraud (corruption, asset misappropriation, and financial statement fraud) and the common fraud types within each category.	7

Frontline	Frontline is an idiomatic term that refers to hands-on people who are responsible for producing and delivering services and goods directly to customers, clients, and stakeholders. They have to achieve targets and deadlines (like factory supervisors). The term provides a distinction between these roles and senior management's broader leadership role, which is more involved in strategic planning, customer and public relations, and oversight, rather than being directly involved in the operational aspects of the business. The analogy is that internal auditors apply a hands-on approach, work to deadlines, and deal directly with clients.	20
Functional Reporting	The chief audit executive will typically have a dual reporting line with functional reporting to the audit committee (and administrative reporting to the chief executive). In this context, functional responsibilities include approving the internal audit charter and forward audit plan, reviewing audit reports and reports on the follow-up of recommendations, and hiring, compensating, performance assessing, and removing the chief audit executive. *See also* Administrative Reporting.	7
Generations	Body of persons born in the same era—traditionalist (1927–1945), baby boomer (1946–1964), Generation X (1965–1980), millennial (1981–2000), Generation Z (born after 2000).	Executive Summary
Goal Setting	An iterative process between the auditor and the team leader aimed at identifying and agreeing the specific results the auditor is required to achieve to help the internal audit activity achieve its objectives. Part of the performance management process.	19
Governance	The combination of processes and structures implemented by the board to inform, direct, manage, and monitor the activities of the organization toward the achievement of its objectives.	5
Graduate	Someone who has successfully completed a tertiary-level course of study or training to achieve an academic degree (or similar).	2

Guest Auditor	Subject matter expert from a technical business area who brings expertise to particular audit engagements, usually for between a few weeks to a year.	2
Hard Controls	Tangible controls involving explicit activities that are usually objective (e.g., approvals, delegations, authorizations, verifications, reconciliations).	5, 12
Hindsight	Assessing a situation, event, or activity that has happened in the past; for internal auditors, reviewing what happened in the past to establish and report a view on control assurance.	11
IIA	*See* Institute of Internal Auditors.	1
Implementation Guidance	Designed to assist internal auditors in applying the *Standards* and promoting good practices by addressing the typical audit approach, methodology, and considerations rather than detailed processes and procedures (part of the IPPF).	8
Independence	Freedom from conditions that threaten the ability of the internal audit activity to carry out internal audit responsibilities in an unbiased manner.	1
Information	Knowledge about a particular topic, subject, event, or activity, and is the result of organizing, processing, presenting, structuring, and/or interpreting data (plain facts) in a way that delivers meaningful insights.	10
Information Technology Assurance Framework (ITAF)	Issued by ISACA to provide the information (including standards) required to meet compliance needs of information systems audit and assurance professionals, as well as providing essential guidance to improve effectiveness and efficiency.	1
Insight	The intuitive understanding of a specific cause and effect in the context in which it is being assessed; for auditors, it encompasses their perspectives on risks facing the organization and control assurance in the here and now.	11
Institute of Internal Auditors, The	Global professional body for internal auditors.	1
Internal Audit	Used to refer to the function or department in an organization.	All
Internal Audit Activity	Used when referring to a generic department.	All

Internal Audit Definition	*See* Definition of Internal Auditing.	1, 8
Internal Auditing	Refers to the overall profession or discipline.	All
Internal Control	*See* Control.	5
Internal Control Framework	Broad grouping of recognized internal control frameworks across the world, including COSO, CoCo, COBIT, and more recently King IV in South Africa.	7
International Professional Practices Framework (IPPF)	Conceptual framework that organizes the authoritative guidance (including the *Standards*) promulgated by The IIA. *See also* Mandatory Guidance and Recommended Guidance in the IPPF.	1
IPPF	*See* International Professional Practices Framework.	1
ISACA	Professional body for IT governance professionals, including information systems auditors.	1
ISO	Activities of the International Organization for Standardization, which is an international body made up of representatives from various national standards organizations with the aim of setting and promoting a range of proprietary, industrial, and commercial standards across the world. ISO is not an acronym, rather it is derived from the Greek word isos, which means equal.	5
ITAF	*See* Information Technology Assurance Framework.	1
Key Performance Indicators (KPIs)	Performance measures that evaluate the success of an organization or specific activities that it undertakes.	3, 19
List of Key Reports	Systematic and structured way to determine, document, prioritize, and review the reliability and integrity of financial, operational, and decision-support information reports.	11
Mandate	*See* Charter.	4
Mind Mapping	A way to visually organize information so major observations are connected to a central concept (e.g., audit objective or business goal) with associated ideas branching out from there. Helps to shape the overall audit conclusion and the structure and content of the report.	14

Mission (in IPPF)	To enhance and protect organizational value by providing risk-based and objective assurance, advice, and insight.	1, 8
Monitoring Recommendations	The systematic follow-up process undertaken by the internal audit activity to evaluate the adequacy, effectiveness, and timeliness of actions taken by management on reported recommendations.	17
Nonconformance to Standards	Result of an internal or external assessment of the internal audit activity as part of the organization's Quality Assurance and Improvement Program (QAIP) where a standard or standards are not being competently applied in practice.	8
Objective	An unbiased mental attitude that allows internal auditors to perform engagements in such a manner that they believe in their work product and that no quality compromises are made. Objectivity requires that internal auditors do no subordinate their judgment on audit matters to others.	1
Observations	*See* Audit Observations.	14
Performance Culture	A systematic model of goal-setting and performance evaluation used for practically managing an organization, its business activities, and its employees, recognizing that culture is a key driver for an organization in achieving its stated purpose.	19
Performance Evaluation	Reflects a constructive performance assessment that involves evaluating the development of an auditor's skillsets and providing structured feedback on their performance annually, every six months, and/or after every audit engagement.	19
Population	Refers to the entire set of data within an internal audit engagement from which an auditor selects a sample in order to arrive at a conclusion against a specified audit objective.	13
Preliminary Client Survey	Structured approach that aids in the familiarization with an operation or activity through the transfer of information, such as answers to specific questions and/or access to specific documentation.	9

Profession	An organized group of people who provide intellectual and conceptual services to their clients, including the general public. It is characterized by specialist knowledge, skills, and expertise acquired through a recognized body of high-level learning and has a code of ethics to govern its activities. *See also* SPACE Features.	1
Professional Development Plan	A structured, systematic, and well-founded plan used as the strategic driver to support an organization's investment in the development of internal audit capability.	19
QAIP	*See* Quality Assurance and Improvement Program.	18
Quality Assertion	Provides explicit confirmation to the audit committee that oblique standards (not evident from routine audit reporting) are understood and have been applied appropriately.	18
Quality Assurance and Improvement Program (QAIP)	A structured and systematic approach for evaluating conformance with professional auditing standards, establishing whether The IIA's Code of Ethics is being applied, and nurturing improvements. Core elements include ongoing monitoring, internal assessments, external assessments, qualitative measures, and quality assertion.	18
Quality Review of Workpapers	Workpapers should carry evidence of a quality review by the team leader (or delegate) with the primary objectives of providing assurance as to the overall quality of the audit, enhancing the value of the audit report, and ensuring staff are professionally developed.	16
Recommendation	Auditors raise recommendations to address audit observations. There are typically five elements to a recommendation: observation, criteria, effect, cause, and specific recommendation to rectify the situation.	14
Record of Interview	Document that reflects the context of an interview, including date, location, participants, main discussion points, outcomes, and further follow-up.	10
Red Book	Colloquial reference to the International Professional Practices Framework (IPPF), which refers to the book's red cover.	4

Regulation	Oversight maintained by an international, global, or local authorized body to ensure laws, rules, directives, statutes, and standards are maintained by organizations and their people.	8
Resourcing Models	Various approaches for the internal audit activity to obtain auditors to undertake audit engagements, including in-house, co-sourced, and outsourced.	6
Right-to-Audit Clause	A clause inserted in tenders and contracts that provides internal and external auditors and other scrutineers access to information, books, records, and assets held by contractors (and third-party subcontractors) for the purposes of their audits of that specific contract.	12
Risk Appetite (Statement)	The broad parameters around the amount and type of risk that an organization's leaders are willing to take in order to achieve its strategic and operational objectives.	5
Risk-Based Auditing	A methodology where auditors consistently apply risk to all elements of the audit process through their mandate, stakeholder management, organizational structure, staffing, planning, fieldwork, reporting, and follow-up.	6, 11
Risk Management	A process to identify, assess, manage, and control potential events or situations to provide reasonable assurance regarding the achievement of the organization's objectives.	5
Risk Register	Record of risks at all levels of the organization identified through a risk assessment process.	5
Root Cause Analysis	An approach to identifying the underlying reason for the occurrence of an error, problem, missed opportunity, or instance of noncompliance.	14
Sampling	Allows conclusions to be reached about an entire population by drawing on an analysis of a portion (less than 100%) of it.	13
Scrutineers	A person or entity from outside the organization that has the power to scrutinize any process or activity that requires rigorous oversight, with a focus on detecting noncompliance, corruption, and errors (e.g., external auditors, regulators, coroner, taxation authority, parliamentary committee, federal or state investigation).	16

SMILE Techniques	Reflects structured interviewing techniques based on structure, meaningfulness, insightfulness, listening, and ending.	10
Soft Controls	Intangible controls that are typically subjective and reflect implicit attitudes (e.g., culture, tone at the top, shared values, morale, integrity, trust, and empowerment).	5, 12
SPACE Features	Features of a profession—status, power, autonomy, capability, and ethics. *See also* Profession.	1
Spreadsheet Risks	Uncontrolled spreadsheets (and similar) used for business-critical purposes. *See also* List of Key Reports.	12
Stakeholders	The people, groups, or organizations that can affect, or be affected by, the internal audit activity.	1
Standards	The *International Standards for the Professional Practice of Internal Auditing* issued as part of the IPPF by The IIA as either attribute standards or performance standards.	8
Substantive Testing	An approach for determining whether data includes a material amount of dollar errors, usually by sampling selected transactions, accounts, or activities.	13
Supplemental Guidance	Provided through a series of publications called Practice Guides, Global Technology Audit Guides (GTAGs), Guides for the Assessment of IT Risk (GAITs), and other detailed guidance for conducting internal audit activities (part of the IPPF).	8
Team Leader	Someone who leads the internal audit engagement on a day-to-day basis. They oversee and allocate the work, provide direction and support, and maintain quality assurance. They may have a variety of titles, such as director of auditing, audit director, audit manager, and audit supervisor.	4
Testing	*See* Compliance Testing and Substantive Testing.	13
Three Lines of Defense	A model that reflects the discrete areas relied upon within the organization to provide assurance, from management controls (first line); to governance, risk, and compliance functions (second line); and ultimately to internal audit (third line).	7

Tone at the Top	Describes an organization's ethical climate, reflecting the board's and senior management's consistent behavioral example, and their meaningful commitment to integrity through their modeling of open, honest, and ethical behavior.	5, 7
Trend Analysis	An analytical review procedure used to determine the reasonableness of recorded data and operational results.	13
Value Proposition	The value proposition of internal audit is based on three core elements of value delivered by internal audit to an organization: assurance, insight, and objectivity.	1
Vision	The preferred future state of an internal audit activity in an organization.	1
Workpapers	Prepared by internal auditors to document the work performed in the planning, performance, and quality assurance review of audits.	13

Internal Audit Foundation
Sponsor Recognition

STRATEGIC PARTNERS

FOUNDATION PARTNERS

Larry Harrington
CIA, QIAL, CRMA

DIAMOND PARTNERS (US $25,000+)

GOLD PARTNERS (US $5,000–$14,999)

The Institute of Internal Auditors Detroit Chapter

The Institute of Internal Auditors Kansas City Chapter

The Institute of Internal Auditors New York Chapter

The Institute of Internal Auditors Northeast Ohio Chapter

The Institute of Internal Auditors Philadelphia Chapter

The Institute of Internal Auditors San Francisco Chapter

The Institute of Internal Auditors Toronto Chapter

Natarajan Girija Shankar, CIA

Paul J. Sobel, CIA, CRMA, QIAL

Internal Audit Foundation
Leadership Society Members

Eric Allegakoen, CIA, CCSA, CRMA

Doug Anderson, CIA, CRMA

Urton Anderson,
CIA, CCSA, CFSA, CGAP, CRMA

Narendra Kumar Aneja, CIA, CRMA

Farah G. Araj, CIA, QIAL

Audley Bell, CIA

Lily Bi, CIA, QIAL, CRMA

Ben Bouchillon, CCSA

Karen Brady, CIA, CRMA

Judith K. Burke, CCSA

Mark Carawan, CIA, QIAL

Raven Catlin, CIA, CFSA, CRMA

Richard F. Chambers,
CIA, QIAL, CCSA, CGAP, CRMA

Angelina Chin, CIA, CCSA, CRMA

Brian Christensen

Daniel Clayton, CIA

Ann Cohen

Andrew Dahle, CIA, CRMA

Gary Daugherty, CIA

Scott Feltner, CIA

Philip E. Flora, CIA, CCSA

Brian Foster, CIA

Michael J. Fucilli, CIA, QIAL, CGAP, CRMA

Steve Goepfert, CIA, QIAL, CRMA

Nancy Haig, CIA, CCSA, CFSA, CRMA

Lawrence J. Harrington, CIA, QIAL, CRMA

Lisa Hartkopf

Eric Hespenheide

Glenn Ho, CIA, CRMA

Pamela Jenkins, CIA, CRMA

Bailey Jordan, CIA, CRMA

Mike Joyce, CIA, CRMA

Tina Kim, CIA, CGAP, CRMA

Deborah Kretchmar, CIA

Michael J. Lynn, CRMA

Betty McPhilimy, CIA, CRMA

Raoul Menes, CIA, CCSA, CRMA

William (Bill) Michalisin

Patricia Miller, CIA, QIAL, CRMA

James A. Molzahn, CIA, CRMA

Naohiro Mouri, CIA

Karla Munden,
CIA, QIAL, CCSA, CFSA, CRMA

Michael Newman, CIA

Frank M. O'Brien, CIA, QIAL

Carey Oven, CIA

J. Michael (Mike) Peppers, CIA, QIAL, CRMA

Cynthia G. Plamondon,
CIA, QIAL, CCSA, CFSA, CGAP, CRMA

Charles Redding

Anthony Ridley, CIA

Michael P. Rose, CIA, CCSA, CRMA

Debra Roth, CIA

Stanley Rubins

Mark Salamasick, CIA, CGAP, CRMA

Thomas Sanglier II, CIA, CRMA

Kimberly Schroeder, CIA

N.G. Shankar, CIA

Alan N. Siegfried,
CIA, CCSA, CFSA, CGAP, CRMA

Harold C. Silverman, CIA, QIAL, CRMA

Paul J. Sobel, CIA, QIAL, CRMA

Jared Soileau, CIA, CCSA, CRMA,
and Laura Soileau, CIA, CRMA

Tania Stegemann, CIA, CCSA, CRMA

Warren Stippich, CIA, CRMA

Carrie Summerlin, CCSA

Gerard Totton, CIA, QIAL

Bonnie L. Ulmer

Dominique Vincenti, CIA, CRMA

Jacqueline Wagner, CIA

Angela Witzany, CIA, QIAL, CRMA

Charles Wright, CIA

Benito Ybarra, CIA

Douglas Ziegenfuss, CIA, CCSA, CRMA

Frank M. O'Brien, CIA, QIAL, *Olin Corporation*

Sakiko Sakai, CIA, CCSA, CFSA, CRMA, *Infinity Consulting*

Anton Van Wyk, CIA, CRMA, QIAL, *PricewaterhouseCoopers LLP*

Yi Hsin Wang, CIA, CGAP, CRMA, *National Taipei University*

Ana Cristina Zambrano Preciado, CIA, CCSA, CRMA, *IIA–Colombia*

Mani Massoomi, CFSA, CRMA, *SoFi*

Joseph A. Mauriello, CIA, CFSA, CRMA, *University of Texas at Dallas*

Mark J. Pearson, CIA

Sundaresan Rajeswar, CIA, CCSA, CFSA, CGAP, CRMA, *Teyseer Group of Companies*

Bismark Rodriguez, CIA, CCSA, CFSA, CRMA, *Financial Services Risk Management*

Hesham K. Shawa, *IIA Jordon – International*

Deanna F. Sullivan, CIA, CRMA, *SullivanSolutions*

Jason Robert Thogmartin, CIA, CRMA, *Santander Holdings USA, Inc.*

Ashley R. Threeton, *ConocoPhillips*

Adriana Beatriz Toscano Rodriguez, CIA, CRMA, *UTE*

Jane Traub, CIA, CCSA, *The Nielsen Company*

Maritza Villanueva, CIA, *Regal Forest Holding*

Paul L. Walker, *St. John's University*

Larry G. Wallis, CIA, *VIA Metropolitan Transit*

Chance R. Watson, CIA, CRMA, *Texas Department of Family & Protective Services*

Klaas J. Westerling, CIA, *Intertrust Group Holding S.A.*